Murder 101

ALSO BY EDWARD J. RIELLY

*Baseball in the Classroom: Essays on
Teaching the National Pastime* (McFarland, 2006)

Murder 101

Essays on the Teaching of Detective Fiction

Edited by
EDWARD J. RIELLY

McFarland & Company, Inc., Publishers
Jefferson, North Carolina, and London

LIBRARY OF CONGRESS CATALOGUING-IN-PUBLICATION DATA

Murder 101 : essays on the teaching of detective fiction /
    edited by Edward J. Rielly.
        p.   cm.
    Includes bibliographical references and index.

    ISBN 978-0-7864-3657-6
    softcover : 50# alkaline paper ∞

    1. Detective and mystery stories, American — History and
criticism — Study and teaching (Higher).   2. Law and
literature — United States— History — Study and teaching
(Higher).   3. Crime in literature — Study and teaching
(Higher).   I. Rielly, Edward J.   II. Title: Murder one hundred
one.   III. Title: Murder one hundred and one.
PS374.D4M853   2009
813'.0872'09 — dc22   2008044841

British Library cataloguing data are available

Cover images ©2009 Shutterstock

Manufactured in the United States of America

McFarland & Company, Inc., Publishers
    Box 611, Jefferson, North Carolina 28640
        www.mcfarlandpub.com

To my wife, Jeanne,
whose love and support make my writing possible

Acknowledgments

I extend my gratitude to all who helped make this volume possible. Foremost, of course, are those excellent faculty who contributed essays, all of whom responded graciously to any suggestions that I had for revision. I am indebted to Saint Joseph's College of Maine for financial support through faculty grants and for the general respect that is a daily element of life on my campus. I have called on the Information Systems staff, especially Eric Tremblay, Skip Williamson, and Kareem Myrick, many times for assistance, and they have always solved my technological problems quickly and courteously. Finally, I thank my wife, Jeanne, whose support is constant, and with whom sharing my work is always a joy.

Table of Contents

Introduction

EDWARD J. RIELLY

Teachers and detectives have some characteristics in common. Both search for truth, typically with the help of others in the case of teachers with their students. The truth that they discover they also share, whether in a courtroom or a classroom. Finding it, both categories of truth-seekers know full well, is often challenging and may invite considerable controversy, but ultimately, in both cases, society benefits.

It seems especially fitting, then, for teachers to use detective fiction in their courses. The close observation and analysis that good detective fiction presents is analogous to the critical abilities that students seek to master, so detective fiction can help students grow intellectually even if, as some traditionalists may complain, the genre is part of popular literature and popular culture.

Being "popular," however, is hardly an intrinsically pejorative concept, or at least it should not be, in a nation founded on the principle that the people — not just a tiny percentage of them, but the collective people, the masses — should control the destiny of the nation. The founding fathers, as teachers and students know, did ignore segments of the populace, such as African Americans and women, but our society has moved much farther toward enfranchising all its members over the past 150 or so years.

In fact, the popularity of certain types of literature, in this case, detective fiction, argues for, not against, including it within our college curricula. The reality that a lot of detective fiction is well written and highly enjoyable as well as intellectually stimulating and informative is all the more reason to use it.

This volume consists of twenty-three essays written by college and university faculty throughout the United States and abroad on how they use detective fiction in their courses. The essays cover a wide range of the college curriculum, from literature to law school courses, from first-year seminars to cultural studies, from composition to gender studies, from architecture to anthropology, and many other courses and disciplines as well. For the purposes of this volume, the definition of detective fiction has been kept as inconclusive as possible. Anyone who solves a crime — professional or amateur, private investigator or official law enforcement figure, an individual within the realm of crime detection or a professional in another field — qualifies as a "detective."

The interdisciplinary nature of the range of courses discussed in these engaging and highly useful essays made simple division into curricular categories seem overly artificial to me, so I merely placed the essays in alphabetical order according to the authors' names. My hope is that readers will browse through the volume, reading whatever essays may stir their interest.

The volume is first of all intended for other faculty; yet those not formally engaged in education but who enjoy detective fiction also will, I am confident, enjoy the essays and learn much about many excellent authors. It is difficult to imagine anyone reading in this collection without making a list of exciting writers of detective fiction to start exploring.

My advice to all educators reading the volume is to look for ways in which you can borrow ideas from these talented, creative faculty for use in your own courses. The essays are primarily descriptive, eschewing polemics. There is no one way to teach effectively, but there are many ways, and certainly using detective fiction to engage students and help them learn the skills and content that you teach can greatly enhance student learning.

Learning, after all, can be fun. In fact, the more fun it is, the more students are likely to learn. So peruse the following essays and discover ways to make your teaching more enjoyable (for both you and your students) and even more effective than it already is. I wish you good reading and good detecting.

Exploring the Origins of American Detective Fiction
Teaching Poe and Dime Novels

PAMELA BEDORE

Detective fiction of the twentieth and twenty-first centuries can be taught as a weathervane of social anxiety around crime and criminality, as a window into representations of group and personal identity, or as an introduction to literary theory, perhaps especially within the fields of gender, genre, and poststructuralist theory. Courses may focus as well on the subgenres of detective fiction — the English cozy, the American hard-boiled, the feminist reclaiming of the genre from the 1970s forward — or may provide a broader survey. Regardless of methodology and text choice, a look to the nineteenth century can help establish the foundations of detective fiction in ways that highlight for students what is at stake in this genre. This chapter provides some strategies for thinking and talking about key moments in the early history of detective fiction, namely the contributions of Edgar Allan Poe and the American dime novel.

As the earliest fully realized exemplars of the detective genre, Poe's detective stories provide an excellent entry into connections between detective fiction and students' everyday and intellectual lives. I like to begin classes on detective fiction by asking students about their own experiences with stories of crime and detection. Which perspective do they prefer — that of the criminal or the detective — and why? What is the difference between the two? Young readers today are often most familiar with Poe's tales of horror — "The Tell-Tale Heart" (1843) and "The Cask of Amontillado" (1846), for example — so setting these up in contrast to his detective stories clearly shows the difference between the detective and criminal perspectives. This discussion can lead to another question that engages students in the study of detective fiction: why is detective fiction so popular?

The explanation put forward by early critics of the genre is that the detective story offers the reader a mediator (the detective or a proximate narrator) in his or her inherent desire to gaze upon the horrific, in this case the criminal. Crime stories force the reader to confront the underbelly of society head-on, and often, using a first-person narrator, put the reader into the uncomfortable psychic space of identifying with the criminal whether or not that criminal has been shown as morally redeemable. Detective stories, on the other hand, place the reader in a more comfortable moral space, focusing on the detective's story rather than the criminal's, and often providing a detective hero who will restore rational or social order. However, as most students are aware, from viewing detective films and television series if not from reading detective fiction, this basic explanation does not fully account for the moral complexity found in detective stories.

Detective characters, both private investigators and police detectives, often question the moral value of their work and express sympathy for the criminal and hatred or disgust for the victim. Further, the genre is not simply about restoring social order, because such order is not always restored; episodes of the well-known television series *Law & Order*, for example, often end with criminals going free despite the detectives' success in identifying and capturing them as perpetrators of heinous crimes. Most readers and viewers recognize that part of their pleasure in the genre also lies in watching the detective repeatedly entering and escaping dangerous situations, perhaps as a proxy for the reader who has neither access to nor courage for such adrenaline rushes in real life.

My students and I have also found it useful to consider throughout the semester whether or not detective fiction should even be treated as serious literature. Early essays demonizing the genre provide some historical context to questions of canonicity and why detective fiction matters. Good essays to teach include any of the early periodical pieces denouncing detective dime novels as dangerous, especially for women and children, such as R.A. Knox's 1958 book *Literary Distraction*, which predicts the imminent demise of the genre, since all detective stories have been told; and Edmund Wilson's three famous *New Yorker* columns (reprinted in *Classics and Commercials*) claiming that detective fiction is the worst kind of addiction: "Why Do People Read Detective Stories?" (1944), "Who Cares Who Killed Roger Ackroyd?" (1945), and "Mr. Holmes, They Were the Footprints of a Giant Hound" (1945).

So what is at stake in the detective genre? What explains the continuing multiplication of detective texts despite the seemingly finite number of available plots? Poe and the dime novels are first in telling many of these classic plots: the locked room mystery, the problem of the lost object, the detective in disguise infiltrating criminal quarters, etc. They also provide the earliest exemplars of several techniques used in making detective fiction palatable (and, according to some, addictive): the use of a narrator close to the detective to tell his story, the competition between reader and detective, connections between philosophical statements and narrative embodiments of epistemology, and tropes of archnemesis and doubling.

Edgar Allan Poe (1809–1848)

Poe is clearly a critical figure in American letters, and a key early player in the development of Gothic, horror, science fiction, and detective fiction. His three detective short stories—"The Murders in the Rue Morgue" (1841), "The Mystery of Marie Rogêt" (1842), and "The Purloined Letter" (1845)— are often considered to be the first fully formed detective stories. They encapsulate many of the aesthetic and narrative moves that will follow in detective fiction. The stories introduce C. Auguste Dupin, the detective figure who uses what Poe called "ratiocination" (deductive reasoning) to deduce seemingly unknowable things about the people he meets. Dupin, an effete problem-solver who embodies the armchair detective, was a major influence on Sherlock Holmes and many of the drawing-room detective figures to follow. In teaching detective fiction, I have found it helpful to spend the first week or two of the semester on Poe's three short stories and to have students write a short paper connecting one aspect of these 160-plus-year-old texts to a detective narrative (print, television, film, or graphic novel) of today. All three stories are widely available online, being long in the public domain, so do not even require the purchase of a text.

"The Murders in the Rue Morgue" introduces students to the narrator-detective relationship we see repeated by Holmes and Watson. The relationship between Dupin and his unnamed narrator is worthy of discussion on many fronts. Perhaps most obviously, the unnamed narrator provides a mediating perspective for the reader, who joins the narrator in first admiring Dupin's uncanny observations and then slowly learning about the methods by which he attains them. Putting the reader directly into Dupin's masterful mind might be overwhelming, or worse, underwhelming, if the reader is unable to follow Dupin's brilliance without the mediating intervention of the narrator, or that brilliance might be diffused by being too readily available.

Tzvetan Todorov, one of the first serious critics of detective fiction, provides a structural analysis of the detective story that continues to define the genre today: a detective story must have doubled narrative strands, with the present-day narrative (perhaps separated only by a few hours) always telling the story of uncovering the narrative of the crime (46). Dupin and his unnamed narrator set the first standard for this structural feature, with the reader accompanying the narrator in imagining multiple explanations for the crime before rejecting the impossible solutions to find the correct one. Students are often familiar with some version of Sherlock Holmes' statement, "When you have excluded the impossible, whatever remains, however improbable, must be the truth" (from "The Beryl Coronet," but repeated with minor alterations throughout Sherlockia), and are often surprised that this principle is explained by Dupin to his narrator a full four decades before Holmes' first foray onto the pages of detective fiction.

Dupin and his unnamed narrator also provide students an entry into discussions of the homoerotics of the detective narrative, especially useful for courses addressing questions of gender. The narrator's clear admiration for Dupin is tinged by attraction, as he characterizes Dupin's friendship as "a treasure beyond price" (143) and sighs that into Dupin's love of the night, as into his other peculiarities, "I quietly fell; giving myself up to his wild whims with a perfect *abandon*" (144, his italics). Erotic implications in the relationship between the detective and his narrator are far from unique; one has but to look at the amount of slash fiction (fan fiction imagining erotic relationships) starring Watson and Holmes to see the pervasiveness of this reading. Dupin, in fact, exists within the framework of the nineteenth-century *flâneur*, the upper-class man who walks the streets of the city at night in order to experience the chaos of society that is unavailable to his more orderly world. The *flâneur*, as construed within the Poe stories, is a voyeur par excellence, and with that voyeurism comes an erotics common to detective fiction. Indeed, students with experience in gender theory may enjoy an assignment to trace the erotic resonances of "Rue Morgue" or other detective narratives through close reading.

As well, in his prefatory remarks to "The Murders in the Rue Morgue," Poe's narrator discourses at length on questions of epistemology — the nature of knowledge — that underlie the whole genre of detective fiction. I often use this relatively obscure statement to hone students' close reading skills. The preface opens with a statement about the difficulty of analyzing analytic abilities, moves through a discussion of the common confusion of the complex with the profound, and ends by suggesting that "the ingenious are always fanciful, and the *truly* imaginative never otherwise than analytic" (143), all within a discussion ostensibly about games. Students must make significant analytic leaps when asked (perhaps in groups if it is early in the semester) to apply one of the epistemological concepts put forward in the preface to an idea embodied in the story of "Rue Morgue."

Advanced students might also read this story through Elizabeth Grosz's notion of monstrous bodies: what, after all, is the aesthetic impact of the female victims' bodies being shoved up a chimney by an orangutan? One might also look to film critics like Laura Mulvey in thinking about the gaze of Dupin and his narrator upon the city and upon the Rue Morgue in particular. Film critics often ask questions that are also of interest to critics of detective fiction: who has access to the power of the gaze? Who gazes and who is gazed upon? What are the pleasures and pains of gazing?

"The Mystery of Marie Rogêt," which develops many of the themes introduced by "Rue Morgue," is perhaps most notable for its exploration of the relationship between reality and fiction. In this story, Poe recasts in Paris the much-publicized story of Mary Rogers, a young cigar girl in New York who disappeared and whose body was found floating in the Hudson River three days later. In "Marie Rogêt," Dupin solves the mystery largely from his armchair, where he listens as the narrator reads aloud newspaper accounts of the case and then puts forward the only plausible explanations. To explore the complexity of this story and its relationship to the real-life story, one might ask students to consider how this story is a "sequel" to "Rue Morgue," what this story says (implicitly or explicitly) about media representations of crime, and why the story is set in Paris instead of New York, where Mary Rogers was actually killed.

One might also use this story to discuss the game between reader and writer that has been codified in detective fiction by the rules of "fair play" that Raymond Chandler outlines in "The Simple Art of Murder" and that many early detective writers and critics reference: the writer must give the reader all relevant information so that a reader could potentially solve the mystery before or alongside the detective. Here Poe puts his fictional detective into competition with real-world New York police detectives, and therefore puts his readers in the position of watching a fictional detective best a real-life detective and/or entering into the competition him or herself, trying to deduce the solution to the mystery more quickly than the narrator, who will not know the solution until Dupin reveals it to him.

"The Purloined Letter," the most technically perfect of Poe's detective tales, expands the theme of private versus public detectives in its overt mockery of the Prefect of Police. The story also introduces the "hidden object" story so thoroughly developed within the English cozy (a type of story in which the crime typically occurs in a village or country house). And perhaps most importantly, this story introduces the archnemesis and the double, themes clearly expanded by Conan Doyle in the creation of Moriarty. The Minister D— is particularly emblematic of the dark doubling so commonly seen in criminals and detectives in most types of detective fiction. For an advanced undergraduate or graduate class, the literary theory devoted to Poe's "The Purloined Letter"—especially the famous articles by Jacques Lacan, Jacques Derrida, and Barbara Johnson—can provide critical rigor to the study of Poe and later detective texts.

Dime Novels

While Poe is acknowledged by most critics to be central to the detective narrative, dime novels, while not as rigorously studied, are also critical in providing students a strong foundation in the roots of detective fiction. Only two decades after Poe, the 1860s saw the arrival of a new format for American fiction: the dime novel. Alternately loved and feared, the dime novel became a mainstay of cultural production in the United States until its demise in the 1910s, sometimes placed at a single moment in 1917 with a change of postal rates, and sometimes seen as more gradual given its morphing into forms like early comic books. The term "dime novel" is actually a trademark, and half-dime novels as well as story papers are generally studied as part of the dime novel industry. Dime novels were printed on cheap paper, priced cheaply, and therefore widely accessible — appropriately so or far too much so depending on one's perspective.

It is within the dime novels that we see hack writers, generally in consultation with publishers who had their finger on the pulse of the public's desire, working out conventions that were adopted or rejected in later exemplars of several of the genre fictions we study today: the western, the adventure, science fiction, and, of course, detective fiction. Several dime novel weeklies were specifically titled *Detective Libraries* or *Stories of Detection*, and these texts, in my opinion, provide a crucial stop on the trajectory of the history of detective fiction in America.

Teaching the dime novel poses some challenges, since all but a few dime novels are long out of print, as befits their ephemeral nature, and much remains to be done within dime novel scholarship. Dime novels have been studied largely as historical artifacts, with *The Dime Novel Round-Up*, a bimonthly journal, and its editor's *The Dime Novel Companion* (Cox) the main source of scholarship. Alongside this approach, we find also socio-cultural explorations of dime novels, especially westerns, as historians and literary critics alike use these texts to better understand the cultural and literary history of the late nineteenth and early twentieth centuries. Classic critical works in this vein include Henry Nash Smith's *Virgin Land* (1950) and Richard Slotkin's *Gunfighter Nation* (1992). Michael Denning's *Mechanic Accents* (1987) changed the face of dime novel studies, employing as it does a cultural theory approach to understanding these ephemeral texts. Denning's study, an excellent introduction to American labor history and Marxist theory, studies dime novels as "a contested terrain, a field cultural conflict where signs with wide appeal and resonance take on contradictory disguises and are spoken in contrary accents" (3). Denning's approach, brilliant and incisive, drew attention to dime novels as a whole but had the unfortunate side effect of discouraging work on specific texts.

Unlike Denning, I believe that individual dime novels have a great deal to teach us. In fact, the dearth of scholarship on individual dime novels provides excellent opportunities for advanced undergraduate and graduate students to do original research. Moreover, the dime novel is a crucial step in the development of detective fiction, and reading a dime novel as a class introduces students to the form of popular fiction in which detective tropes were developed. If one's school library has a dime novel collection, introducing students to Rare Books will be invaluable. Teachers who do not have ready access to a dime novel collection, though, are likely to find librarians at their own or other institutions helpful at gaining copies of dime novels for study. Like the Poe short stories, almost all dime novels are in the public domain, so making copies of these texts (often thirty-two small-print pages) or directing students to online full-text archives falls within fair use.

I discuss here three types of detective dime novels, but numerous others would also be well suited for teaching. In a recent upper-level undergraduate class focusing on gender and epistemology in American detective fiction, I taught a fascinating dime novel, *The Broken Blackthorn; or, Hunting the Race-Course Robbers* (1883), from the "Allan Arnold" corpus. Dime novel publishers often used house names in which a number of writers contributed stories all published under a single name (usually an invented name, as "Allan Arnold" is) that functioned as a brand, alerting readers to the type of story they could expect. The Allan Arnold books tend to deal with gender in intriguing and forward-looking ways that anticipate later developments in the genre; other good titles for teaching include *The Dandy Detective* (1883), *A Diamond Ear-ring; or, Nina the Female Detective* (1888), and *Belle Boyd, the Girl Detective; or, A Story of Chicago and the West* (1891).

The Broken Blackthorn features Gay Gus Giles, a strong and effeminate detective who becomes embroiled in a plot full of Gothic elements as well as nascent detective conventions including disguise, the tension between physical and mental approaches to detection, the relationship between private and police detectives, and the construction of masculinity within detective work. The novel allowed us to discuss competing notions of gender performance in the story, as Gus, who can be seen as queerly performing his masculinity, is set up against a hypermasculine male villain and a morally complex female opponent whose femininity is often in question. In addition, the story can be much enhanced by reading it through the lens of Gayle Rubin's essay "The Traffic in Women: Notes toward a Political Economy of Sex," which argues that male bonds are often forged and maintained by the exchange of women through the institution of marriage. This is a common theme in early detective fiction, where the male detective often earns as his prize a young bride somehow attached to the victim. *The Broken Blackthorn* also raises questions of epistemology, since even within the framework of detective work that involves making deductions (borrowing from but less intellectual than Dupin's) and engaging in physical confrontations with suspects (gesturing forward to the hard-boiled), the status of knowledge is at stake. The talisman of the title introduces superstition as a legitimate way of knowing; the talisman's power is so great, in fact, that it must be destroyed at the end of the story, suggesting that superstition is both powerful and dangerous as a strategy for processing knowledge.

Another fine detective to explore with students is Nick Carter, by far the most famous dime novel detective. The Nick Carter series ran in various forms in the pulp magazines for a full fifty years, from 1886 to 1936. J. Randolph Cox, the leading expert on Nick Carter, estimates that there are approximately 1465 different Nick Carter stories, taking into account the habit of publishers to reissue stories, sometimes with a new title, without indicating their original publication date ("The Dime Novel Detective"). Numerous radio plays, films, and comic books featuring both Nick Carter and his apprentice/adopted son, Chick Carter, were produced well into the twentieth century. In fact, the *Nick Carter: Killmaster* series issued 261 paperback spy novels featuring the famous detective between 1964 and 1990. Over 100 authors have contributed Nick Carter stories, so it is not surprising that he is not an entirely consistent character. He is, however, centrally involved in the creation of an American heroism that marks him as very different from Sherlock Holmes, whose fictional career is almost exactly contemporaneous with Nick's.

Nick is a clear precursor to hard-boiled detectives. A text like *The Turn of a Card; or, Nick Carter Plays a Skillful Game* (1911), for example, allows a class to make the transition from nineteenth- to twentieth-century detective tropes, as this fascinating novel presents as Nick's adversary a femme fatale known only by her stage name of The Ace of Hearts. In his labyrinthine journey to better understand the woman who constantly eludes him, Nick is, like the James Bond figure he will become in the 1970s, placed in numerous tight situations from which his escape seems impossible and yet is managed. We find here the same combination of shrewd guesswork and adventure–driven legwork that marks the American hard-boiled narrative.

The dime novel is finally important in demonstrating to students that the fluidity of the detective genre is a defining feature even from its origins. Some of the most morally complex dime novels are those that cross genres, perhaps most importantly between detective stories and outlaw stories. Narratives about the outlaw brothers, Frank and Jesse James, and their gang of bandits were extremely popular throughout the 1880s and 1890s and even into the new century. Although most dime novel serials specialized in either outlaw stories or detective stories, a surprising number focused on the intersection between the two types of heroes, an ambivalence proclaimed in series titles like *The Jesse James Stories: A Weekly Dealing with the Detection of Crime* and *The New York Detective Library*, for a time subtitled, *The Only Library Containing True Stories of the James Boys.* The inclusion of outlaw stories in these detective publications shows not only far-reaching public interest in such stories; it also demonstrates a conceptual link between the story of the detective and that of the outlaw. Exploring any of the hundreds of detective-outlaw stories available among the dime novels helps students understand that it is partly the moral complexity of the detective figure, who can be effectively doubled by the outlaw, that accounts for not only the genre's popular appeal, but also its ability to sustain rigorous and ongoing critical attention from scholars.

WORKS CITED

Arnold, Allan. *Belle Boyd, the Girl Detective; or, A Story of Chicago and the West. The New York Detective Library* 457. New York: F. Tousey, 1891.

_____. *The Broken Blackthorn; or, Hunting the Race-Course Robbers. The New York Detective Library* 22. New York: F. Tousey, 1883.

_____. *The Dandy Detective. The New York Detective Library* 31. New York: F. Tousey, 1883.

_____. *A Diamond Ear-ring; or, Nina, the Female Detective. The New York Detective Library* 298. New York: F. Tousey, 1888.

Carter, Nicholas. *The Turn of a Card; or, Nick Carter Plays a Skillful Game. New Magnet Library* 1305. New York: Street & Smith, 1911.

Chandler, Raymond. "The Simple Art of Murder." *The Art of the Mystery Story: A Collection of Critical Essays.* Ed. Howard Haycraft. New York: Carroll & Graf, 1946. 222–37.

Cox, J. Randolph. *The Dime Novel Companion: A Source Book.* Westport, CT: Greenwood, 2000.

_____. "The Dime Novel Detective and His Elusive Trail: Twenty Years of Dime Novel Research." *Dime Novel Round-Up* 54.6 (1985): 90–94.

Denning, Michael. *Mechanical Accents: Dime Novels and Working-Class Culture in America.* London: Verso, 1987.

Derrida, Jacques. "The Purveyor of Truth." Trans. Willis Domingo. *Yale French Studies* 52 (1975): 31–113.

Grosz, Elizabeth. *Volatile Bodies: Toward a Corporeal Feminism.* Bloomington, IN: Indiana University Press, 1994.

Johnson, Barbara. "The Frame of Reference: Poe, Lacan, Derrida." *Yale French Studies* 55–56 (1977): 457–505.

Knox, R.A. *Literary Distractions.* New York: Sheed and Ward, 1958.

Lacan, Jacques. "Seminar on 'The Purloined Letter.'" Trans. Jeffrey Mehlman. *Yale French Studies* 48 (1972): 39–72.

Mulvey, Laura. "Visual Pleasure and Narrative Cinema." *Screen* 16.3 (1975): 6–18.

Poe, Edgar Allan. *Complete Tales and Poems*. New York: Vintage, 1975.

Rubin, Gayle. "The Traffic in Women: Notes Toward a Political Economy of Sex." *Toward an Anthropology of Women*. Ed. Rayna Reiter. New York: Monthly Review P, 1975. 157–210.

Sedgwick, Eve Kosofsky. *Between Men: English Literature and Male Homosocial Desire*. New York: Columbia University Press, 1992.

Slotkin, Richard. *Gunfighter Nation: The Myth of the Frontier in Twentieth-Century America*. New York: Atheneum, 1992.

Smith, Henry Nash. *Virgin Land: The American West as Symbol and Myth*. Cambridge, MA: Harvard University Press, 1950.

Todorov, Tzvetan. *The Poetics of Prose*. 1971. Trans. Richard Howard. Ithaca, NY: Cornell University Press, 1984.

Wilson, Edmund. *Classics and Commercials: A Literary Chronicle of the Forties*. New York: Farrar and Strauss, 1950.

Detective Fiction, Cultural Categories, and the Ideology of Criticism

STEPHEN BRAUER

In 1930, Sinclair Lewis, author of such novels as *Main Street*, *Babbitt*, and *Arrowsmith*, won the Nobel Prize for Literature. Although at the time he was seen as among the foremost American novelists, along with such writers as Edith Wharton, F. Scott Fitzgerald, and Ernest Hemingway, eighty years later it is difficult to find any of Lewis's novels on a college or high school syllabus for a course in American literature. That same year, 1930, Dashiell Hammett published *The Maltese Falcon*, the third of his five hard-boiled detective novels. Although the genre of detective fiction was commercially successful at the time, it had not received much critical support or plaudits. Moreover, the hard-boiled school was merely a niche in the genre and nowhere near as successful as the style known as the "puzzle story." Nonetheless, *The Maltese Falcon* (or *Red Harvest*, Hammett's first novel) is often present on college syllabi today, and not just for courses in detective fiction. What happened to Lewis's reputation since his heyday in the 1920s and 1930s? And how did Hammett become so established in an American literary tradition? To answer these questions, we need to consider the evolution in critical taste, and in the case of these questions, we especially need to explore the evolution of cultural categories and hierarchies. After all, in 1999, *Motherless Brooklyn*, a detective novel written by Jonathan Lethem, won the prestigious National Books Critics Circle Award. That is quite a change for how critics read a genre that Edmund Wilson — in his diatribe against detective fiction entitled "Who Cares Who Killed Roger Ackroyd?"— once dismissed as "rubbish" (153).

Looking at detective fiction and its critical reception over the last one hundred years can serve as a valuable means of getting at the changes in critical reputations and the changes in how critics have responded to different genres. During the Golden Age of Detective Fiction, in the 1920s and 1930s, such luminaries in the genre as Agatha Christie, Dorothy Sayers, Ellery Queen, Hammett, and others published a number of important novels.[1] While critics once saw these detective novels as exercises in a limited genre, they now treat them as a reflection of the culture in which they were produced, especially in relation to issues of gender, race, sexual orientation, and ideology. Tracing the historiography of criticism of these books and writers reveals the way in which critics have responded in fundamentally different ways than they did when the novels were first published. This not only demonstrates how critics treat the genre in a different way, but also demonstrates how ways of reading have developed over the last eighty years. A course on the evolution of cultural categories through the lens of detective fiction and its critical reception, then, can not only reveal changes in reader response to the genre; it can also illuminate the ideological battles at stake in the very act of reading.

I have placed at the heart of this investigation a research project that asks students to gather contemporaneous reviews of a detective novel written during the Golden Age and then to track the critical reception of that novel from that time period, through the different schools of thought and theory, to the present. Because of the wealth of information now available to us through research databases, locating and gathering these texts is much less onerous than it would have been before the onset of digital technology. Nonetheless, this is an extensive project that encompasses research, writing, and conceptual skills that many of my students do not possess before beginning the course, and helping students not only to integrate these materials into a single paper but also to synthesize them into an overall argument poses a challenge. Accordingly, I structure my syllabus so that I offer the students opportunities to develop these skills and competencies while also introducing them to literary concepts with which they are not familiar.

A useful way to begin such a course is by assigning a series of readings that debate ways of reading. Jonathan Culler's "Beyond Interpretation," M.H. Abrams's "How to Do Things with Texts," and Stanley Fish's "Is There a Text in This Class?" offer compelling examples of critics articulating varying approaches to a text, often in explicit opposition to one another's ideological position. If students have not had exposure to these types of debates before taking this class—as is the case with my students—having them read these spirited essays can demonstrate some of the complications and implications of reading according to a theoretical framework. Most of my students, for example, believe that the critic's job is to explicate the text, how it works, and what it means—and that these things have an essential or absolute quality to them. For them, a close reading that leads to an illumination of the author's intention is the sole appropriate manner of reading. Assigning Culler, Abrams, and Fish places my students in a discomfiting position that destabilizes their expectations of critical work, let alone their expectations of fiction, poetry, and drama.[2] That destabilization can serve quite well to set up the rest of the course — not only because the students will start to recognize that critics have agendas of their own, but because the students will begin to have a more complicated approach to the written word. This is especially valuable in a course that looks deeply at the workings of detective fiction, which, at its core, has a likewise deep-seated ambivalence with reading and writing. Reading these essays, in which established critics debate how best to read and interpret a text and the relationship between the writer and the reader, shows students how meaning is not something set in stone but is something negotiated and determined — much like solving a case.

We begin our reading of detective fiction with three stories by Edgar Allan Poe — "The Murders in the Rue Morgue," "The Mystery of Marie Rogêt," and "The Purloined Letter." These three stories feature the character Auguste Dupin, a lay detective and a character often cited as the first detective in the genre. These stories allow students to locate the origins of detective fiction and to introduce them to what is involved in the project of detective fiction. Poe begins "The Murders in the Rue Morgue" with a disquisition on observation and analysis, which sets the tone for the story that follows, which hinges a great deal on what Dupin gleans from a newspaper account of two murders. Dupin's close attention to detail allows him to discern a pattern in the testimonies of witnesses that all have a similar "peculiar" — the word is his — quality (155). This observation, and his pursuant analysis of that peculiarity, leads him to the stunning conclusion that an orangutan had committed the murders and escaped from the chambers in such a way that seemed to defy understanding. For Dupin, however, it was a matter of deductive reasoning: of determining the meaning through observation and rumination. The focus of each Dupin story is on the act and the process of ratiocination. Both the act and the process are central. As highlighted in "The Purloined Letter," Dupin tries to put himself in the mind of the criminal, to identify with him, and to perceive how the criminal perceives. This, he believes, enables him to solve the crime. In the case of "The Purloined Letter," a minister has stolen a private letter with potentially damaging information. After hearing the details of the protracted and perfectly thorough search that the police have undertaken of the minister's home, Dupin goes there himself and almost immediately spots the letter, which is hidden in plain sight and not in an especially ingenious hiding place. Achieving something close to the criminal's way of seeing the world allows Dupin to recognize the types of choices he would make if her were the criminal and therefore is able to locate the letter. Indeed, the focus on the process of deductive reasoning in each of the Dupin stories demonstrates that the act of detection is — at least in part — about the very act of constructing meaning. Often, the clues to solving the crime come from something written: the testimonies of the murder that were published in the newspaper, and the very letter itself. Reading and writing and the fundamental elements of language have a great deal to do with the solving of the crime for Dupin; moreover, because of our reliance on him to move us toward resolution, reading and writing — and the construction of meaning — are primary for us as readers as well. Like Poe's nameless narrator in the stories, these stories that track the resolution to a puzzle ultimately leave us to wonder how we ourselves determine meaning from a text.

After we discuss the stories, I assign a number of brief reviews and critical essays that focus on Poe's detective stories and ask students to write a paper in which they construct an argument about a single Poe story that considers an element of the story in relation to at least two of the critical perspectives.[3] I have found that selecting the criticism for the students allows them to focus on analyzing the argument and ideological position that the critic takes or enacts, and frees them from the difficulties of having to locate the criticism on Poe. Since the students begin by engaging with varying approaches to reading, and since Poe's stories themselves dramatize the act of making meaning, having the students recognize the act of criticism as an ideological one in relation to Poe himself serves well to connect the first parts of the course. This paper provides the students with an opportunity to begin to place critical perspectives in relation to one another, thereby helping them recognize an evolving critical consciousness about a text and preparing them for what they will do in their final project for the course.

Presenting students with the origins of detective fiction began to pay off for me as a professor when I learned to counterpoint Poe's stories with a more modern writer. An especially useful model for this is Ellery Queen's first novel, *The Roman Hat Mystery*.[4] This novel, published in 1929, is a classic example of the puzzle story, with a perfect crime that seems to have no possible solution. The book contains a "Lexicon of Persons Connected with the Investigation," a map of the scene of the crime, and other elements that allow the reader to garner as strong a sense as possible of the murder, the suspects, and the motive. In short, the novel is constructed to entice the reader to try to solve the crime, including the inclusion of an "interlude" in which the reader is challenged to name the killer. As such, it nicely represents the dominant mode of detective fiction in the 1920s and 1930s. *The Roman Hat Mystery* features Ellery Queen, a highly educated young man who operates much in the tradition of Dupin and Arthur Conan Doyle's Sherlock Holmes, an amateur sleuth who solves seemingly perfect crimes through a close attention to details, inconsistencies, and rigorous deductive analysis. Moreover, the novel seems also invested in Poe's interest in reading and writing. After all, Ellery Queen is the author of the novel but is also the main character in the novel, a young man who is a detective novelist. The complications of this structure, highlighted in the Foreword by an unknown "J.J. McC.," call attention to how meaning is determined through the process of laying out a narrative — much the same way that Dupin's stories operate.

Poe's stories and Queen's novel enact the construction of meaning, and through looking at the texts students can recognize how this is central to the genre of detective fiction. The differences between Poe and Queen, though, help students also distinguish the genre from a broader American literary tradition. Queen's novel ultimately serves to encourage the reader to participate in the solution to the mystery, in the construction of an answer that will make sense of what seems impossible. Poe's stories, however, do not offer this same sort of invitation. Indeed, the solutions to Poe's mysteries are ones that no readers could guess— an orangutan did it? This is not Poe's concern. Poe is much more invested in the very questions of logic and deduction, in what it means to construct meaning, than in concocting a situation that would entice a reader into a game of detection. (Indeed, much of Poe's writing in the detective stories focuses not on details of the mysteries but on disquisitions on observation, analysis, logic, deduction, and mathematics.) Placing Queen next to Poe, in other words, not only puts the genre of detective fiction into relief by looking at its origins and then its evolution in the twentieth century. That placement also helps us recognize how Poe is involved, in his detective stories, in a project that connects to writers like Charles Brockden Brown, Emerson, Henry James, Ralph Ellison, and others. How meaning is determined is not only a concern of detective fiction but is deeply embedded in the project of American literature. Making connections to these writers and others— especially Hawthorne in *The Scarlet Letter*, which takes the battle over determining the meaning of and impact of the "A" as a significant part of its very subject — helps students see how the genre is invested in many of the same forms found in canonical American literature, and helps students discern how even commercially minded writers like Ellery Queen can be invested in questions similar to those raised by the titans of the American canon.[5]

When it comes to helping students think further about cultural categories, reading commercially minded detective fiction like Ellery Queen next to writers like Poe and Hawthorne can very much push at students' expectations of texts and their presuppositions about the highbrow, middlebrow, and lowbrow. Indeed, following the linking of Queen and Poe, I try to show my students some of the writing on these categories that cultural critics produced in the early to middle twentieth century: including Van Wyck Brooks, "'Highbrow and 'Lowbrow'"; Gilbert Seldes, "People and the Arts"; Clement Greenberg, "Avant-Garde and Kitsch"; Dwight MacDonald, "Masscult and MidCult"; Leslie Fiedler, "The Middle Against Both Ends"; and Irving Howe,

"Notes on Mass Culture." These essays are often difficult for students, who frequently need a fair amount of historical context to make sense of the ideological arguments at play in the debates; however, these essays help to broaden my students' understanding of what can be at stake in cultural categories and how we approach a text, and they do so in a way that nicely complements the critical readings that we begin the semester with. The essays prompt the students to think about how critics contextualize cultural production for the public, as well about the ways that the public — and critics — consume those products. By the time the students make it through these essays, they usually want to engage more forcefully in discussions about who determines the value of a novel or genre, let alone who determines the meaning of them.

At this point in a course, it makes sense to turn back to detective fiction to further interrogate our expectations of the genre and of particular texts. Dashiell Hammett's *The Maltese Falcon* was published in 1930, a year after *The Roman Hat Mystery*, but though this novel features a detective, it bears little resemblance to the Queen novel. Sam Spade, Hammett's protagonist, is a hard-boiled detective and is nothing like Dupin; instead, Hammett modeled Spade on actual detectives he had known, and the characterization owes a debt to the portrayal of rugged individualism in western literature and the dime novels of the previous fifty years. The plot, moreover, is nothing like the puzzles of Queen and other contemporaries, but is grittier, more violent, and reflective of actual crimes. Hammett does not neatly fit student expectations of detective fiction that they acquire from reading Poe and Queen, and complicates what they think about the genre.

A particular episode in the novel highlights the way in which the novel is engaged in a project different from that of the puzzle writers: when Spade takes a moment from the investigation to tell the story of Flitcraft to Brigid O'Shaughnessy. Flitcraft was a married man who, one day, just managed to avoid having a falling beam hit him on the head. He immediately left town, his family, and his job and moved to a new city. Spade says that Flitcraft "felt like somebody had taken the lid off life and let him look at the works... .He knew then that men died at haphazard like that, and lived only while blind chance spared them.... What disturbed him was the discovery that in sensibly ordering his affairs he had got out of step, and not into step, with life" (63–64). Soon, though, Flitcraft established a new career and new family and carried on his life as if nothing had happened. After telling this story to Brigid, Spade returns to the investigation, and the whole vignette has no impact on the rest of the novel. Students tend to be stumped with this odd episode in the novel and are not sure how to make sense of it, but examining the episode with the students can help them recognize how Hammett seeks to situate himself in an American literary tradition, in this case by the story's allusion to Hawthorne's "Wakefield" and to the American tradition of naturalism, with its emphasis on chance and an individual's lack of agency. This episode takes the narrative outside the genre of detective fiction itself. It forces readers to consider how we can make sense of this odd episode in and of itself, but also how we can make sense of it within the novel proper. When we consider that the role of the detective in the genre is not only to determine meaning but to articulate it, this episode forces readers to interrogate how this role operates both within the plot itself and also in the very form of the novel. Hammett, then, seems interested not only in questions of genre in *The Maltese Falcon*, but in questions of narrative and in questions of the novel. Unlike Queen and the puzzle story writers, he seems to imagine himself within a tradition that exceeded that of detective fiction.[6]

It is valuable as a writing assignment to ask students to research the critical reception of Hammett from the time of his publication to the present. This enables them to build on the work of the Poe assignment, which asked them to contextualize critical work that they read in class, by directing them now to locate and select criticism.[7] It also serves as practice for the Final Project, in which they must choose their own author and track his critical reception from the time of his publication to the present.[8] These assignments, I have found, do a great deal to help students recognize the shifting critical reception of detective fiction, and especially help students grapple with shifting ideas about cultural hierarchies and categories from the 1920s and 1930s to the present. Moreover, it is in these assignments that the students best come to understand the ideological battles over literature that they first considered at the start of the semester. Now those battles center around an individual writer and a particular genre, and that focus helps them perceive the stakes of the debates more clearly.

In the last few weeks of the semester, I try to assign a couple of novels that clearly owe a debt to the detective genre but which also push at the bounds of that genre even further. Thomas Pynchon's *The Crying of Lot 49* is not a detective novel per se but does involve an investigation and an attempt on the part of Oedipa Maas to grapple with the complexity of the estate of Pierce Inverarity. Her task, then, is very much one of constructing knowledge and meaning. As she travels throughout California, pursuing clues that might help her unravel the mystery of Pierce's estate, Oedipa comes upon a series of signs— many of them literal ones, others tied up in plays, songs, and pamphlets— and tries to make sense of them in the context of the estate. As she proceeds, she eventually seems to realize that there is no way for her to make sense of all the myriad clues and signs that her investigation uncovers. The novel ends before the revealing of what she hopes will be the final clue, as if Pynchon is signaling that the search for meaning can never be realized. Pynchon, in other words, makes the construction of meaning, which has been the implicit work of the detective in the detective novel, the explicit work of this novel, literalizing it both for his protagonist and also for his readers.

Finally, Jonathan Lethem's *Motherless Brooklyn*, which operates as a straightforward detective novel, brings many of the threads of the course together. Although clearly genre fiction, Lethem's novel is also an award-winning literary novel and sits firmly within the American literary tradition established by Brockden Brown, Poe, Hawthorne, and other writers who explored issues of how we determine meaning and how language itself is the means through which we both formulate and articulate that determination. The novel begins with the protagonist, Lionel Essrog, listening to a wiretap and unable to make sense of the conversation he hears—setting up the novel's interest in our desire to make meaning and the way that language can actually shape the very way that we make meaning. Lionel is a detective with Tourette's Syndrome, and because of the way that this verbal tic occurs he makes meaning through the act of association. He says:

> The ducks were on the pond, the monkeys were in a tree, the birds wired, the fish barreled, the pigs blanketed: However the players in this tragic fever dream ought to be typed zoologically, I had them placed together now. The problem wasn't one of tracing connecting. I'd climbed into my Tracer and accomplished that. Now, though, I had to draw a single coherent line through the monkeys, ducks, fish, pigs, through monks and mooks—a line that accurately distinguished two opposed terms [274].

Lionel's process of making meaning—linguistic association—complements the act of detection. He realizes the inherent limitation in this—the book begins with the phrase, "Context is everything"—but also must operate accordingly, for he has no other choice (1). Lionel, for all his limitations, is rather sophisticated as to the foundation of his work—as well as to the fundamentals of the detective-fiction genre. Near the end of the novel, after he has solved the murder, he says, "Assertions are common to me, and they're also common to detectives.... And in detective stories things are always *always*, the detective casting his exhausted, caustic gaze over the corrupted permanence of everything and thrilling you with his sweetly savage generalizations" (307). Like Dupin, like Spade, like so many of the detectives that came before him, Lionel makes assertions of meaning, and readers accept the logic of the solution because the act of assertion serves to resolve the uncertainty and instability that the original crime initiated.

Along with Pynchon, Lethem's self-consciousness about language and detection makes his novel a fitting place to end this course and serves to complicate the students' expectations of the genre of detective fiction as they are working on their historiographic rendering of the critical reception of a single detective writer from earlier in the twentieth century.[9] Students recognize that writers like Pynchon, Lethem, Paul Auster, and Michael Chabon — all of whom have written detective fiction — belong in a literary tradition that is not tied simply to a genre. They start to comprehend that these writers use the genre to pursue literary goals, much the same way that critics read novels based on particular ideological approaches. Teaching detective fiction can help students understand the evolution of cultural categories and the ways in which the genre has moved from the literary margins to a space firmly within the canon of American literature, and it can help students adopt a more sophisticated, and self-conscious, approach to any literary text.

NOTES

1. Although one could choose detective fiction that originates from many different countries, I have chosen in my course to limit the readings to American fiction so as to more easily help students recognize and grapple with the literary and cultural contexts at play in the literature.

2. Indeed, one student in my class broke down in tears during class in the fall of 2007 when we discussed these essays. She felt she had been misled for so many years— from junior high, through high school and into college — by teachers and professors who had implied that the new criticism was the sole way to read. The challenge that these critics posed to her was not in the complexity of their arguments but in the realization that she had been taking an ideological position in her reading practice her whole life without ever having realized it.

3. I detail this assignment in Appendix A. I try to assign critical perspectives that take students through a historical time span, so that they can experience different types of critical perspectives and different types of critical approaches to the literature. For Poe, the articles include John Robert Moore, "Poe, Scott, and 'The Murders in the Rue Morgue'"; Howard Haycraft, "Time: 1841— Place: America," from *Murder for Pleasure*; Liahna Armstrong, "The Shadow's Shadow: The Motif of the Double in Edgar Allan Poe's 'The Purloined Letter'"; and John T. Irwin, "Detective Fiction as High Art: Lacan, Derrida, and Johnson on 'The Purloined Letter.'"

4. Ellery Queen was the pseudonym for two cousins, Manfred Lee and Frederick Dannay, who wrote the novels collaboratively. For simplicity's sake, though, I will refer to Queen as one writer and will do my best to distinguish Queen the writer from Queen the character within the novel.

5. For this reason — the ability to see connections to lots of other American writers and literary movements— I have found that this course works best if students have already received a grounding in American literature and can recognize many of these links.

6. Using Raymond Chandler would work to this effect as well, especially with *The Big Sleep* and its use of the romance as a complementary (or even counter) genre to detective fiction. Chandler's interest in the chivalric tradition, and his linking of it to the rugged individualism of hard-boiled detective fiction, not only had a huge influence

on other writers, it also pushed at the boundaries of the genre and of readers' expectations of the genre.

7. See Appendix B for this assignment.

8. I have copied the final project assignment in Appendix C. In this assignment, I try to help the students by giving them some suggestions as to which writer they should choose. Because many of these writers are no longer very much in print, I have found that identifying them for the students gets them started more quickly and helps move them more readily into the research process.

9. Paul Auster's *The New York Trilogy* is another valuable text to have students read near the end of the semester, as these three stories very nicely complement the work of earlier writers such as Poe and Hawthorne, as well as Hammett.

WORKS CITED

Abrams, M. H. "How to Do Things with Texts." *Critical Theory Since 1965*. Ed. Hazard Adams and Leroy Searle. Tallahassee: Florida State University Press, 1986. 436–49.

Armstrong, Liahna. "The Shadow's Shadow: The Motif of the Double in Edgar Allan Poe's 'The Purloined Letter.'" *The Selected Writings of Edgar Allan Poe*. Ed. G.R. Thompson. New York: Norton, 2004. 863–73.

Auster, Paul. *The New York Trilogy*. New York: Penguin, 1990.

Brooks, Van Wyck. "'Highbrow' and 'Lowbrow'" from "America Comes of Age." *Three Essays on America*. New York: E.P. Dutton, 1934.

Chandler, Raymond. *The Big Sleep*. New York: Vintage, 1988.

Culler, Jonathan. "Beyond Interpretation." *The Pursuit of Signs: Semiotics, Literature, Deconstruction*. Ithaca, NY: Cornell University Press, 1981. 3–17.

Fiedler, Leslie. "The Middle Against Both End." *Mass Culture: The Popular Arts in America*. Ed. Bernard Rosenberg and David Manning White. New York: Free Press, 1964. 537–47.

Fish, Stanley. "Is There a Text in This Class?" *Is There a Text in This Class*? Cambridge: Harvard University Press, 1980. 303–21.

Greenberg, Clement. "Avant-Garde and Kitsch." *Mass Culture: The Popular Arts in America*. Ed. Bernard Rosenberg and David Manning White. New York: Free Press, 1964. 98–110.

Hammett, Dashiell. *The Maltese Falcon*. New York: Vintage, 1989.

Haycraft, Howard. *Murder for Pleasure*. New York: Appleton-Century, 1941.

Howe, Irving. "Notes on Mass Culture." *Mass Culture: The Popular Arts in America*. Ed. Bernard Rosenberg and David Manning White. New York: Free Press, 1964. 496–503.

Irwin, John T. "Detective Fiction as High Art: Lacan, Derrida, and Johnson on 'The Purloined Letter.'" *The Selected Writings of Edgar Allan Poe*. Ed. G.R. Thompson. New York: Norton, 2004. 941–52.

Lethem, Jonathan. *Motherless Brooklyn*. New York: Vintage, 1999.

MacDonald, Dwight. "Masscult and MidCult." *Mass Culture: The Popular Arts in America*. Ed. Bernard Rosenberg and David Manning White. New York: Free Press, 1964. 59–73.

Moore, John Robert. "Poe, Scott, and 'The Murders in the Rue Morgue.'" *American Literature* 13 (Mar. 1936): 52–58.

Poe, Edgar Allan. *Complete Stories and Poems of Edgar Allan Poe.* New York: Doubleday, 1984.

Pynchon, Thomas. *The Crying of Lot 49.* New York: Perennial, 2006.

Queen, Ellery. *The Roman Hat Mystery.* New York: Signet, 1979.

Seldes, Gilbert. "People and the Arts." *Mass Culture: The Popular Arts in* America. Ed. Bernard Rosenberg and David Manning White. New York: Free Press, 1964. 74–97.

Wilson, Edmund. "Who Cares Who Killed Roger Ackroyd?" *Mass Culture: The Popular Arts in America.* Ed. Bernard Rosenberg and David Manning White. New York: Free Press, 1964. 149–53.

APPENDIX A

Paper on Poe's Detective Stories

In a paper of at least five pages, construct an argument about a single Poe story that considers an element of the story in the context of the varying critical perspectives you have read in the last week or so. Please include a Works Cited Page.

As part of your argument about the story, you need to analyze key passages and situate them within the critical perspectives on the story. Be sure to engage with at least two of the critical responses we have read, and to quote directly from them. Be sure to accurately represent each writer's position and thinking.

APPENDIX B

Critical Review Paper

In an essay of at least six double-spaced, stapled pages, trace the critical reception of *The Maltese Falcon* from its publication to the present. In the essay you will need to analyze individual responses to the novel and to summarize the overall nature of the critical reception. Be sure to use MLA citation style and to include a Works Cited List.

To complete this essay, you need to locate *four* writers who critique the novel, analyze each critical take on the novel, and evaluate how that critical position fits into the larger reception of the novel. Quote from each of these critics to illustrate their position and to demonstrate the validity of your analysis of their critique.

Be sure to offer a brief summary of each critique, to analyze its critical position in relation to the novel (and perhaps in relation to the genre), and to place the critique in the context of the others you are discussing.

APPENDIX C

Final Project

For a final project, I would like you to choose a writer from the list below and trace the critical reception of this writer from the time of first publication to the present.

Construct an argument about how critics have read and where they have placed this writer in terms of the detective genre or the broader literary canon.

You will find it necessary to read some of the writer's novels to give you a sense of the work and so that you can have a strong grasp on the critical reception of the writer. Do not wait too long to do this, as some of these novels may be somewhat difficult to locate and you may need to use interlibrary loan or to order these books online in order to locate them.

You will also need to search databases and library catalogues to locate critical sources. Put the databases to good use and always be sure to check out the footnotes, citations, and bibliographies of any critical sources for what they might offer in terms of other sources you can pursue. Again, you may need to utilize interlibrary loan to do some of this work.

This paper should be at least twelve double-spaced, typed, stapled, and numbered pages, with a title. You must include at least four critical sources in addition to any primary sources you utilize in your paper. Be sure to quote from your sources and to cite using MLA style. You will need to include a Works Cited page.

Novelists to choose from:

John Dickson Carr
Raymond Chandler
Carroll John Daly
Erle Stanley Gardner
Ellery Queen
Rex Stout
S. S. Van Dine

Teaching International
Detective Fiction

PATRICIA P. BUCKLER

If there were only one reward for studying and teaching detective fiction from around the world, it would be the discovery of Edogawa Rampo, Japan's first mystery writer. Edogawa Rampo, whose pen name is a play on "Edgar Allan Poe," was Hirai Taro (1894–1965), a writer whose earliest works developed the Gothic forms of Poe into Japanese models. His first story, "Nisen-Doka" ("The Two-Sen Copper Coin," 1923), employs a cryptogram using Japanese Kanji. He virtually created the crime and mystery genre in Japan, and before the wars in Asia and the Pacific, his dark and grotesque fiction found a large audience. Eventually the censorship of the war years turned him away from the Gothic and toward detectives featured in adventure tales. His detective, Akechi Kogoro, is seen as the counterpart of Sherlock Holmes. Rampo founded the Japan Association of Mystery Writers. His influential and popular works remain in print and are still used in film, television, and theater.

Rampo demonstrates the idea that the mystery and detective genre, although created and popularized in the United States and Europe, appeals directly across cultures, sharing human traits of attraction to the mental challenge of puzzle solving, fascination with deviant/criminal behavior, the satisfaction of closure, the discovery and punishment or elimination of the guilty, admiration for the detective hero, and the enjoyment of suspense and surprise.

American students find mysteries appealing for all the same reasons. When they read mysteries set in foreign countries, they recognize the same fundamental quest that they find in English and American mystery stories with the added value of seeing the journey through the eyes of a different culture.

Rampo is only one example of international authors who have introduced the American or British model of the ratiocinative detective into their national literatures. Successful examples can be found in most European countries, Latin America, Asia, and Australia. Frequently these models have been succeeded by a hard-boiled brand of sleuth. But in almost all cases, once the imitative detective has succeeded, national authors have developed their own national detective typologies.

Once you start delving into international detective fiction, you will find that selecting from so many intriguing works and fascinating contexts will be the hardest task. Among the many issues to address, first of all is whether the selected text is available in English (unless you are teaching the course in a foreign language) and in print. Even the books of popular American writers such as Marcia Muller are not always available, so often pedagogy must submit to practicality.

Naturally, students who know nothing about the genre to begin with need to be exposed to the basic requirements of the detective story along with useful terminology. (See the appendices at the end of this essay.) After all, they cannot determine if an Israeli detective follows the hard-boiled, ratiocinative, or cozy pattern if they do not understand the difference. Personally, I begin every detective fiction course with Edgar Allan Poe's three stories "The Murders in the Rue Morgue," "The Purloined Letter," and the "Mystery of Marie Rogêt." They provide a base from which to build whatever house of mystery I'm planning.

Another important choice is the unifying idea of the course. For instance, my course in 2004 attempted to use detectives from more familiar European countries and English-speaking countries before turning to the more exotic locales of Japan and Botswana. (Although, for sure, the Australian aboriginal setting of Arthur Upfield's novels is pretty alien.) A professor may choose to use detective stories from a specific part of the world (European Union countries, for example); or a particular culture (such as Latin American and Hispanic, Asian, or Jewish); an explicit type of detective (female, hard-boiled, cozy, Marxist, blue-collar, intellectual, and so forth); or simply a smorgasbord of offerings such as my own. High school and middle school teachers look for stories that meet curricular guidelines and avoid objectionable language and explicit sex. (Alexander McCall Smith's series, The No.1 Ladies Detective Agency, set in Botswana, has proved a good choice at these levels.)

My detective fiction courses in the past were offered at the advanced undergraduate-graduate level during an eight-week summer session, so the selection of works depended on type of student and time allotted. Since detective novels are fast reading for me, I originally overestimated how many books my students could manage in eight weeks. Some English majors later confessed that they finally finished the reading list over the Thanksgiving break!

Besides placing my syllabus at the end of this chapter, I will also include some of the assignments I use to help the students become more involved in the literature, including a "Create Your Own Detective" exercise and a list of authors suggested for oral reports. I find this latter assignment works well for exposing the class to many authors we just do not have time to cover, and, of course, it gives students an opportunity to explore their own interests. Two English majors actually proceeded to develop their assignments into full-blown senior capstone projects. One wrote her own detective story, and another wrote a paper on Paul Mann's India novels.

My hope for this essay is to give other teachers some ideas and methods for constructing their own courses about international detective fiction. Approaches to teaching international detective fiction are as numerous and varied as there are teachers. You can focus your course on them as literature, culture, sociology, popular culture, or history. Traditional literary analysis of plot, character, theme, and other formal elements can be used. Current critical theories always apply. In making my own choices, I hold one rule above all others — teach only the mysteries that I myself admire and enjoy. The worldwide fascination with this genre is phenomenal, it is part of mainstream culture, and it is a valuable mirror of current life. The following discussion should offer some doors into this literature of the world.

Poe's "The Murders in the Rue Morgue," "The Purloined Letter," and the "Mystery of Marie Rogêt" take place in a foreign venue and with a foreign detective. Although C. Auguste Dupin is considered to be more like Poe himself than a French detective (Dorff), these stories established the international spirit of the genre.

In her comprehensive article "The French Connection: A Short History of the *Roman Policier* from Vidocq (the real-life founder of the Sûreté) to Simenon's Maigret to France's Currently Bestselling Crime Writer, Frédéric Dard," Susan L. Dorff points out how the native French detective developed from the work of the first detective police force, founded in 1811 by François Eugene Vidocq. Consequently, the police detective became the template for French detectives. In the 1930s, Georges Simenon created the most popular and well-known French detective hero, Maigret. Still a bestseller around the world, Maigret represents a deeply French yet decipherable detective for American students.

More interesting yet, but also more advanced, would be consideration of the Nouveau Roman detective novel. This type of work "calls into question most of our expectations of what a narrative should be — in terms of plot, psychology, character, logical and chronological sequences" (Sirvent). Michel Sirvent, in fact, argues that the "post–Nouveau Roman detective novel" is a hybrid of the early Nouveau Roman with traditional detective novel features. He refers to works by Jean Lahougue (*Comptine des Height*), Benoit Peeters (*La Bibliothèque de Villers*), and George Perec (*53 Jours*) as examples of this new breed of fiction.

For a very different approach to crime fiction on the continent, there is

Boris Akunin (Grigory Chkhartishvili), whose Russian series featuring Erast Petrovich Fandorin is set in 1876. The story of Chkhartishvili and his work offers insights into the transformation of Russian literature along with the Russian state since the early 1990s. He is a philologist and translator whose highly intellectual works are deep but not popular. Akunin's books have only begun to be translated into English since 2004, but they provide students with a double experience — the literary movements in modern free Russia and the atmosphere and attitudes of Czarist Russia. Chkhartishvili has started two other series — one with a crime-solving nun set in the nineteenth century, and one featuring Fandorin's grandson set in modern times. According to T.J. Binyon, another value to the novels is their many allusions to Russian history and literature. Students who so desire (or professors who desire them to do so) can research these topics. The novels, Binyon adds, are not as dull as they sound: "They are extraordinarily readable, full of incident and excitement, swift-moving, at times hilariously funny, and told with a sparkling light-heartedness which is impossible to resist."

Another fascinating look at post–Soviet literature is provided by Alexandra Marinina (Marina Anatolyevna Alexeveya), an author extremely popular in Russia whose works are now appearing in English. Her heroine is Anastasia Kamenskaya, a detective from the Moscow CID. Marinina has written over thirty novels and plays, some of which were turned into a smash television series. Although best sellers, her books have been criticized as showing a Soviet sensibility and even for trying to portray KGB officers as heroes (Ivanova). Nevertheless, an examination of emerging literatures in former Soviet bloc countries would be worthwhile for students.

Numerous other detective writers from Nordic and Baltic countries as well as Russia offer stories to consider for an international course. In fact, a group of authors and fans gathered in 2005 in Vilnius, Lithuania, to explore Nordic crime fiction at the Vilnius Alibi Festival. Writers in attendance included Arne Dahl (Sweden), Leif Davidsen (Denmark), Raidas Dubrė (Lithuania), Leena Lehtolainen (Finland), Birutė Mackonytė (Lithuania), Aleksandra Marinina (Russia), Jo Nesbø (Norway), Eeva Park (Estonia), Jānis Ivars Stradiņš (Latvia), and Árni Thórarinsson (Iceland). The Festival published an online book of mystery stories set in Vilnius by seven of the authors, and as of December 14, 2007, the stories in English were still available online at <http://www.vilniusalibi.lt/index.php/book_of_the_festival/240>.

Latin America's supply of detective fiction is widespread. According to Latin-American scholar Ilan Stavans, himself a writer of detective novels, "Art and literature in Latin America are, have always been, richly, ethnically diverse, ideologically explosive. Proof of it is the incredible output, since the late nineteenth century, of literary private eyes and time-travelers; one very few readers abroad know about." Besides the highly intellectual private eye created by Jorge Luis Borges, there are more accessible detectives in works by Hernando Tellez, Rodolfo J. Walsh, Enrique Anderson Imbert, Maria Elvira Bermudez, Antonio Helu, and Pepe Martinez de la Vega. Detective fiction in the Hispanic world, Stavans says, is morally ambiguous, and "good doesn't triumph over evil ... [but it] is about intellectual tricks and corrupt authority figures, not about reason mastering the chaos of nature" (2–5). Argentina, especially, is considered the birthplace and nursery of Latin American detective stories.

The most popular Spanish language detective writers are Manuel Vázquez Montalbán (Spain) and Paco Ignacio Taibo II (Mexico). They have found a true Spanish voice in the *novela negra,* based on the noir hard-boiled formula. According to José F. Colmeiro, the legitimate incorporation of detective fiction into Spanish literature comes from the hard-boiled genre's ability to focus more on motivation, social context, and "the unmasking and indictment of a corrupt social order" (55). Montalban is credited with bringing the noir novel into Spanish culture. The spread of this new, uniquely Spanish style detective story to Latin America shows "a communion of interests, experiences, and cultural practices" (Colmeiro 57). Montalban's works are matched by those of Mexican author Taibo. Both produce culturally authentic characters and situations, although Taibo's are very Mexican while Montalban's reflect his own Catalan and Galician roots. "Taibo's detective, Belascoaran Shayne, has working class and democratic sensibilities and relies on becoming personally involved in other peoples' lives" (Martin 17).

With over 44 million Americans classifying themselves as of Latino or Hispanic descent, and more than 2½ million enrolled in high school and nearly 2 million in college (U.S. Census Bureau), the study of detective novels in the Spanish and Latin American cultures would be productive, valuable and exciting. Teachers of English or Spanish would find students more readily engaged in detective stories that reflect their own backgrounds.

Italy shares the international enthusiasm for detective stories, called *gialli,* written by both Italians and foreigners. (The term *il giallo* [yellow] comes from the mass of early detective novels published in yellow covers by Mondadori Press.) The fascist Italian government fostered the creation of indigenous Italian detectives by decreeing in the 1930s that at least one-third of all publications must feature Italian detectives. Furthermore, the books were to have pleasant, straightforward, nice characters while the victims and perpetrators had to be foreigners. All Italian characters had to be portrayed as good, hard-working, and upstanding citizens, and no contemporary politics were allowed.

The first "national detective" was invented by Alessandro Varaldo, who in 1931 introduced Ascanio Bonichi, a Dupin/Poirot type ratiocinative sleuth, with a superior intellect, egg-shaped head, Toscano cigars, bowler hat, trench coat, and correct forensic methods (Lombardi). He appeared in eight novels between 1932 and 1941, beginning with *Le Scarpette Rosse* (*The Red Slippers*). However, the author credited with introducing a distinctively Italian approach to the genre is Augusto De Angelis, with the creation of a "serious and talented Italian police procedural set in Milan. His detective/commissioner, De Vincenzi, was a literate and clever hero who attempted to get inside the criminal's mind" (Somigli 71). Two other Italian authors, Sicilians Leonardo Sciascia and Andrea Camilleri, initiated a watershed of modern Italian detective writers. Both writers deal frankly with the sociopolitical landscape of Sicily, exposing and criticizing the vicious operations of mafia families.

Two outsiders who created Italian detectives are American Donna Leon and Briton Michael Dibdin. Dibdin's Aurelio Zen is a special cases officer who moves to different cities in order to pursue criminal investigations. Commissario Guido Brunetti, on the other hand, remains anchored in Venice. Both writers have foreign readers in mind, and Leon has actually never been translated into Italian. Native Italians and foreigners share a fascination with the unique and flawed criminal justice system in Italy.

In the early twentieth century, China had its share of fictional detectives based on Western stereotypes. Huo Sang, created by Cheng Xiaoqing, first appeared in 1914 in *The Human Shadow in the Lamplight*. Based on Sherlock Holmes, his Watson was a former boxer named Bao Lang. Huo Sang does not use cocaine or play the violin, but he is noted for using scientific method in solving cases. He repeatedly battles the same criminal enemies such as Hairy Lion and his Five Blessings Gang, has informants in the underworld, and maintains contacts with the local police force. He is well informed like Holmes and is very "Westernized, dressing in Western-style suits and ties, packing guns, smoking cigarettes and wearing a brimmed felt hat" ("Huo Sang").

China today is emerging from a long, bleak, anti-literary and anti-intellectual era, but some new Chinese detectives are on the scene already. Qiu Xiaolong and Diane Wei Liang have created modern Chinese detectives who are forced into cases that draw them into the brutal Maoist period of labor camps, Red Guards, famine, and slaughter. Every investigation can potentially lead there, since the present is only a surface supported by the legs of this nightmare past. Qiu Xiaolong's series commenced in 2000 with *Death of a Red Heroine*, quickly followed by *A Loyal Character Dancer* (2002), *When Red Is Black* (2004), and *A Case of Two Cities* (2006). Chief Inspector Chen Cao of the Shanghai Police Bureau treads deftly through the political quagmire of Shanghai, struggling to sustain his personal integrity while avoiding a career catastrophe. Like P. D. James's detective, Adam Dalgliesh, he is a poet whose immersion in police work does not prevent him from appreciating the rich significance of China's past and present culture. This series is beautifully written with a wealth of information and insight into China's ongoing transformation.

Diane Wei Liang's series featuring Mei Wang has only two entries so far, but they reveal much about Beijing and its modern generation. Mei runs her own private investigation business and even has a male secretary. *The Eye of Jade* is an elusive mystery that is driven by her family's past and the Cultural Revolution. Her second mystery, *Paper Butterfly*, will be out in 2008. Although both of these Chinese series are written by expatriates, they offer realistic impressions of life in China today and are especially relevant in relation to the Beijing Olympic Year, 2008.

My expectations for Israeli mysteries, I confess, were originally along the lines of the book and film *Exodus*— thrilling plots with deep underground operations and political consequences, starring agents of the Institute for Intelligence and Special Operations (the Mossad). Instead, there are two rather normal detectives in modern Israeli detective literature, Lizi Badichi, created by Shulamit Lapid, and Michael Ohayon, created by Batya Gur. Most of Lapid's books so far have not made it into English, but five of Gur's books have been published in the United States: *The Saturday Morning Murder* (1992), *Literary Murder* (1993), *Murder on a Kibbutz* (1994), *Murder Duet* (1999), and *Bethlehem Road Murder* (2003). Gur's books have been widely read in English, and Margalit Fox wrote in a *New York Times* obituary for Gur in 2005: "While Ms. Gur's novels were ostensibly police procedurals, they were no ordinary whodunits. Her mysteries were less about the death of the body than they were sustained, thoughtful explorations of the life of the mind."

The vast supply of high quality fiction in the detective genre makes covering the world impossible in a few pages here or even in a full-semester course. But teaching this fiction has led me on a challenging and fascinating journey into the unknown, and I have had a splendid trip. You will too.

WORKS CITED

Binyon, T.J. "A Criminal Talent." *Rusnet.nl. Print version.* 13 May 2003. 12 Dec. 2007 <http://www.rusnet.nl/news/2003/05/17/print/culture01.shtml>.

Colmeiro, José F. "The Hispanic (Dis)Connection: Some Leads and a Few Missing Links." *Journal of Popular Culture* 34.4 (Spring 2001): 49–65.

Dorff, Susan L. "The French Connection: A Short History of the *Roman Policier* from Vidocq (the real-life founder of the Sûreté) to Simenon's Maigret to France's Currently Bestselling Crime Writer, Frédéric Dard." *The Armchair Detective* 22.4 (1989): 374–80.

The Edogawa Rampo Reader. Kurodahan Press. Intercom LTD 2007. 12 Dec. 2007 <http://www.kurodahan.com/e/catalog/titles/j0020.html>.

Fox, Margalit. "Batya Gur, Mystery Writer and Critic, Is Dead at 57." *New York Times.* 30 May 2005 *nytimes.com.* 14 Dec. 2007 <http://www.nytimes.com/2005/05/30/obituaries/30gur.html?>.

"Huo Sang." *Pulp and Adventure Heroes.* 14 Dec. 2007 <http://www.geocities.com/jjnevins/pulpsh.html>.

Ivanova, Natal'ia. "Why Russia Chose Putin: Alexandra Marinina I Contexts Literary and Otherwise." *Russian Social Science Review* 46.1 (Jan.-Feb. 2005): 65–80.

Lombardi, Patrizia. "The Persona of the Italian Detective Then and Now." Conference Presentation. Murder and Mayhem in Mare Nostra Conference. Monash University Prato, Prato, Italy. 6 July 2004.

Martin, Jorge Hernandez. "On the Case." *Americas* (English Edition) 47.2 (March–April 1995): 16–21. InfoTrac Web. Expanded Academic ASAP. Purdue University North Central Library, Westville, IN. <http://www.infotrac.galegroup.com>.

Myers, Steven Lee. "A Russian Intellectual Turns to Crime (Fiction)." RUSNET.NL. Print version 17 May 2003. 28 June 2004 <http://www.rusnet.nl/news/2003/05/17/print/culture01.shtml>.

Sirvent, Michel. "Reader-Investigators in the Post-Nouveau Roman: Lohogue, Peeters, and Perec." *The Romanic Review* 88.2 (March 1997): 315–21. InfoTracWeb. Expanded Academic ASAP. Purdue University North Central Library, Westville, IN. 13 March 2004. <http://www.infotrac.galegroup.com>.

Somigli, Luca. "The Realism of Detective Fiction: Augusto de Angelis, Theorist of the Italian *Giallo.*" *Symposium* 59.2 (Summer 2005): 70–83.

Stavans, Ilan. "Introduction"Private Eyes and Time Travelers." *The Literary Review* 38.1 (Fall 1994): 5–16. Expanded Academic ASAP. Purdue University North Central Library, Westville, IN. 12 June 2004. <http://web4.infotrac.galegroup.com/itw/info-mark/869/281/52352941w4/purl=rc1_EAIM_0>.

U.S. Census Bureau. "American FactFinder." 14 Dec. 2007 <http://factfinder.census.gov/servlet/DTTable?_bm=y&-geo_id=01000US&-ds_name=ACS_2006_EST_G00_&-mt_name=ACS_2006_EST_G2000_B03001>.

_____. "American FactFinder." 14 Dec. 2007 <http://factfinder.census.gov/servlet/DTTable?_bm=y&-geo_id=D&-ds_name=D&-_lang=en&-redoLog=false&-mt_name=DEC_2000_SF3_U_P147H>.

Appendix A

SYLLABUS FOR SUMMER COURSE 2004
(International Detective Fiction)

The goal for this course is to look seriously at detective fiction both as literature and as cultural artifact (nay, cultural phenomenon). We will establish the conventions of detective fiction and then examine how the genre is used in novels from different countries and cultures.

Reading List

Maj Sjöwall & Per Wallöö. *The Laughing Policeman.* Tr. Alan Blair. Vintage Crime/Black Lizard, 1992. ISBN 0–679–74223–9.

Leonardo Sciascia. *To Each His Own*. Tr. Adrienne Foulke. New York Review Books
  Classics, 2000. ISBN 0–940–32252–8.
Alexander McCall Smith. *The No. 1 Ladies' Detective Agency*. Anchor Books, 2002. ISBN
  1–4000–3477–9.
Arthur W. Upfield. *Murder Down Under*. Scribner, 1998. ISBN 0–684–85059–1.
Michael Dibdin. *Blood Rain*. Vintage/Black Lizard, 2001. ISBN 0–375–40915–7.
Seichi Matsumoto. *Inspector Imanishi Investigates*. Tr. Beth Carey. Soho, 1989. ISBN
  1–56947–019–7.
M.C. Beaton. *Death of a Charming Man*. Mysterious Press, 1994. ISBN 0–446–40338–5.
Georges Simenon. *Maigret and the Wine Merchant*. Harvest Books, 2003. ISBN 0–156–
  02844–1.
Gail Bowen. *Murder at the Mendel*. McClelland & Stewart, 2000. ISBN 0–771–01492-9.
Boris Akunin. *The Winter Queen*.

Requirements

6 Mini-Papers (2–3 pages or 500–750 words) (30%)
Mid-term Exam (20%)
Final Exam (20%)
1 Oral Presentation (15%)
Quizzes & Homework (15%)

Reading — First and foremost, you must keep up with the reading. Since the course will
include much class discussion, you must be familiar with the texts if you are to participate fully. Have all novels read before class on the first day assigned and prepare to discuss them. A factual reading quiz will be given for each work. (Most of these books are
"quick reads" so it should be possible to keep up.)

Quizzes — Will be given on each assigned reading the day it is due. Missed quizzes cannot be made up. Homework assignments such as informal writing assignments, bits of
research, etc., will be made as the class progresses.

Papers — Six short papers written outside of class. Papers will be 2–3 pages (500–750
words). Papers must be formatted and documented following the requirements of the
Modern Language Association (MLA).

Oral Presentation — You will have the opportunity to report to the class on a mystery
writer of your choice. A list of recommended authors will be provided upon request.

Graduate Credit — Students registered for English 596 will meet additional requirements, to be discussed.

Tentative Calendar

JUNE

M 7   Introduction and overview of course. You already know a great deal about
        mysteries!

W 9   Read Early Crime Classics: "Murders in the Rue Morgue" / "Purloined Letter"
          / & others (Can be Found on I-Drive in Buckler/Detective Fiction Folder)

M 14   Read. M.C. Beaton. *Death of a Charming Man*

W 16   *Mini-paper #1*

M 21   Read Georges Simenon. *Maigret and the Wine Merchant*

W 23   *Mini-paper #2* Read Maj Sjöwall & Per Wallöö. *The Laughing Policeman*

M 28   Read Boris Akunen. *The Winter Queen*

W 30   *Mini-paper #3* Read Leonardo Sciascia. *To Each His Own*

JULY

M 5   NO CLASS — INDEPENDENCE DAY OBSERVED

W 7   Mid-Term Exam; Read Michael Dibdin. *Blood Rain*

M 12   *Mini-paper #4* Read Arthur W. Upfield. *Murder Down Under*

W 14   Read Alexander McCall Smith. *The No. 1 Ladies' Detective Agency*

M 19   Read Seichi Matsumoto. *Inspector Imanishi Investigates Mini-paper #5*

W 21   Read Gail Bowen. *Murder at the Mendel*

M 26   *Mini-paper #6* Last Class

W 28   Final Exam, 9:00–11:00 A.M., in regular classroom

Mini-Paper #4 Create a Detective

Modern detectives such as Kinsey Millhone, Easy Rawlins, and V.I. Warshawski are fully realized characters whose stories are driven by them as much as by plot or circumstances.

Your task in this assignment is to play Author. Create a character from birth to serve as protagonist and/or narrator in a proposed detective story written by you. Let Sue Grafton's biography of Kinsey Millhone serve as your inspiration (http://www.sue grafton.com). After reading the attached bio, start at the beginning with your own character and write two to three pages of your detective's life story.

The list of categories below is just to get you started. Make full use of your own imagination and have fun!

Name
Age
Gender
Physical description
Mental description
Occupation
Parents
Where does the character live?

Does he or she have an accent?
Hobbies
Favorite food
What is his or her dream?
What does he or she most fear?

APPENDIX B

Useful Detective Fiction Terms

Amateur Detective— Works for free and often earns a living in other ways. Is not likely to have any training or education in sleuthing. Sometimes the amateur is retired or wealthy with free time to spend on cases.

Caper Mysteries— Not as serious as murder mysteries. Usually the investigation focuses on a theft and has a light-hearted or even comic tone.

Cozy or Traditional Mysteries— The so-called "cozy" is most commonly connected with Agatha Christie. It usually features an English village that has been disordered by the commission of a murder, frequently committed through clever methods. The amateur's job is to solve the puzzle and restore order and well-being. Little or no overt violence is seen.

Crime Fiction— Refers to any fiction about crime, including mystery and suspense. Police procedurals, private eye stories, cozy or traditional mysteries are types of crime fiction.

Dime Novels—1860–1901 in America, cheap and light paperbacks that sold for 10 cents and were extremely popular because they could be mailed inexpensively. They were shipped in large quantities to soldiers during the Civil War.

Dr. Watson— Sherlock Holmes's assistant who witnessed and recorded the stories of Holmes's cases. Refers today to any helper or sidekick who often also narrates the tale of the case.

Edgar Allan Poe (1809–1849)— Considered the inventor of the detective story. His first detective story, published in 1841, was "The Murders in the Rue Morgue." It was set in Paris.

Edgar Awards— The Mystery Writers of America give awards each year in various categories. The award is a statuette of Edgar Allan Poe.

Gothic Mysteries— Have a dark tone and often involve ghosts or other supernatural elements. Settings are frequently abandoned houses, castles, churches, or cemeteries.

Hard-Boiled Mysteries— An American invention, the hard-boiled detective is usually a cynical loner who is willing to use violence to solve cases. Dashiell Hammett, Raymond Chandler, and Ellery Queen are the classic authors of this type of mystery. Female hard-boiled detectives made their debut in the 1970s.

Heist— This tale involves a theft rather than a murder, but is usually more serious than a caper. The author describes the plan and execution of the crime as well as its solution.

Howdunits— These stories focus on the *how* of a crime, especially if the technique is devious or obscure.

Locked Room Mysteries— A Howdunit in which the crime seems impossible to solve since the victim is found inside an apparently locked and sealed area.

McGuffin— Alfred Hitchcock invented this term for the thing in the story that the characters are all out to get.

Penny Dreadful— A type of cheaply produced novel in Britain in the 1870s. Writers were paid a penny a line and then later a penny a word. The content of these stories was sensational, featuring adventure, violence or crime.

Police Procedurals— Mystery stories in book, film, or TV form that deal with the work of the police in solving crimes. Considered to be "realistic."

Private Investigators— Licensed, paid detectives who have been trained in the methods of investigation.

Pulp Fiction— Cheap books printed on low quality paper that usually contained lurid and sensational cases.

Red Herring— When training dogs for the hunt, a herring was dragged across the trail to try to confuse them. Thus this term refers to false clues.

Scotland Yard— The Metropolitan Police Force responsible for Greater London. The C.I.D. is the Criminal Investigation Department.

Shamus— This term originated in the 1920s and is slang for private eye or detective.

Sherlock Holmes— Created by Arthur Conan Doyle, Holmes follows a purely logical and scientific approach to solving cases. His stories have been continued by other writers.

True Crime Stories— are just what they seem — nonfiction stories about real crimes and real criminals.

Tuckerize— The practice of naming characters after friends and acquaintances. The term comes from Bob Wilson Tucker, who wrote science fiction in the 1950s and 60s and named characters after friends and acquaintances.

Whodunits— The detective tries to find out *who* did the murder.

Whydunits— The detective tries to find out *why* the murder took place — also called psychological mysteries.

Appendix C

English 396A-596A
International Detective Fiction
Dr. Patricia P. Buckler
Summer 2004

International Detective Novelists for Oral Reports

Argentina

Jorge Luis Borges
Rodolfo J. Walsh
Enrique Anderson
Imbert
Marco Denevi

Botswana

Alexander McCall Smith

Brazil

Ruben Fonseca

China

Qiu Xialong
Diane Wei Liang
William Marshall
(Hong Kong)

Colombia

Hernando Tellez
Gabriel Garcia Marquez

Cuba

Daniel Chavarria
Jose Latour
Thomas Sanchez
Randy Wayne White

Czech Republic

Josef Skvorecky

Denmark

Leif Davidsen

Estonia

Eeva Park

Finland

Leena Lehtolainen

France

Georges Simenon
Frederic Dard
Dean Fuller
Emile Gaboriaux
Maurice Leblanc
Gaston Leroux

Germany

Jakob Arjouni

Iceland

Árni Thórarinsson

India

Paul Mann Manuel

Israel

Batya Gur
Jon Land

Italy

Andrea Camilleri
John Spencer
Donna Leon
Michael Dibdin
Magdalen Nab
Italo Calvino
Umberto Eco

Japan

Edogawa Rampo
Koji Suzuki
Natsui Kirino
James Melville

Latvia

Jānis Ivars Stradinš

Lithuania

Raidas Dubrė
Birutė Mackonytė

Mexico

Maria Elvira Bermudez
Antonio Helu
Pepe Martinez de la Vega
Paco Ignacio Taibo II

The Netherlands

Janwillem van de
    Wetering

Norway

Pernille Rygg
Jo Nesbø

Pakistan

Cheryl Bernard

Russia

Boris Akunin
Alexandra Marinina
Martin Cruz Smith

Spain

Manuel Vazquez
    Montalban(Catalonia)
Maria-Antonia Oliver
    (Catalonia)
Roderic Jeffries

Sweden

Arne Dahl
Henning Mankell

Undergraduates and Hispanic Sleuths

The Importance of University Cor(ps)e Requirements in a Liberal Learning Curriculum

Benjamin Fraser

> *"Education never ends, Watson."*
> — Sherlock Holmes, "The Adventure of the Red Circle"

Detective fiction is a superb device for stimulating undergraduates' interests in social problems due to both its appearance of accessibility and its pertinence to questions of race, class, gender, and sexuality posed by recent theoretical approaches to literature. First, on account of its roots as a popular form of literature whose early structural elements adhered to a widely accepted standardization, detective fiction today retains the appearance of accessibility. Elements of the detective plot are quite common in popular major-network television shows that today's university students are familiar with, even if they themselves do not watch such programs (*CSI*, *Law & Order*, etc.). This appearance of accessibility persists to some degree even in the most convoluted permutations of and departures from that structure by authors who have brought the detective novel closer to the stylistic and conceptual rebellions of the avant-garde. Second, detective fiction offers itself up as a catalyst for discussion of an extensive range of social topics. This is particularly true for detective fiction in the Hispanic world. Depending on the specific novel that is incorporated into the course, detective fiction may open the undergraduate classroom up to polemical battles over gender (the female protagonist of Lourdes Ortiz's *Picadura Mortal*), sexuality (the alternative Cuban sexualities of Leonardo Padura-Fuentes's *Máscaras*), race (the indigenous struggles of Paco Ignacio Taibo II's *Desvanecidos difuntos*) and class (the urban speculation underlying Manuel Vázquez Montalbán's *Los mares del sur*). Together, both the appearance of accessibility and the versatility of Hispanic detective fiction allow the instructor to craft a syllabus that balances the needs of a rigorous university education with the comfort afforded his or her students by their initial familiarity with the subject.

In a university setting grounded in a mission that strongly advocates the importance of liberal learning, the advantage of using detective fiction in the undergraduate classroom increases exponentially. Like many other universities focused on undergraduate education, Christopher Newport University in Newport News, Virginia, has recently instituted a liberal learning curriculum whose

> [...] ultimate aim is to produce empowered, informed, and responsible learners, whose key intellectual and personal attributes are enumerated below [see website]. All coursework at CNU — whether in the Liberal Learning Core, in the major, or in the advanced program of integrated study — seeks to develop, reinforce, and advance student aptitude in these primary domains [http://liberal-learning.cnu.edu/foundations.html].

As part of this Liberal Learning Core, all students must take at least eighteen hours in "Liberal Learning Foundations," twenty-two hours in "Areas of Inquiry," and six hours in a "Liberal Learning Emphasis." In this context, it is advantageous to allow students hoping to major/minor in Spanish to pursue the needs of the university-wide Liberal Learning Core in a class from their major/minor department (Modern & Classical Languages and Literatures), thus meeting the Core requirement at the same time that they earn credits toward their major/minor.

A course on Hispanic detective fiction, such as the one whose syllabus is appended to this essay ("Hispanic Sleuths and the State: Detective Fiction in Spain and Latin America"), can be easily tailored to meet university-level requirements. The description that follows provides one example of how this can be done through specific reference to the university-level requirements of a liberal learning curriculum. While this course was designed to be conducted in Spanish, the following discussion also includes readings in English and references to English translations of Spanish-language works. These readings and references should prove useful for those designing a course to be conducted in English on Hispanic detective fiction or even instructors not specifically focusing on the Hispanic world. In the specific context of Christopher Newport University's focus on undergraduate education, "Hispanic Sleuths and the State" meets the university-wide "Area of Inquiry" requirements and focuses on one of those Area requirements titled "Western Traditions." (See <http://liberallearning.cnu.edu/core.html> for more information.)

In order to highlight its relevance to university requirements and procedures, the present essay includes revised excerpts of the information originally submitted for approval of this course by the CNU Undergraduate Curriculum Committee. The bracketed information constitutes the general list of what a student should be able to do after taking a "Western Traditions" course. Each item is followed by a brief description of how this course on Hispanic Sleuths accomplishes this goal with references to specific aspects of the class. The reader may find it helpful to refer to the syllabus included in the appendix to this essay. Included are references to short stories, critical essays, important figures, and even class activities. Following this information-driven list of student objectives is a sequential elaboration of how this course attempts to accomplish those objectives.

Student Objectives for a Western Traditions Course

1. Critically examine the thought processes that have evolved in Western culture (Required)

This course encourages students to explore the connection between literary forms and their historical, political, and sociocultural context. This exploration takes on subjects very important to Western culture as a whole such as the rise of the modern state in the nineteenth century, the role of the appropriation of foreign literary forms within nineteenth- and twentieth-century national discourse, and the transition from a Romantic to a Realist literary aesthetic — all through an exploration of detective fiction. To this end, the selections by Kaemmel, Alewyn, and Woods contextualize the detective phenomenon in literary and social history. These readings introduce students to the rise of the private detective out of the formation of the modern police force (Alewyn, Woods), bourgeois patterns of readership and the relevance of socioeconomic models to the production and consumption of detective fiction (Kaemmel), and the detective's connection not only to rationality and objective realism but also to the marginality often associated with romanticism (Alewyn). They also make reference to important figures such as criminal anthropologist Caesare Lombroso (1836–1909) and, of course, English-language authors including Sir Arthur Conan Doyle, Wilkie Collins, Edgar Allan Poe, and Agatha Christie. The breadth of these readings and their important introductory qualities help students from the first day of class to start thinking about possible topics for their future final papers. The selection by Mariano José de Larra (1809–1837; born the same year as Poe) titled "La policía," is a crowd-pleaser as he lambastes the modern police force with wry wit and caustic irony perhaps only equaled in English by the late Lenny Bruce.

2. [Analyze primary works within the framework the course provides (Required)]

This class allows students to engage with representative works of the detective literary tradition by men and women authors of both Spain and

Latin America. The study of these works emphasizes basic literary analysis and places them within specific sociocultural frameworks of the Hispanic world. Students have the opportunity to pursue the study of primary works in this tradition not covered in class in either a comparative or context-based manner. Possible primary works are included in the class syllabus and mentioned in the contextualizing readings provided not only by Alewyn, Kaemmel and Woods but also by Englekirk, Colmeiro, Compitello, Díaz Eterovic, Hart, and Planells. Comparative study is introduced by the essays that root the detective phenomenon in the English-speaking world and is supported by the choice of *The Usual Suspects* as an accompanying film for the course (along with *La cripta*). If the course being constructed is oriented more toward the English-language, instructors may want to discuss Agatha Christie's *The Murder of Roger Ackroyd*. The latter presents remarkable similarities with *The Usual Suspects* in terms of narration. S. S. Van Dine's "Twenty Rules for Writing Detective Stories," which in the late 1920s attempted to preserve the "pure" experience of stories in the classical model in the face of the shift to hardboiled fiction, is also applicable here. Consulting this list, constructed by the famed detective author Willard Huntington Wright, whose pseudonym was S. S. Van Dine, reveals that both the film and the novel go against the spirit of "fair play" that ran through much of late-nineteenth-century detective fiction.

> 3. [*Place one or more of the historical, artistic, or intellectual traditions of the West in its cultural context*]

Students in this class delve into the origins of a Western artistic, historical, and intellectual form occurring frequently in both literary circles and popular culture. They have the chance to discuss the adaptation of the form to temporal changes in literary style as well as to specific spatially rooted Western circumstances. Regarding this aspect of the course, students might be encouraged to report on the development of detective fiction in a given country for their final paper. The collection by Yates is useful for suggesting paths of investigation to interested students, as is Simpson's *New Tales of Mystery from Latin America*.

> 4. [*Describe how the material under study has influenced the development of Western culture*]

Students in this course discuss the role of detective fiction not only as a reflection of the historical, political, and sociocultural context in which it was written but also as an expression of the tensions of racial, gender, and class inequality that have been an integral part of the development of the West. Paco Ignacio Taibo II's *Algunas nubes/Some Clouds* (a splendid novel also available in English translation) proves to be an investigation of Mexican history just as it is an investigation of a specific crime. Particularly poignant in this regard is the novel's key incorporation of the student protests of 1968 in Mexico City that were brutally repressed by the government of President Díaz Ordaz as well as its reference to the twentieth-century legacy of a single political party's control of the Mexican government (the PRI, Partido Revolucionario Institucional/Institutional Revolutionary Party, in power from 1929 to 2000). The novel is also a good choice for its humor, accessible symbolism (the clouds representing corruption), mention of popular culture (Kalimán), metafictional device (Paco Ignacio appearing as a character in his own novel), and intriguing narrative shifts. Two chapters in particular (IV, IX) depart from the standard narrative style of detective fiction. Instead of the narration following the detective as a camera would, thus limiting the reader's knowledge to only those things experienced by the detective, in these two chapters the reader is exposed to extensive background information of which Taibo II's detective is unaware. Of course, by replacing Taibo II's novel with another, the emphasis of the class can be easily shifted to cover another particular aspect of the development of Western culture (for suggestions see this essay's first paragraph, above).

5. [*Connect the historical roots of phenomena
with later aspects of the tradition*]

The course charts the complex evolution of the detective form from its origins in the stories of Edgar Allan Poe in the mid–nineteenth century ("La carta robada"; Englekirk, "Introduction") through the late-nineteenth-century short stories of Spaniard Emilia Pardo Bazán ("La cana," "La gota de sangre," Hart), through the mid–twentieth-century cerebral stories of Argentine Jorge Luis Borges ("La muerte y la brújula"/translated into English as "Death and the Compass") to the resurgence of the detective form in late-twentieth-century Spain and Latin America (Colmeiro, Compitello, Díaz Eterovic). Along the way, students are encouraged to collaborate in comparative discussions that draw upon their experience of this genre in its very popular present-day format on American television (*CSI*, *Law & Order*, etc.).

Methods for Meeting Course Objectives

1. [*Participating in class discussion and debate*]

Students respond to themes and participate in discussions and debates organized by the professor on a regular basis. Since the topic of the detective is so familiar to undergraduate students, it is helpful to have a discussion on what they already know. After pair-discussion of this previous knowledge, one student steps to the board to record a list of detective figures, shows, images, stories, novels, etc., suggested by the pairs of students. Much of what the students suggest can be unknown to the instructor (a student once mentioned the young children's show *Blue's Clues*, for example). Explaining the basic characteristics of the classical vs. hard-boiled model of detective fiction and having students attempt an initial characterization of the list into one camp or the other engages them with a key categorization of the course (see "Week 6" in the appended syllabus). Inevitably there are items on the list that do not fall cleanly into one camp or the other.

This discussion introduces students to the legacy of the explosion in detective fiction that departed from closed, classical models of clear, rational distinctions and univocal clues. This is an important discussion to have when following the appended syllabus because it paves the way for the ambiguity of the novel *Algunas nubes/Some Clouds* (Taibo II), which incorporates aspects of both the classical detective model and the hard-boiled model. Using S. S. Van Dine's "Twenty Rules for Writing Detective Stories" to help students make this determination grants a degree of confidence to those students who shy away from the seeming ambiguity of literary study.

2. [*Engaging in teamwork and other collaborative exercises*]

In groups, students have the opportunity to lead discussions on a given short reading, prepare and distribute appropriate and original questions, and manage the participation of the other students on a rotating basis. Given that this class is taught in Spanish, which as any language professor knows has its own issues regarding the pedagogical "affective-filter"(read: comfort level), students benefit from leading discussions during the latter third of the course, after they have all had ample opportunity to engage with the vocabulary of detective fiction and get to know their peers. Taibo II's novel lends itself to this discussion-leading task as students can focus either on the plot development or on more literary aspects of the work — depending on their language abilities and experience with literary analysis.

3. [*Writing analytical or evaluative papers, perhaps incorporating original research*]

Students have the opportunity to write short analytical and evaluative papers throughout the semester. Each student completes a final project according to his or her own interest and enthusiasm. Suggested projects may include but are not limited to a research paper on an Hispanic detective novel, a research paper on an Hispanic author of short stories in the genre, a study of the detective as popular culture in a Spanish-speaking nation, the creation of an original short story conforming to one of the detective form's subgenres studied in class, or a comparative study of a text covered in class with one of the student's own choosing. The appended syllabus provides ample opportunity for students to learn about writers that are not specifically included in the course.

4. [*Making oral presentations*]

As part of their responsibilities leading discussion (see appended syllabus), students give a brief oral presentation on the work to be discussed (the essays or even chapters of the novel). Students also give brief oral presentations on their final projects at the end of the semester.

5. [*Creating an artistic product or a performance*]

The creative/artistic option for the final project is to create an original short story that highlights the components of the detective genre's form as discussed in class. All instructors know that while some students invariably opt for more traditional papers rather than engage in a creative activity, there are just as many who prefer creative writing to more "academic" papers. Requiring the student who opts for this creative alternative to display knowledge of the characteristics of the classical detective story as identified by S. S. Van Dine, for example, assures that this original work is rooted in what they have learned in the class.

6. [*Participating in fieldwork*]

Since Newport News, Virginia is only approximately seventy miles from Richmond, Virginia, students have the opportunity to visit the Edgar Allan Poe Museum in Richmond, with or without the professor, and write a response as one of the requirements for this class. This necessarily optional response paper (some students may find it difficult to make time outside of class for a day-trip to Richmond) substitutes for one of the two short papers. For those instructors who are interested in developing a similar class (or just intrigued by the museum), but for whom a trip to the museum would be too costly or inconvenient, the museum's website (http://www.poemuseum.org) offers educational resources (a sample lesson, an online quiz, and links to Poe websites), selected works by the author, biographical information, and even an online store. The museum itself boasts one of the largest collections of Poe memorabilia in the world and explores his specific connection to Richmond.

Conclusion

The course on "Hispanic Sleuths" outlined above, and whose basic syllabus appears in the Appendix, is intended for the university student who seeks a rigorous and yet accessible course to fulfill his or her requirements in the Spanish major/minor and at the same time complete one of the University-wide Core requirements of a Liberal Learning Curriculum. The readings I have selected cover a range of difficulty, from straightforward English-language introductory texts to Spanish-language literature that can often prove quite difficult for even advanced students of literature. The works of two authors are particularly difficult: Pardo-Bazán's short stories—for their use of Gallician regionalisms, and Borges's "La muerte y la brújula"/"Death and the Compass"—for its cerebral character. On the other hand, *Algunas nubes*/*Some Clouds* is a solid midlevel text that affords those students inexperienced with Hispanic/Spanish-language literature a plot-driven narrative in straightforward prose while still offering the rich social commentary and eclectic vocabulary expected by more advanced students. Perhaps most importantly for courses that meet university-level requirements, the novel is an intensely readable one.

Overall, students' familiarity with the figure of the detective and the eclectic mixture of readings in both Spanish and English help prevent students from being as intimidated as they might be in a more standard (Spanish-language) Hispanic literature class. The films (*The Usual Suspects*, *La cripta*) and optional field trip (The Poe Museum) keep students engaged with the theme of the course through a variety of formats. Having a creative option for the final paper encourages more artistic students to succeed in their own milieu. The accessibility and versatility of the detective theme really does present something of interest to each student, regardless of their interest in high literature, their Spanish abilities, and their previous college experience. Whether one is teaching an undergraduate class on Hispanic detective fiction in English or in Spanish, turning a core requirement into a cor(ps)e requirement should prove to be a great experience for both students and instructors alike.

NOTES

For more information about some of the works mentioned here and other works of interest to the course, see my "Narradores contra la ficción: La novela detectivesca como estrategia política" (2006).

I am indebted to my colleague Steven Spalding for suggesting the play on words provided by the fusion of core/cor(ps)e.

WORKS CITED

Alewyn, Richard. "The Origin of the Detective Novel." 1974. *The Poetics of Murder: Detective Fiction and Literary Theory.* Eds. Glenn W. Most and William W. Stowe. San Diego, CA: Harcourt, 1983. 62–78.

Bermúdez, Maria Elvira. "El Embrollo del Reloj." *El cuento policial latinoamericano.* Ed. Donald A. Yates. Mexico City: De Andrea, 1964. 67–77.

Borges, Jorge Luis. "Death and the Compass." *Collected Fictions.* Trans. Andrew Hurley. New York: Penguin, 1999. 147–56.

_____."La muerte y la brújula." *Ficciones.* Madrid: Alianza, 1982. 147–63.

Christie, Agatha. *The Murder of Roger Ackroyd.* New York: Dodd Mead and Company, 1975.

Colmeiro, José. *La novela policiaca española: teoría e historia crítica.* Barcelona: Anthropos, 1994.

Compitello, M. A. "The Contemporary Spanish Detective Novel and the Question of Form." *Revista Monográfica* 3 (1987): 182–91.

La cripta. Dir. Cayetano del Real. Fígaro Films, 1981.

Díaz Eterovic, Ramón. "Una mirada desde la narrativa policial." <http:letras.s5.com/eterovicramon.htm>.

Englekirk, John Eugene. "Introduction." *Edgar Allan Poe in Hispanic Literature.* New York: Instituto de Las Españas, 1934. 15–22.

Fraser, Benjamin. "Narradores contra la ficción: La novela detectivesca como estrategia política." *Studies in Latin American Popular Culture* 25 (2006): 199–219.

Hart, Patricia. "Detective Beginnings in Spain." *The Spanish Sleuth: The Detective in Spanish Fiction.* London and Toronto: Associated University Presses, 1997. 17–25.

Hernández Martín, Jorge. "Paco Ignacio Taibo II: Post-Colonialism and the Detective Story in Mexico." *The Post-Colonial Detective.* Ed. and introd. Ed Christian. Basingstoke, England: Palgrave, 2001. 159–75.

Kaemmel, Ernst. "Literature Under the Table: The Detective Novel and Its Social Mission." 1962. *The Poetics of Murder: Detective Fiction and Literary Theory.* Ed. Glenn W. Most and William W. Stowe. San Diego, CA: Harcourt, 1983. 55–61.

Larra, Mariano José de. "La policía." *Artículos de costumbres.* Ed. Luis F. Díaz Larios. Madrid: Espasa-Calpe, 2001. 297–304.

Ortiz, Lourdes. *Picadura Mortal.* Madrid: Alfaguara, 1996.

Padura Fuentes, Leonardo. *Máscaras.* Barcelona: Tusquets, 1997.

Pardo Bazán, Emilia. "La cana." *Cuentos policíacos.* Ed. Danilo Manera. Madrid: Bercimuel, 2001. 167–77.

_____."La gota de sangre." *Cuentos policíacos.* Ed. Danilo Manera. Madrid: Bercimuel, 2001. 25–82.

Planells, Antonio. "El género policíaco en Hispanoamérica." *Monographic Review/Revista Monográfica* 3.1–2 (1987): 148–62.

Sebreli, J. J. "Dashiell Hammett o la ambigüedad." *Quimera: Revista de Literatura* 119 (1993): 48–53.

Simpson, Amelia. *New Tales of Mystery from Latin America.* Cranbury, NJ; London; Mississauga, Ontario: Associated University Presses, 1992.

Taibo II, Paco Ignacio. *Algunas nubes.* México: Alfaguara, 1995.

_____. *Desvanecidos difuntos.* México: Planeta Mexicana, 1999

_____. *Some Clouds.* Scottsdale, AZ: Poisoned Pen Press, 2002.

Todorov, Tzvetan. "The Typology of Detective Fiction." *The Poetics of Prose.* Trans. Richard Howard. Ithaca: Cornell University Press, 1977. 42–52.

The Usual Suspects. Dir. Bryan Singer. PolyGram Filmed Entertainment, 1995.

Van Dine, S. S. "Twenty Rules for Writing Detective Stories." <http:gaslight.mtroyal.ab.ca/vandine.htm>. [Originally published in *American Magazine* (1928)].

Vázquez Montalbán, Manuel. *Los mars del sur*. Barcelona: Planeta, 1997.

Woods, Robin. "'His Appearance Is Against Him': The Emergence of the Detective Novel." *The Cunning Craft: Original Essays on Detective Fiction and Contemporary Literary Theory*. Ed. Ronald Walker and June M. Frazer. Macomb: Southern Illinois University Press, 1990. 15–24.

Yates, Donald. *El cuento policial latinoamericano*. México: De Andrea, 1964.

APPENDIX

Basic Course Syllabus

SPAN 397: HISPANIC SLEUTHS & THE STATE:
DETECTIVE FICTION IN SPAIN & LATIN AMERICA

Course Description

This course will trace the evolution of the detective genre from its origins in America/England to its proliferation in Spain and Latin America through such literary forms as the short story, novel and film. Students will review the historical and political circumstances of the nineteenth century that gave rise to the genre as part of modern state formation and will explore the adaptation of the detective form to the specific political, economic and sociocultural realities of Spanish-speaking countries throughout the nineteenth and twentieth centuries. Students will have the opportunity to create a final project under the direction of the professor. Such projects may include but are not limited to: a research paper on an Hispanic detective novel, a research paper on an Hispanic author of short stories in the genre, a study of the detective as popular culture in a Spanish-speaking nation, the creation of an original short story conforming to one of the detective form's sub-genres as studied in class, or a comparative study of a text covered in class with one of the student's own choosing. This course will be taught in Spanish.

Learning Objectives

By the end of this course students will be able to:

1. Critically examine the connection between the detective genre as a literary form and its evolving historical, political and sociocultural contexts
2. Comment on the sociocultural and literary origins of the detective genre
3. Distinguish between the traditional and contemporary forms of the detective story
4. Describe the adoption of the detective genre by the Hispanic World
5. Analyze primary works of detective fiction in Spanish (i.e., short story, novel, film)
6. Recognize the importance of the detective genre in contemporary popular culture
7. Assess the importance of socio-cultural inequalities to the Hispanic detective story

Course Grade

Participation: 20%
Discussion Leadership: 10%
Midterm Exam: 20%
Exam on *Algunas nubes:* 10%
Short Papers: 10%
Final Project: 30%

Required Books— Taibo II, Paco Ignacio, *Algunas nubes*, México: Alfaguara, 1995. Students must purchase a course packet of readings

Recommended— Good Spanish/English dictionary

Participation— Students will be expected to regularly attend all class meetings, to have done the assigned readings and homework, and to participate in Spanish in discussions of assigned reading materials.

Discussion Leadership— In groups of 2–3, students will lead discussion on the reading material for that class day. This will include an introduction to the reading, a group discussion on an aspect of the work chosen by the discussion leaders, and an interactive class activity designed and led by the presenters. Total time 15–20 minutes in Spanish.

Midterm Exam— The midterm exam will cover the origin of the detective genre, the transition to the Hispanic World, the difference between the classical and hard-boiled narrative models, and the short stories covered in class.

Exam on *Algunas nubes*— The second exam will cover *Algunas nubes* and S.S. Van Dine's rules of detective fiction and will be based on class discussions.

Short Papers— Students will have the opportunity to write two short analytical and evaluative papers throughout the semester. Each paper will be 2–3 pages in Spanish. Topics will be assigned based upon the class readings. A short reaction paper on a visit to the Edgar Allan Poe Musuem in Richmond, VA with or without the professor may substitute for one of the two short papers.

Final Project— Each student will complete a final project according to their own interest and enthusiasm. Such projects may include but are not limited to: a research paper on an Hispanic detective novel, a research paper on an Hispanic author of short stories in the genre, a study of the detective as popular culture in a Spanish-speaking nation, the creation of an original short story conforming to one of the detective form's subgenres studied in class, or a comparative study of a text covered in class with one of the student's own choosing. 5–7 pages in length with bibliography in MLA format. (20%)

Each student will prepare a 250-word abstract for their final paper due in class shortly after the midterm exam. (5%) Each student will also give a brief (5–7 min.) oral presentation on the final project at the end of the semester. (5%)

Optional Field Experience— Students may visit the Edgar Allan Poe Museum in Richmond with or without the professor and write a 2–3 page response in Spanish in lieu of one of the short paper assignments.

Class Schedule

All readings will be available in a course packet. Readings will be in both Spanish and English. All class sessions will be held in Spanish.

WEEK 1: Introduction to the Course, Vocabulary of Detection, Origins of the Genre E. Kaemmel, "Literature under the Table: The Detective Novel and its Social Mission"

R. Alewyn, "The Origin of the Detective Novel"

R. Woods, "'His Appearance Is Against Him': The Emergence of the Detective Novel"

WEEK 2: Early Readings in Detective Fiction

M. J.de Larra, "La policía"

J. Englekirk, *Poe in Hispanic Literature*, "Introduction"

Edgar Allan Poe, "La carta robada"

WEEK 3: The Detective Story in Spain

P. Hart, "Detective Beginnings in Spain"

E. Pardo Bazán, "La cana"

E. Pardo Bazán, "La gota de sangre"

WEEK 4: The Detective Story in Latin America

A. Planeéis, "El género policíaco en Hispanoamérica"

D. Yates, *El cuento policial latinoamericano*, selecciones

TURN IN SHORT PAPER ONE

WEEK 5: The Detective Story in Latin America

María Elvira Bermúdez, "El embrollo del reloj"

Jorge Luis Borges, "La muerte y la brújula"

WEEK 6: Classical vs. Hard-boiled Models of Detective Fiction

T. Todorov, "The Typology of Detective Fiction."

S. S. Van Dine, "Twenty Rules for Writing Detective Stories"

J.J. Sebreli, "Dashiell Hammett o la ambigüedad"

Film *The Usual Suspects*

TURN IN SHORT PAPER TWO

WEEK 7: The Detective Novel Revival in Spain and Latin America

R. Díaz Eterovic, "Una mirada desde la narrativa policial"

M.A. Compitello, "The Contemporary Spanish Detective Novel and the Question of Form."

WEEK 8: The Detective Novel Revival in Spain and Latin America

J. F. Colmeiro, *La novela policiaca española*, excerpt

REVIEW FOR MIDTERM EXAM

MIDTERM EXAM

WEEK 9: The Mexican Detective Novel: Paco Ignacio Taibo II's *Algunas nubes*

TURN IN ABSTRACTS FOR FINAL PROJECT

J. Hernández Martín, "Paco Ignacio Taibo II: Post-Colonialism and the Detective Story in Mexico"

A. Simpson, *New Tales of Mystery from Latin America*, selections

WEEK 10: Paco Ignacio Taibo II's *Algunas nubes*

Paco Ignacio Taibo II, *Algunas nubes, Chs. 1–3*

WEEK 11: Paco Ignacio Taibo II's *Algunas nubes*

Paco Ignacio Taibo II, *Algunas nubes, Chs. 4–6*

WEEK 12: Paco Ignacio Taibo II's *Algunas nubes*

Paco Ignacio Taibo II, *Algunas nubes, Chs. 7–9*

WEEK 13: Paco Ignacio Taibo II's *Algunas nubes*

Paco Ignacio Taibo II, *Algunas nubes, Chs. 10–13*

WEEK 14: Paco Ignacio Taibo II's *Algunas nubes*

EXAM-*Algunas nubes*

Workshop final projects for final changes

Film *La cripta/(El misterio de la cripta embrujada)*/Film Discussion

WEEK 15: PRESENTATIONS OF FINAL PROJECTS

Contemporary Detective Fiction Across the English Curriculum

GENIE GIAIMO

Detective fiction is an accessible, media-rich genre; as such, it is a particularly apt pedagogical tool for introductory-level English courses and upper-level English seminar courses alike. Detective fiction, in particular the hard-boiled fiction of the late 1920s and early 1930s that defined the early development of the genre, works well as an introduction to textual analysis and composition because of the linear narrative structure that it follows. Dashiell Hammett's *The Maltese Falcon* and Raymond Chandler's *The Big Sleep* are excellent examples of how linear narrative structure and the hero myth operate in literature. These texts are a great place for first-year college students to begin their development as critical readers, thinkers, and writers. Detective fiction also offers effective examples for more advanced students to learn about the origins of a genre and how a genre develops over time. Detective fiction forms the perfect basis for students to learn how to deconstruct a text because even the most conservative, structurally formulaic texts in the genre can be read with political, social, and racial intent.

I teach English courses at the advanced level as well as at the introductory level. In my seminar course, which is devoted solely to the progression of the detective genre from Edgar Allen Poe to Walter Mosley, I offer historical, political, and aesthetic analysis of the genre, pulling in threads of discussion about minority rights, postmodern philosophy, and filmic versus textual analysis. The numerous discussion topics that detective fiction elicits allow for every student in the course to contribute an opinion, observation, or remark to classroom discussion. In my expository writing courses I use elements of the detective genre to teach critical reading and writing because this popular literary form has been picked up and re-imagined by various media outlets. It is a familiar genre that is accessible and pervasive enough for students to analyze effectively and to enjoy as well. Detective fiction brings the nuances of textual analysis and theoretical thinking to students who are largely unaccustomed to reading for the underlying messages, political ideologies, and symbols in a text.

Accessibility is a crucial element in training students to engage critically with literature. The story outline for older detective fiction is relatively conventional and easily recognized by students of all ages due to the pervasive treatment of the genre, both seriously and satirically, in various media sources such as cartoons, films, and, of course, popular fiction. The order of events for Poe's stories and the later hard-boiled writings of Hammett and Chandler (among others) has a rather standard structure: we are introduced to the detective; we witness or learn, secondhand, about the crime; the detective begins inspecting the clues; the detective is threatened or implicated in some way; the detective pieces together the clues and solves the case. Ultimately, moral order, which is absent at the beginning of the story, is restored and the villains are soundly punished for their crimes. Although the narrative of early detective fiction is relatively predictable and linear, the plot is not simple. Hard-boiled fiction and American film noir, which is based on the hard-boiled tradition, use various symbols and storylines that are laden with racist, sexist, and xenophobic ideologies. These ideologies manifest in characters such as the sexually and racially ambiguous villain Joel Cairo and in the aggressive and womanizing hero-detective Sam Spade, both from Hammett's *The Maltese Falcon*. Hard-boiled detective fiction offers complexly constructed political ideologies, informed by the historical and social atmosphere of late 1920s and early 1930s America, in a fast-moving and accessibly structured way. The familiar narrative structure, punctuated by the complex and often subtle markers of conservative politics, makes this an ideal genre with which to introduce students to college-level reading, writing, and analysis. This also works effectively for more advanced students, because the traditional narrative allows them to familiarize themselves with the common themes of the genre and then to move quickly to the highly complex, largely interdisciplinary detective stories created for venues such as cinema, graphic novels, fiction, and video games; most of which students are familiar with on an informal, noncritical level.

The expository writing course that I teach is designed to train first-year college students the basics of textual analysis, scholarly research, argumentation, composition, and grammar. At the beginning of the semester I use detective fiction in order to draw students into engaging with critical thinking and writing. I do this because detective fiction, while having an accessible and recognizable narrative form, conceptually engages with serious issues such as prejudice and violence in our society. Detective fiction and film noir adaptations of hard-boiled texts are tools that make complex concepts such as cognitive organization and critical analysis clear while also offering a comprehensive perspective on the ever-changing, yet eerily familiar, political landscape of America. In particular, I encourage students in my expository writing courses to engage in political discussions that explore issues of class, gender, race, and ethnicity in our society. The setting, the language, and the character development in hard-boiled fiction is rooted in a specific moment in American history, in this case that of post–World War I and pre–World War II America. They are small pieces of Americana, informed by the relatively conservative, sexist, racist, and cynical mores of the time. As such, this fiction is a particularly apt tool with which to teach how the political and the historical moment influence the philosophies that drive a text.

Many of the students enrolled in this course have not deeply contemplated the myriad forms that inequality takes in America. Detective fiction, especially the hard-boiled tradition, allows for students to consider, analyze, and write about the semiotic clues that inform the white-washed, male dominated vision of the world that authors such as Raymond Chandler and Dashiell Hammett upheld in their writing. I show specific clips from the film versions of *The Big Sleep* and *The Maltese Flacon* to highlight the legacy of xenophobic and Nativist sentiment throughout American history and prompt my students to explore whether or not the fear of the ethnic "Other" (embodied by Joel Cairo in *The Maltese Flacon*), which was so prominent prior to World Wars I and II, is still present in our society today. This genre, and the noir tradition specifically, is an excellent venue with which to begin an introductory writing course because the conservative political agenda of the older texts prompts students to consider the ways in which the social climate of the time can strongly influence the content of literature and film. And as students continue to read more recent texts and observe and analyze modern-day forms of media, the seeming polarization between political thought of the late 1920s into the early 1930s and current-day political thought begins to blur and they are left to confront the lingering prejudice in our society in a much more historically based and self-aware manner.

This genre is not only useful in teaching expository writing students about how ideological motivations can drive a text, but also in teaching how structural principles can drive a text, and, more broadly, an entire genre. The relatively linear narrative construction of detective fiction helps students to define and examine narrative myth structures. Myth structures are patterns that are easily recognizable in a text because they recur in literature (and various other forms of media) throughout history (Seger 320), and they offer students who are unaccustomed to analyzing a text a story pattern to follow and various character types (archetypes) and symbols to identify. The hero myth is a common myth structure that we find repeatedly in literature. Hard-boiled detective fiction, which falls under the auspices of the hero myth (320), features the lone private eye, characterized by Sam Spade and Philip Marlowe; this noble, yet largely impotent archetype of the American outlaw hero

(Paradis 95), is a crucial component of the narrative myth structure. These detectives go on a quest, face resistance, hit rock bottom, but eventually fulfill their mission: solving the case and restoring moral order (Seger 321); yet their anachronistic and slightly twisted employment of chivalry, and their apparent refusal to secure aid from outsiders, leaves them unable to maintain the restoration of moral order, thus shaping the archetype of the American hard-boiled hero as a tenuous one, fraught with ineffectuality.

After the students learn the elements of narrative myth structures and how to conduct a filmic analysis, they write a response journal, highlighting the recurring narrative elements and political ideologies in detective fiction. They then write a three-to-five-page analysis paper that either explores the semiotic markers of political ideology in a novel or a film created within the last decade or that analyzes the myth structure and archetypes in a novel or a film created within the last decade. This letter-graded paper allows students to branch out into other genres of literature and film in order to discuss and analyze political ideologies or narrative structure. Before they jump into this first expository writing assignment, however, I use detective fiction to teach them how to do a textual or a film analysis with a focus on political ideologies, and how to write about these critical ideas in a cogent manner. The section of the course on the analysis of political ideologies and narrative myth structures segues smoothly into the section where students have to do comparative textual analysis. Detective fiction helps students ease into understanding and analyzing various forms of "texts" and serves as the foundation with which they build up their own particular writing style and critical approach.

The seminar I teach solely on detective fiction is radically different from that of my expository writing courses. It is an upper-level English seminar offered through the Continuing Education Department at Clark University. Conceptually, the class is centered on the development of the detective fiction genre beginning with Edgar Allen Poe, one of the first American authors to write in the genre, and moving to Walter Mosley, one of the foremost contemporary authors of ethnic detective fiction. But the course does not stop at the more traditional venues in which the detective fiction genre has been treated, such as literature. The class also examines filmic interpretations of the detective genre by the Coen brothers and David Lynch's *Mulholland Drive*, postmodern-inspired detective fiction by Haruki Murakami, noir-inspired episodes of the Japanese anime series *Cowboy Bebop*, and Allen Moore's take on mystery writing with the graphic novel *Watchmen*.

In this course, I do not focus heavily upon the rudiments of composition but rather on historically contextualizing the development of the detective genre in America, offering various theoretical opinions on the role of popular culture in academia, and highlighting the political and therefore thematic shifts the genre has undergone from its inception until now. I begin with Tzvetan Todorov's *Typology of Detective Fiction*, a comprehensive but somewhat polemical and restrictive categorization of the detective fiction genre. In class, I discuss definitions of genre and the limitations of solely studying canonical texts. I attempt to set up genre as more fluid and complex than Todorov (43). I then move into the historical trajectory of the genre. I end with the disruption of the detective fiction genre and its amalgamation with various other genres across multiple forms of media.

Because this is an advanced adult education course, I can focus less on preparation for the collegiate and the professional world, and more on textual analysis and theoretical discussion. I assign only two papers: a midterm and a final. The midterm is a five-to-seven-page analysis of two texts from the course, with no outside sources necessary, and the final paper is a seven-to-ten-page research paper on two texts from the course with five to seven outside sources necessary. I plan in the future to assign a weekly journal, two to three typed pages double spaced per week, asking students to reflect on the thematic and structural elements of the texts they read. Students have responded well to the relatively sparse writing assignments and focus their energy on the two papers while engaging with political or structural issues in detective fiction. It is important, however, to ensure that the students begin researching well in advance of the date their second assignment is due because the relatively little amount of scholarship done on the contemporary texts I assign can be an issue for their final essays.

The structure of the detective fiction course is not the only way in which the seminar differs from the expository writing course; the background of the students who enroll in the seminar course is radically different as well. Students vary greatly in their educational level, motivation for taking the course, and knowledge of the detective genre. The enrollment includes traditional college students looking to get ahead on their coursework but also nontraditional students, such as one seventy-five-year-old woman who took my course because she had a deep interest in the detective fiction genre. The dynamic of a classroom changes dramatically depending on the department and the semester in which I teach my detective fiction course. I try to remain flexible with the reading assignments and how long I spend on each topic, as many of these students are nontraditional college students who work full time and commute to class. I also take into account the classroom demographic when I design my syllabus, and I adjust it according to the level of familiarity students have with detective fiction, literature-based courses, and scholarly research and writing. One semester I might get through every text and all the supplemental material, and the next semester I might have to drop two texts and focus heavily on the Todorov article. Flexibility and a willingness to gage the aptitude of the particular class produce the most worthwhile learning experience for students and teacher alike.

Most students, even the ones who have completed a large number of English courses, will initially be hesitant about reading theoretically sophisticated material, but once we review it in class and apply it to a specific text or texts, they realize that it is as important to theoretically ground texts as much as it is to historically contextualize them. Pairing the text versions of *The Big Sleep* and *The Maltese Falcon* with the film versions is one way of giving students who are unfamiliar with thinking and writing critically about texts a more tangible structure with which to think about the ways in which the detective genre operates. Analysis of the similarities and the differences between text versions and film versions of the same story highlights how narrative conventions, symbolism, and character development vary greatly from medium to medium; this dual analysis also reveals how the direction, production, and marketing of hard-boiled detective fiction and films were rooted in the historical and cultural period in which they were produced, even if the date of publication differed from the production of the film by approximately ten years.

Media culture, and this genre in specific, helps to teach students how to engage critically in discussions on canonicity, to explore the significance of popular culture, to conduct seminar-level research, and to develop a final project at the end of the semester; detective fiction does all of this effectively because a lot of it has a largely recognizable narrative and symbolic structure. These more traditional elements in detective fiction allow for students of all ages and educational backgrounds to engage freely and quickly with the more traditional material. After they engage with the genre's seminal texts, they move to the complex postmodern interpretations of the genre. It is then that I bring in the Murakami text, the Moore graphic novel, and the Coen brothers and Lynch films. Students in my seminar have already engaged with Todorov's classification of detective fiction; they have examined the origins of detective fiction in America with the writings of Edgar Allen Poe; and they have read and analyzed the influential hard-boiled texts produced during the late 1920s and early 1930s in America. At this point, they are well equipped to recognize plot structure, character development, and metaphoric language in the text; they are also able to recognize the political ideologies in operation in older texts of the genre. Introducing narratives such as Murakami's *Hard-Boiled Wonderland*, which merges science fiction with mystery and suspense in a double, simultaneously occurring narrative, and David Lynch's *Mulholland Drive*, which uses fantastical events and an inherently unstable storyline to convey a mysterious case of murder and confused identity, opens students up to the creative and critical possibilities of current genre fiction and prompts them to reconsider the role of popular fiction and media culture in a classroom setting.

Students are typically not trained to deconstruct a text before they enter college; rather, they are loosely trained to recognize elements of plot development, character development, and imagery. In my composition-based courses and in my continuing education courses, I have met with a lot of resistance when I have prompted my students to consider the multiple meanings (a number of which are politically and socially informed) a text can contain. Many students, particularly the traditional ones, seem to ascribe to a more conservative view of what constitutes literature and what literary elements comprise a text. So to begin my composition courses and my continuing education seminar with the more rigid exemplifiers and classifiers of detective fiction, such as myth criticism and Todorov-informed readings, gives students a solid handle on how the genre operated in its initial stages and allows them to begin thinking, analyzing, and writing about detective fiction with a developed structure. It is then that my two courses diverge in their scholarly direction: my expository writing course uses the textual and ideological analysis students learned with detective fiction to branch out and explore narrative myth structures and political philosophies that drive other genres and media sources. My seminar course rapidly reviews the rudiments of how narrative and character development in this genre operate, and then students break out of traditional interpretations of detective fiction and begin to think about the films, graphic novels, cartoons, video games, and texts that resist simple classification as "detective story" because they cross over into the science fiction genre, the memoir genre, the ethnic genre, and the African-American genre, but also because they merge elements from these other sources together into a highly self-conscious, politically driven, re-envisioned genre. Detective fiction offers these students insight into how a genre can develop over time from a relatively straightforward and politically uniform medium to one that is complexly interwoven with other genres, political ideologies, and references from popular culture. The detective genre, in its many stages of development and in the many forms it takes in the media, is useful in training students of all academic levels to become more politically aware thinkers and more self-aware writers.

WORKS CITED

Chandler, Raymond. *The Big Sleep.* New York: Vintage Books, 1992.
Derrida, Jacques. "The Law of Genre." *Critical Inquiry* 7.1 (1980): 55–80.
Hammett, Dashiell. *The Maltese Falcon.* New York: Knopf, 1930.

Klein, Kathleen Gregory, ed. *Diversity and Detective Fiction.* Bowling Green, OH: Bowl-
    ing Green State University Popular Press, 1999.
Paradis, Kenneth. "Warshawski's Situation: Beauvoirean Feminism and the Hard-Boiled
    Detective." *South Central Review* 18.3–4 (2001): 86–101.
Seger, Linda. "Creating the Myth." *Signs of Life in the USA: Readings on Popular Cul-
    ture for Writers.* Boston: Bedford St. Martin's, 2006.
Smith, Johanna M. "Hard Boiled Detective Fiction: Gendering the Canon." *Pacific Coast
    Philology* 26.1–2 (1991): 78–84.
Todorov, Tzvetan. "The Typology of Detective Fiction." *The Poetics of Prose.* Ithaca, NY:
    Cornell University Press, 1977.
Wilson, Edmund. *Classics and Commercials: A Literary Chronically of the Forties.* New
    York: Vintage Books, 1950.

Appendix: Course Syllabus

*Let's Talk Turkey! Detective Crime Fiction
from Hard Boiled to Multi-Ethnic Voices*

Professor Genie Giaimo

Course objectives

Of mystery novels, Edmund Wilson famously wrote, "With so many fine books
to be read, so much to be studied and known, there is no need to bore ourselves with
this rubbish." In spite of his criticism, however, serious students of literature have continued to read and value mystery and detective fiction. We will begin this course with
Poe, the precursor to modern detective fiction. From him we will move on to the hard-
boiled tradition, examining both fiction and films that responded to the genre. We will
then explore the intersection of feminism and detective fiction as well as critical race
studies and detective fiction. We will complete this course with exploring the influences
of detective fiction on contemporary media, including the postmodern novel and cinema. The study of mystery and detective fiction should lead you to a deeper understanding of how literature works overall, what characteristics are common to all
significant literary works, how history and culture influence the development of a genre,
and how literary critics assess works of literature, i.e., how a writer or a genre becomes
labeled as "major" or "minor," "belletristic" or "low-brow."

Texts

Chandler, R. *The Big Sleep* ISBN: 0–394–75828–5
Grafton, S. *"A" Is for Alibi: A Kinsey Millhone Mystery* ISBN: 0553279912
Hammett, D. *The Maltese Falcon* ISBN: 0–679–72264–5
Mosley, W. *Devil in a Blue Dress* ISBN: 0–393–02854–2
Murakami, H. *Hard-Boiled Wonderland and the End of the World.* ISBN:0–679–74346–4
Paretsky, S. *Indemnity Only* ISBN:0–440–21069–0

Poe, E.A. "The Murders in the Rue Morgue" (1841), "The Mystery of Marie Rogêt" (1843), and "The Purloined Letter" (1844) (Handout).
Todorov, T. "The Typology of Detective Fiction," *The Poetics of Prose* (Handout).

Participation

It is expected that all students participate during in-class exercises and class discussions. I understand that it is difficult for some people to speak up in class, but without input from 100% of the students, the class cannot be 100% productive.

Test Policies: There will be no formal exams; however, there will be two papers, a midterm and a final that I expect everyone to complete and return to me by the listed deadline. On the midterm you do not need to use outside sources; however, for the final paper you must incorporate five to seven outside sources into your paper. The topics for your papers will be left up to you; however, I will provide a list of potential thesis topics as well. I also require a weekly journal response and an in-class response to the films we view.

Grades/Assessment

The overall grade for this course will be based on the two papers, preparation for the course, attendance, and participation.

Attendance and other policies: Attendance matters. Arriving late or leaving early will count as ½ of an absence. 2 unexcused absences is an automatic failure. Please turn off cell phones and pagers. Drinks and food are fine during class.

PROCEDURE FOR EXTRA HELP! If there are concepts that you have trouble grasping, or you feel that my comments on your written work are unclear, please do not hesitate to approach me before or after class.

*Please note that plagiarism is unacceptable. If you hand in plagiarized work I will be compelled to turn your work over to academic advising and you will fail the course.

Course Schedule

— Introduction to Detective Fiction
— Introductions; review course syllabus; some basics of detective writing (Todorov handout to be read for next class); handout and Edgar Allan Poe's "The Murders in the Rue Morgue" (1841), "The Mystery of Marie Rogêt" (1843), and "The Purloined Letter" (1844).
— A template for detective fiction? Poe continued; Todorov, Tzvetan. "The Typology of Detective Fiction."
— The Hard-boiled tradition in America
— Dashiell Hammett, *Maltese Falcon*; view 1941 film starring Humphrey Bogart
— Raymond Chandler, *The Big Sleep*; view 1946 film starring Humphrey Bogart
— Midterm paper due 5–7 pages.
— Feminism and Detective Fiction
— Sue Grafton, "A" Is for Alibi
— S. Paretsky, *Indemnity Only*
— Ethnic Detective fiction

— Walter Mosley, *Devil in a Blue Dress*; view 1995 film starring Denzel Washington
— Influences of the Hardboiled tradition in Postmodern media
— H. Murakami, *Hard-Boiled Wonderland and the End of the World*; view *Cowboy Be-Bop*
— Last Class: View Coen brothers film, *The Big Lebowski*
— Final paper due 7–10 pages with five to seven outside sources

Holmes Is Where the Art Is
Architectural Design Projects

DERHAM GROVES

Two Architectural Design Projects

I have been hooked on Sherlock Holmes ever since Mrs. Vines, my seventh grade English teacher, read "The Adventure of the Speckled Band" by Sir Arthur Conan Doyle out loud in class one day in 1969. I began a bachelor of architecture degree at Deakin University (Australia) in 1976. For my final-year project in 1981, I designed a Sherlock Holmes Centre — a building devoted to the study of Holmes, comprising a cinema and a theatre on the ground floor, a museum on the first floor, and a library on the second floor. Since I started teaching architecture in 1988, a continuing interest of mine has been exploring sense of place through the Holmes stories. What I mean by "sense of place" is the story-telling — even "autobiographical" — potential of architecture.

Conan Doyle was expert at creating literary houses that truly reflect the personalities of the fictional characters who inhabit them. One of the best is 221B Baker Street — the London abode of Holmes. The detective's quirky personality is revealed through small details about 221B, such as keeping "his cigars in the coal-scuttle [and] his tobacco in the toe-end of a Persian slipper" (*New Annotated Sherlock Holmes* 1: 528). However, there is a wealth of good examples in the sixty Holmes stories: Deep Dene House in "The Adventure of the Norwood Builder," Nathan Garrideb's house in "The Adventure of the Three Garridebs," Pondicherry Lodge in *The Sign of the Four* — to name just three. Furthermore, the titles of six Holmes stories feature houses: Abbey Grange, The Copper Beeches, the empty house (i.e., Camden House), Shoscombe Old Place, The Three Gables, and Wisteria Lodge. Conan Doyle was acutely aware of the importance of place in the Holmes stories.

Crime fiction writers may be better at describing places than writers of other types of fiction, if for no other reason than solving a mystery usually depends on the detective (closely followed by the reader) knowing exactly where everyone and everything were when the crime occurred. But Conan

Doyle's architectural imagination may not have been solely due to his skills as a crime fiction writer; the fact that his father was an architect might have also contributed to it. Indeed, when summing up his body of writings in his autobiography *Memories and Adventures,* Conan Doyle even likened himself to "some architect or builder who, having laboured long to complete his edifice, finally stands back to survey it in its entirety."[1]

Given that architects and crime fiction writers share an interest in "character" and "place," and that Conan Doyle learned a great deal from his father who was an architect, perhaps architects can also learn a lot from crime fiction writers like Conan Doyle. Two architectural design projects that I sometimes have run at RMIT University (Australia), where I used to teach, and the University of Melbourne (Australia), where I now teach, use the Holmes stories as starting points. In "Better Holmes and Gardens," groups of first- and second-year architecture students designed contemporary houses for characters in the Holmes stories, while in "Holmes Away from Home" they designed a hotel with a Sherlock Holmes theme. Following is a sample of what they came up with.

Better Holmes and Gardens

In *The Hound of the Baskervilles* brash young Sir Henry Baskerville inherits Baskerville Hall following the unexplained death of his uncle, Sir Charles Baskerville. "In the fading light I could see that the centre was a heavy block of building from which a porch projected," observes Holmes' colleague and friend Dr. Watson, as he views the Hall for the first time. "The whole front was draped in ivy, with a patch clipped bare here and there where a window or a coat of arms broke through the dark veil. From this central block rose the twin towers, ancient, crenulated, and pierced with many loopholes. To right and left of the turrets were more modern wings of black granite. A dull light shone through heavy mullioned windows, and from the high chimneys which rose from the steep, high-angled roof there sprang a single black column of smoke" (3: 466–67). Sir Henry vows to carry out his deceased uncle's plans to modernize their gloomy ancestral home.

Andre Konarski (RMIT) thought of Sir Henry as showy and vain, so he designed a large imposing house that resembled a peacock. It had a central cluster of brick and stone towers, more Disneyland than medieval in style, with two wings of glass and metal on either side. The central entrance porch was shaped like the toe of a shoe — a reference to the theft of Sir Henry's boots, an incident in the story that helps Holmes solve the case. The towers housed a lounge room on the ground level, a master bedroom with an adjoining bathroom on the first level, a garden atrium on the second level, and a turret on the third level. The north wing of the house contained a dining room, a kitchen and a rumpus room on the ground level, and a sunroom, a bedroom with an adjoining bathroom, and an outdoor deck on the first level. The south wing contained a billiard room, a bathroom, two bedrooms adjoining another bathroom, and a garage on the ground level; and a study, a bedroom with an adjoining bathroom, and an outdoor deck on the first level. The towers represented the peacock's body and old Baskerville Hall, while the wings represented the peacock's tail and modern Baskerville Hall.

Sir Henry's neighbours— Jack Stapleton, a keen amateur entomologist, and his sister Beryl — live at Merripit House, which is not described in detail in *The Hound of the Baskervilles.* When Sir Henry falls in love with Beryl, Jack unaccountably becomes jealous. However, it turns out they are not siblings, but husband and wife. It also emerges that Jack is actually a long-lost member of the Baskerville family who desperately wants to inherit Baskerville Hall, so he revives the curse of the hound of the Baskervilles, setting a vicious dog first on his uncle, Sir Charles, resulting in the old man's death, and then on his cousin, Sir Henry, who barely survives the attack.

Sebastiano Ghezzi (RMIT) designed a brick house in the form of a butterfly, symbolizing Stapleton's hobby — entomology. A patio and an outhouse, which doubled as a kennel for the hound, separated the two wings of the butterfly/house. One wing had hardly any windows, representing Jack's dark side, while the other let in the light, symbolizing his public face. The single-story dark wing had a living room and a circular study hidden by a fireplace, while the two-story bright wing had a bathroom, a kitchen, and a dining room on the ground level; and a bedroom on the first level. The roof was clad with timber shingles and swept up to a sharp point, expressing the flight of a butterfly.

In "The Adventure of Black Peter," Peter Carey, the retired captain of the steam-sealer *Sea Unicorn,* is stabbed to death with a harpoon inside "a little, single-roomed hut, sixteen feet by ten.... He had called it a cabin, and a cabin it was, sure enough, for you would have thought that you were in a ship. There was a bunk at one end, a sea-chest, maps and charts, a picture of the *Sea Unicorn,* a line of log-books on a shelf, all exactly as one would expect to find it in a captain's room" (2: 981). Carey's cabin is located a few hundred yards from his house, a long low stone building, where the drunk and violent captain's long-suffering family lives.

To indicate that Carey was a seal hunter, the plan of the house designed by Eric Yu (Melbourne) was shaped like a decapitated seal. Its body was at one corner of the site and its head was diagonally opposite. Carey's cabin was in the seal's head. On the ground floor was his den with a large seascape on one wall, and in the basement was his bedroom. Carey's house was in the seal's body. The front door was in the fin; the foyer, featuring an aquarium where Carey raised baby seals to eat, according to Eric, was in the stomach; the bathroom, bedrooms, kitchen, laundry, and living room ran along the spine; and the garage was in the tail. Undulating arches that ran the length of the house symbolized the seal's skeleton, ocean waves, and the lurching gate of a drunken sailor.

In "The Adventure of the Man with the Twisted Lip," Holmes looks into the mysterious disappearance of Neville St. Clair, a well-dressed man about town who lives comfortably with his wife and two children at The Cedars, "a large villa which stood within its own grounds" (1: 178). Mrs. St. Clair is convinced that Hugh Boone, a well-known hideous-looking beggar who lives alone above the opium den the Bar of Gold, "the vilest murder-trap on the whole river-side" (1: 168), is responsible for kidnapping her husband. But Holmes discovers that St. Clair and Boone are one and the same person.

The house designed by Jessie McCudden (Melbourne) reflected Neville's daily transformation from respectable businessman to squalid beggar while attempting to hide from his family how he made a living. It consisted of four rectangular boxes arranged like "a cascade of children's bricks" (1: 172–73) similar to those Neville promised to buy his children on the day that he disappeared. The family lived in the first three boxes, which were linked to each other by a pair of enclosed bridges. The first contained a bedroom and an en suite bathroom and toilet for Neville and his wife; the second had a dining room, a kitchen and a lounge room for the family; and the third contained two bedrooms and an en suite bathroom and toilet for the children. Hugh Boone lived in the fourth box. While it appeared to be isolated from the rest of the house, it was actually connected to the first box by an overhead wire-cage bridge that was almost invisible. Every morning Neville entered his bathroom, climbed a hidden staircase, crossed the wire-cage bridge, opened a trapdoor, and descended a ladder into the fourth box where he dressed as a beggar and left via a secret back door.

In "The Adventure of the Final Problem," Holmes is chased by his nemesis, Professor James Moriarty, to Switzerland where they fight above the treacherous Reichenbach Falls, resulting in the Professor tumbling to his death below. Moriarty is "a man of good birth and excellent education, endowed by nature with a phenomenal mathematical faculty," Holmes tells Watson. "At the age of twenty-one he wrote a treatise upon the binomial theorem.... On the strength of it he won the mathematical chair at one of our smaller universities.... But the man had hereditary tendencies of the most diabolical kind.... He is the Napoleon of crime.... He is the organiser of half that is evil and nearly all that is undetected in this great city" (1: 718–19).

Rosalyna Wee (Melbourne) designed a house in the form of a long narrow strip, which comprised a row of abstract sculptures that fitted into the suburban park site extremely well and—most importantly—hid the underground house below, where Moriarty lived completely out of sight. It was divided into two zones at opposite ends of the house: one for work/day, which included his office, and one for rest/night, which included his bedroom. There were also interactions of light and dark and voids and solids between the park and the house. For example, an ornamental pool at ground level allowed light into the work/day zone below. According to Rosalyna, Moriarty's house was a play of opposites. Holmes, the perfect hero, needs Moriarty, the perfect villain, to exist in the same way that light needs dark and voids need solids.

In "The Adventure of the Veiled Lodger," Holmes and Watson hear the tragic confession of ex-circus performer Eugenia Ronder. She was married to the owner of a circus, "a human pig, or rather ... wild boar" (2: 1700), who constantly abused and mistreated her. This forced her into the arms of Leonardo, the circus strong man, and together they plotted to murder her "ruffian, bully, beast" (2: 1700) of a husband. Leonardo beat the circus owner to death using a nail-studded club, hoping that it would appear that a lion had mauled him. However, when Eugenia opened the lion's cage to conceal their crime, the creature smelled blood and viciously attacked her. After that she always wore a heavy veil to hide her badly disfigured face.

Daniel Kumnick (Melbourne) designed a long narrow house that represented the course of Eugenia's life. The front wall of the house was decorated with multiple full-height images of Andy Warhol's painting of Marilyn Monroe, *Orange Marilyn,* which represented Eugenia's face. At one point Marilyn-Eugenia's face was savagely cut by two large shards of glass and thereafter her face was blurred almost beyond recognition. This symbolized Eugenia being mauled by the lion. Inside the house fractured glass walls that provided varying levels of transparency represented this horrific event.

In "The Adventure of the Speckled Band," Dr. Grimesby Roylott attempts to murder his stepdaughter, Helen Stoner, by coaxing his pet swamp adder to bite her while she sleeps. Two years earlier he murdered her sister, Julia, in the same way. Fittingly, his house, Stoke Moran, is one of the most sinister-looking houses in the Holmes stories. It has "a high central portion, and two curving wings, like the claws of a crab, thrown out on each side," observes Watson. "In one of these wings the windows were broken, and blocked with wooden boards, while the roof was partly caved in, a picture of ruin. The central portion was in little better repair, but the right-hand block was comparatively modern, and the blinds in the windows, with the blue smoke curling up from the chimneys, showed that this was where the family resided" (1: 246). Furthermore, the devil lurks in the details, as Stoke Moran is built not simply of stone but "grey, lichen-blotched stone," and Helen's bedroom is lined not just with oak but "brown, worm-eaten oak, so old and discoloured that it may have dated from the original building of the house" (1: 246–47).

The house designed by Madeleine Scarfe (RMIT) matched Watson's description of Stoke Moran fairly closely. However, she added some interesting touches of her own to the residential wing of the house, including a gold-coloured roof and Indian style roof decorations, which reflected Roylott's past as a doctor in Calcutta where he acquired a menagerie of exotic pets that not only included the poisonous snake but also a baboon and a cheetah.

The house designed by Lucas Riley (Melbourne) looked nothing like Stoke Moran in the Holmes story, reflecting instead Roylott's total domination of Julia and Helen. Roylott occupied four guard-towers arranged in a square block and linked by elevated walkways resembling a prison camp. He overlooked Julia and Helen's bedrooms, which were shaped like coffins and connected to each other by an underground serpentine passage. Roylott could access this passage via a rope ladder symbolizing the dummy bell pull that helped Holmes solve the case. The ceiling (lid) of Julia's bedroom (coffin) was completely closed because she was already dead while Helen's lid was only half-closed because her fate still hung in the balance.

Sir Arthur Conan Doyle's characters make fascinating architectural clients—to say the least—and the designs of their houses constitute a unique manifestation of the world of Sherlock Holmes. Most of the students took to the Holmes stories like seasoned aficionados, even though many came from Asian countries where Holmes is not an intrinsic part of the popular culture. These projects allowed the architecture students to explore a number of important issues concerning sense of place, including the consequence of small details, the function of materials, the role of storytelling, and the significance of symbolism. They also gave students the opportunity to hone their place-recording skills through drawing, model-making and writing. However, they could not resolve for certain which is mightier: the writer's pen or the model-maker's saw.

Holmes Away from Home

Instead of running the "Better Holmes and Gardens" project again in 2004, I asked the second-year architecture students at the University of Melbourne to design a hotel with a Sherlock Holmes theme for the Baker Street Irregulars (BSI), the world's oldest Sherlock Holmes appreciation society. The BSI was founded in the early 1930s by the American writer Christopher Morley, who named it after a group of street urchins in *A Study in Scarlet,* the very first Holmes story. Membership in the BSI was initially restricted to Morley's inner circle, but in December 1934 it was opened up to anyone who could solve a cryptic Holmes crossword puzzle published in his column in *The Saturday Review of Literature.* While only six people did it correctly, the ranks of the BSI grew steadily from then onwards. Currently it has about three hundred members. The BSI holds an annual dinner in New York City on the Friday closest to the 6th of January — Holmes' birthday.

I was concerned that designing a multistory hotel might be beyond the abilities of some students, but then I read of a plan to convert a dowdy office building in the heart of Melbourne into a boutique hotel, and figured that it might be easier for them to renovate this rather than starting from scratch. (While Melbourne is not New York City, I decided that for the sake of this project it was close enough.)

A few students had never read a Holmes story (egad!), so I suggested they start with "The Adventure of the Speckled Band" (described earlier) and "The Adventure of the Red-Headed League." In the latter story, flame-haired Jabez Wilson joins the mysterious Red-Headed League to receive a generous salary for sitting in the League's office all day and copying out the *Encyclopaedia Britannica,* only to discover later that it was merely a ruse to get him away from his pawnbroker's shop during the day. I chose these two because in 1927 Conan Doyle declared "The Speckled Band" to be his best Holmes story and "The Red-Headed League" to be second best, while in 1944 the BSI judged them to be his best and third-best, and in 1954 his best and fourth-best.

Several architecture students based their designs on one or more of Holmes' famous symbols — his deerstalker hat, his Inverness cape, his magnifying glass, and his (apocryphal) meerschaum pipe. While this was perhaps an obvious approach to take, successfully making architecture from everyday articles like these is more difficult than it perhaps sounds, since the articles usually have to undergo drastic changes of scale and materials in the process.

The BSI Hotel designed by Gladys Chan was dotted with conical bay windows that symbolized Holmes' magnifying glass, which she believed was a talisman because it changed the way people saw and understood things. The front of the building was imprinted with two sets of concentric circles, which looked like the ripples caused by dropping a stone in a pond and represented a Sherlock Holmes investigation, since it also radiated out in all directions from a central starting point and caused ripples or waves. The circles also looked like shooting targets, which was perhaps a reference to Holmes' habit of adorning "the opposite wall [of his sitting room] with a patriotic V.R. done in bullet-pocks" (1: 529). The hotel also appeared to be swathed in fabric, like a criminal wearing a mask to conceal his identity. This also resembled the sheet used to cover a murder victim at the scene of the crime.

I was not surprised that "The Speckled Band" featured in so many of the architecture students' designs. This was not merely because Holmes and Watson pretend to be architects in the story, but mainly for the reason that the snake provided the students with a very good opportunity to experiment with curves— an architectural form that they often discover in the second year of their course. To give the feeling of snakes winding through the building, Sky Yi weaved a serpentine plane through the length of the Jetset building, which was made up of different-sized coloured-glass discs that represented the markings of the deadly snake. As the plane zigzagged from floor to floor it created a series of interesting and unusual interior spaces. The walls and ceilings were curved; even the furniture was curved. The top two-thirds of the hotel's north facade and the bottom two-thirds of its south facade were covered with black metal louvres with different sized holes in them, which represented the air vent through which the "speckled band" silently passed from Dr. Grimesby Roylott's bedroom to his stepdaughters' rooms. The holes also functioned like huge peepholes, which allowed the people inside the hotel to look out and the people outside it to look in.

The BSI Hotel designed by Jacky So looked like an open volume of the *Encyclopaedia Britannica* as well as a newspaper. The Red-Headed League's advertisement announcing "there is now another vacancy open which entitles a member of the League to a salary of four pounds a week for purely nominal services" (1: 45) was written on the north facade of the building, while lots of bright red metal poles, which symbolized Wilson's fiery red hair, pierced the south facade, dramatically carving up the hotel's interior, including the banquet hall and the lobby.

A number of architecture students incorporated puzzles into their hotel designs because they viewed the Holmes stories as puzzles for the detective and the reader to solve. Some students also wanted to acknowledge the important role played by Christopher Morley's 1934 crossword puzzle in the history of the Baker Street Irregulars.

The hotel designed by Caroline Stawell looked like a huge crossword puzzle because a hotel designed for the Baker Street Irregulars must reflect their society she said. The building's structural grid of columns and beams doubled as the crossword puzzle's square grid, which not only controlled spaces in all directions, but also the design of the furniture and fittings contained within them. On the outside of the building clear glass formed the white squares and tight wire mesh made up the black ones, while inside the hotel the floors formed the white squares and the walls made up the black ones. Open plan architecture making use of open spaces was the result of this strict design methodology according to Caroline. In addition, twisted copper handrails ran between some floors on the outside of the building, which resembled the snakes in a game of snakes and ladders as well as the snake in "The Speckled Band."

A number of students designed hotels that symbolized the various stages of a crime investigation. Jeanniffer Andriana's BSI Hotel, for example, had asymmetrical panels arranged higgledy-piggledy on the outside of the building, which were either black to represent the mysteries depicted in the stories or red as a reminder of how Holmes solves the mysteries, often through bold action. The panels were attached to a crystalline truss, which also formed the ceiling of the banquet hall at the top of the building. Light entered through the gaps between the panels and washed down the walls to the public circulation areas. Many of the interior walls were also irregularly shaped, and there was a crystalline tiling pattern on the floors as well. Jeanniffer adopted this deconstructed design to capture the sense of drama that is present in the Holmes stories, referring to the distress, enthusiasm, confusion, and thrills experienced by Holmes.

It was very interesting to watch the second-year architecture students from the University of Melbourne interpreting literary concepts in bricks and mortar. However, this project presented them with some difficult challenges. The BSI Hotel was the largest and most complex building they had designed to date. Also, the drawing skills of some students had not yet developed sufficiently to do justice to their ideas, which often were very difficult to represent through drawings and models anyway.

The idea that a building can tell a story underpinned both "Better Holmes and Gardens" and "Holmes Away from Home." However, books have the power to impart new information, whereas buildings can evoke only what is already known — albeit in a new, perhaps more profound, way. That is why reading a building requires a lot more speculative imagination than reading a book.

NOTE

1. This quotation is from Conan Doyle's *Memories and Adventures*, page 447. All other documentation refers to *The New Annotated Sherlock Holmes*.

WORKS CITED

Conan Doyle, Arthur. *Memories and Adventures*. London: John Murray, 1930.
_____. *The New Annotated Sherlock Holmes*. 3 vols. Ed. Leslie S. Klinger. New York: Norton, 2005–06).

Southern Crime

The Clash of Hero and Villain in a Writing Course

MARY HADLEY

"An effective private eye short story will have all the qualities of good short fiction, and in addition will feature artistry in foreshadowing, theme and the planting of clues and will involve a chemistry that adds interest and meaning to the clash of the hero and villain" [Lutz 175].

Many people feel that they have within them a story just waiting to be written, perhaps because since childhood they have told stories and entertained their friends with imaginative flights of fancy. Writing fiction can be a perfect outlet for such students, but what about crime fiction? As teachers of this genre, we aim to tap into their enthusiasm but also into their evil character traits. These darker sides to their imaginations are the most enjoyable to unlock since the students will admit that they never dared voice the wicked scenarios which now flood their minds.

At Georgia Southern University crime fiction is taught as a writing class, not, as is the case at many universities, as literature.[1] Even though mine is substantially a creative writing class, I decided to incorporate a historical overview. Without an idea of where the genre began, how it evolved, and especially how societal changes on both sides of the Atlantic have influenced it, students cannot fully understand the different types of crime fiction and write stories that respond to or react against this tradition. In addition, the class is titled "Crime Fiction" rather than "Detective Fiction" or even "Mystery Writing," since the focus is not only on "whodunit" (mystery) or on the use of professional or amateur detectives (detective fiction), but also on *why* and *how* crime is done.

The types of students who choose Crime Fiction 5631 as one of their electives vary. Some semesters there are mainly creative writing majors taking the class as a final elective; other times the class is composed of students with a variety of majors who love to read crime fiction and want to try writing in the genre. Although some students see Crime Fiction as simply a fun class, they soon learn that the writing component of the class is just as rigorous and demanding as that of creative fiction or creative nonfiction.

Not only is the writing rigorous, but for many the reading is also. One of the problems with some of the students is that they have not read a lot, and in some cases have not read at all in the genre. Since I am a firm believer that students need to read in the genre if they want to write in it, I include several short stories in the class notes packet (see Appendix A) and at least one novel to show the students the huge variety of possibilities in the crime fiction genre.

Although not very familiar with the mystery/detective/crime genre, many students are totally hooked on writing science fiction or fantasy and want to write only about crimes that also incorporate these other elements. Over the years, I have learned that in order to prevent several students from immediately dropping the class, I have to be flexible. To this end, I allow one or two of their stories to include fantasy or sci-fi aspects; I nevertheless encourage them to see how exciting traditional crime fiction can be.

The assessment of this class is twofold. The students critique each other's writing in small or large groups in a workshop environment. After the initial criticism, the students will edit their work and then hand it in to me for my suggestions. At this point, I do not put any grade on the piece. At the end of the semester, the students pick whichever stories and exercises they think best reflect their progress with a minimum requirement of thirty pages and present them to me in a portfolio which is assigned a grade.

Crime Fiction 5631 starts with a historical overview both to show the development of the genre and to make sure that the students read some of the classic crime stories of our time. Beginning with Poe's "The Murders in the Rue Morgue," students move to Sir Arthur Conan Doyle's "The Adventure of the Speckled Band" and watch the movie *The Hound of the Baskervilles*. They also watch an A & E biography of Conan Doyle with footage of an interview with him.

Because writing in the crime fiction genre is new to all the students, their early assignments include having them imitate stories they have read. Since these earlier stories use language which is very different from today's slang, it is important to familiarize the students with it. The first writing assignment is made easier by having heard Conan Doyle speak, seeing Sherlock Holmes and Watson in the movie, and reading Conan Doyle's short story. The students then have to write a two-page dialogue between Holmes and Watson, which takes place either at the start, the middle, or the end of a crime. The reason why they do not write a complete mystery in the style of Conan Doyle is because the focus of this first assignment is on voice and tone. At this point in the semester, they cannot pull all the threads of a mystery

together, but they can imitate what they have read and heard and be successful in this simple exercise. It is important to build up to the writing of a complete story of ten or more pages in length, and students always say that
exercises of this kind work well for them. (See *Teach Yourself Writing Crime
Fiction* by Lesley Grant-Adamson for more of these sorts of exercises.)

The next assignment is to read Agatha Christie's "The Chocolate Box"
and learn some interesting facts about the Golden Age of mystery fiction.[2]
Though Raymond Chandler criticized these writers in his "The Simple Art
of Murder," Christie's puzzle-formula plots[3] moved the detective genre forward and bear studying if students want to use the still popular closed-room
technique (where there is a limited number of characters in one location) in
their crime stories. Her huge popularity and amazing book sales make her
an author that crime fiction courses do well to include.

At different times the course has included a Christie movie such as *The
Mirror Crack'd* (1980), or as it moved onto the American hard-boiled genre,
The Maltese Falcon (1941) or *Farewell, My Lovely* (1975). Having read "The
House in Turk Street" by Dashiell Hammett, students discuss the rise of the
American hard-boiled genre and why the "mean streets" appealed more to
the urban American reader of the 1930s and 1940s than the cozy countrified
stories of Agatha Christie, Dorothy Sayers, and others. *Farewell, My Lovely*
and the short story lend themselves to the next assignment, a dialogue
between a vamp female and Philip Marlowe.

The contrast in voice and tone between this assignment and the previous dialogue helps make the students aware of their own narrative strengths
and weaknesses. Many love this exercise and describe both characters with
ease. Focusing on characters that are very different from today's male private
investigators and women forces the students to consider details which make
their dialogues realistic. For example, they research some of the slang words
of the period and describe both characters with attention to the types of
clothes worn at that time. When the exercise is complete, the students read
both of their dialogues to the whole group, who critique them. Later I collect the dialogues and add my input.

Some crime fiction teachers may wonder if it is important to have a historical component in a creative writing class. Crime fiction has changed a great
deal in the past one hundred and fifty years, and today's novels and short stories are less likely to contain puzzles and focus on who did the crime. In his
book *The Reader and the Detective Story*, George Dove describes the detective story as "transitory, without long-range goals or purposes; it is fundamentally an intellectual undertaking; it is recreational, intended primarily
to relax, and it is a disciplined, delimited literary form" (2). He makes a good
case for the early authors following this pattern, but those who teach crime

fiction would likely disagree when he adds Sara Paretsky's *Guardian Angel* to his list. Many of today's detective stories are neither "fundamentally an intellectual undertaking" nor "a disciplined, delimited literary form." They are far more complex, and it is because of this fascinating complexity that students should study how far and in what different directions today's crime fiction has traveled.

Paretsky, along with the other feminist hard-boiled writers who began writing in the early 1980s, added a great deal to crime novels. By knowing the history behind such writers as Sara Paretsky and Sue Grafton, students will learn how and why the genre has changed so much. Priscilla Walton and Manina Jones claim: "Feminist hard-boiled detective novels provide their readers with fictional narratives that have repercussions beyond their immediate textual performances" (112). In "Writing a Series Character," Paretsky says: "I'm interested in such social questions as how large institutions affect the lives of ordinary people, and how the criminal justice system treats large-scale white-collar crime" (74). Even though Paretsky was familiar with the earlier male hard-boiled writers, she did not want her protagonist to be like theirs, nor did she want someone like Miss Marple. Thus the female private eye was born. Openly sexual, working in urban areas, using physical violence, but rarely resorting to guns, and easily able to defend themselves, the women "display a deep fascination with human motivation, with the searing emotional drama of splintered relationships, with the corrosive friction between the individual and society" (Albert 100). Because the female hard-boiled authors so changed the crime genre, it is essential that students not only read stories by these authors, but that they learn the extent of the social consciousness raising which has ensued and, if possible, incorporate some themes into their own work to make their stories reflect the norms of today's writers.

George Dove describes detective fiction that is a far cry from the crime fiction of today, when most authors are concerned with the psychology of the criminal and the detective and continue to shine light on contemporary social problems. British author Minette Walters, for example, whose first novel, *The Ice House*, was published in 1992, has tackled such problems as the far-reaching consequences of a lack of education, racism, child abuse, homelessness and the use of torture in wartime within stand-alone novels that are exciting psychological crime thrillers. As students read stories by such authors as Walters, and the class's historical perspective moves from the early writers to the important female hard-boiled writers, students see how the focus of the genre has changed from who has committed the crime to why and how he or she did it; they learn how today's female protagonist is very different from her earlier male counterpart and that they too can blend serious issues within the framework of a work of fiction.

The next assignment asks the students to write an initial two-page detailed description of a main character, following suggestions from the text *Teach Yourself Writing Crime Fiction* by British author Lesley Grant-Adamson. At this point many of the female students choose to make their protagonist a strong female in the style of the stories they read by Paretsky and Grafton, but some of the male students return to a Philip Marlowe type. Since this activity and the following one are leading to their first five-ten page short story, it is necessary for the students to have a fully fleshed out main character to bring verisimilitude to their story. Once all the students have decided that they really like their main character, they gather in small groups and read the descriptions. They then critique the portraits and give helpful suggestions for possible alterations. At this point, individuals are encouraged to justify why they have created a certain type of character and give a brief overview of the story they are working on. And then I take in the descriptions to add my own advice.

Next the class examines the importance of setting and plotting by reading chapters two and four in *Teach Yourself Writing Crime Fiction*. Students are encouraged to use a setting with which they are familiar. Since many of them come from Georgia, some choose either a rural setting or the urban complexities of Atlanta. Both work well as the background for their first longer mystery. However, as they know that they will have to write a Georgia mystery later in the semester, some of them choose another setting at this point for greater variety in their stories. Having practiced writing dialogue, and having a detailed description of their protagonist and a good idea as to where they will set their first story, the students are able to incorporate these elements into a fast-moving plot. Although *Teach Yourself Writing Crime Fiction* is a self-guided text, it is eminently practical and packs a huge number of important details into each chapter. The students are able to make good use of it because it answers most of their questions but does not talk down to them.

After every assignment, the students meet in a workshop setting to discuss what they felt was successful and where they had problems with their stories. They read them aloud to get feedback from their peers and to get help with details like titles, and major aspects like characterization, plot twists, endings, etc. The workshop format is fairly standard for creative writing classes, and most students feel comfortable giving and receiving criticism. Teachers can be more facilitators than directors and can work with the suggestions of the students and add their opinions rather than be the only voice of authority. Very quickly students learn who are the stronger writers and will listen carefully to their suggestions while giving help to those who are clearly having the greatest difficulty.

The next assignment begins the reading of a full-length novel. Over the years I have used novels of local authors who will visit the class to talk about their craft. Beginning authors such as Tanya Tienne (*Control*) and Rowan Wolfe (*The Trial of Evan Gage*) have talked to the class as well as highly successful local author Karin Slaughter (*Blindsighted* and others), and as yet unpublished authors, including Tina Whittle, a former student and winner of *Gulf Stream Magazine*'s 2004 Mystery Fiction Contest. In addition, I have used the books I have co-authored with my husband under the name Mary Charles. Using my own books is very successful since I can tell the students all the difficulties we had, and especially when the students read *Casey's Revenge*, I can talk about the particular problems of writing a first novel in a series. Since many of the students envisage a time when they will write a novel and want to be published, these visits by an author can answer many of their questions and concerns.

Since *Casey's Revenge* is set in the Savannah, Georgia, area and has a local flavor, the next assignment, of ten to fifteen pages, is for the students to write a Georgia mystery. For those who had a Georgia setting in the previous story, this assignment is different in that not only is the setting local, but the characters are also typically Georgian. This leads to a discussion on stereotypes and the use of dialect. Over the years in this course, students have written such diverse stories as one based in the Okefenokee Swamp with hunters as the main characters and a story based in downtown Atlanta with gang members as the characters. Georgia is such a large state that the variety of characters and the diversity of crime are endless.

The next assignment, again ten to fifteen pages in length, focuses on a distinct subgenre of crime fiction, the police procedural, because this is such a popular genre on television. Most students have a favorite television show they watch regularly and find it interesting to write this type of story. Since it is important for students to pay attention to details in their writing, this story with a police detective as the main protagonist reinforces what they had to do for the hard-boiled dialogue and asks them to research police terminology and procedure to gain accuracy and verisimilitude.

From writing stories of ten to fifteen pages, students move to a very short story of no more than three pages in length with a surprising twist in the ending. Students read at least one story from Roald Dahl's excellent book *Tales of the Unexpected*. These stories are compactly crafted with fascinating, unexpected endings. In addition, they read some *Five Minute Mysteries* by Ken Weber. Many students find it hard to plot in only a few pages, so this assignment helps them tighten their style and make every word count. Students who have taken a flash fiction course, where students write only one to three pages total for each story, have no problems writing only two or three crisp pages, but those who tend to be verbose find this a tough task. In all of the assignments, I try to balance a focus on writing style with creating an exciting, fast-paced plot.

The last assignment is possibly the class's favorite since it usually results in excellent research, personal satisfaction, and a lot of fun for the students and for all who hear their stories. The students have to write a "Perfect Crime." This means that whatever the crime, not necessarily murder, the perpetrator must get away with it. Over the years, the students have written the most amazing stories for this assignment. Because this assignment proved to be so successful, I began the habit of having the students choose either this story or an earlier one to put in a class collection for them to keep as a memento of the class. This has worked well, and I give a copy to my department chair and college dean. The collections have been used to recruit creative writing majors at Georgia Southern's open houses.

As this essay shows, a crime fiction class with a historical base and a great deal of creative writing can be enormously satisfying for both teachers and students. The choice of which readings to include is a hard one, but having a packet of class readings (see Appendix A) that can be changed each time the class is offered is one solution. In this way, as the teacher I can remain enthusiastic and current, and the students can learn about the conventions while being exposed to the latest innovations. Over the years students have usually been committed to reading the materials, industrious in their research, and extremely creative in their writing. Several have gone on to MFA programs, two have novels being considered by publishers, and many have had their stories published online or in competitions. This is a course that allows them to be successful even as they are plotting a character's demise.

NOTES

1. A website entitled *Courses: General Introductions to Crime Fiction* gives details of many crime fiction classes in universities in England and Canada as well as the United States. All save one of the universities described — Cardiff, Lancaster, Leeds, University of Western Ontario, Notre Dame, Buffalo University, and others— teach crime fiction by tracing its development and analyzing it within historical, philosophical, aesthetic, social, and other contexts. Of all the courses described on this site, only Alverno, in Milwaukee, Wisconsin, adds a creative writing component in the form of journal writing. However, the amount of writing appears far less than what students are expected to do at Georgia Southern.

2. The Golden Age is that period of mystery fiction which runs from about 1920 to the late 1930s. Authors such as Agatha Christie, Dorothy Sayers, Margery Allingham, Nagaio Marsh, and others are considered Golden Age authors. The mysteries of this period followed certain conventions, in particular that the focus of the mystery was for

the readers to discover the identity of the murderer "whodunit" as opposed to being concerned with why or how the crime was committed

3. The puzzle formula allowed the author to create several puzzles or false leads to encourage the reader to consider certain characters to be the murderer while in fact the least likely suspect usually turned out to be the perpetrator. The Golden Age mysteries were considered mind games or puzzles for the readers of that period. Author and critic Alison Light in *Forever England: Femininity, Literature and Conservatism Between the Wars* explains why detective writers needed to write in a soothingly entertaining fashion as a reaction to the traumas of World War I:

> The whodunit between the wars came rapidly to be as insensible to violence as it could be. As a literature of convalescence it developed a strongly meditative framework, relying upon a kind of inturned and internal ratiocination rather than on what would stir or shake the reader.... Fleshiness [of characters] either figuratively or literally, was perhaps in gross bad taste after the butchery many had witnessed. Violence is literally bad form [70].

WORKS CITED

Albert, Susan Wittig. 'Tough Girls, Hard Cases: Strong Women in Mystery." *Deadly Women*. Ed. Jan Grape, Dean James and Ellen Nehr. New York: Carroll & Graf, 1998.

Charles, Mary. *Casey's Revenge*. Tunbridge Wells: Twenty-First Century Publishers, 2003.

Courses: General Introductions to Crime Fiction. <http://www.crimeculture.com/Con tents/Courses-GenIntros.html>.

Dahl, Roald. *Tales of the Unexpected*. New York: Vintage Books, 1990.

Dove, George N. *The Reader and the Detective Story*. Bowling Green, OH: Bowling Green State University Popular Press, 1997.

Grafton, Sue. " Introduction." *Writing Mysteries*. Ed. Sue Grafton. Cincinnati: Writer's Digest Books, 2002.

Grant-Adamson, Lesley. *Teach Yourself Writing Crime Fiction*. Chicago: McGraw-Hill, 1996.

Light, Alison. *Forever England: Femininity, Literature and Conservatism Between the Wars*. London: Routledge, 1991.

Lutz, John. "Short and Shamus." *Writing the Private Eye Novel*. Ed. Robert J. Randisi. Cincinnati: Writer's Digest Books, 1997.

Paretsky, Sara. "Writing a Series Character." *Writing Mysteries*. Ed. Sue Grafton. Cincinnati: Writer's Digest Books, 2002.

Popular Fiction at Stonecoast. University of Southern Maine. <http://www.usm.maine. edu/stonecoastmfa/PopularFictionatStonecoast.htm>.

Walton, Priscilla L., and Manina Jones. *Detective Agency*. Berkeley and Los Angeles: University of California Press, 1999.

Weber, Ken. *Five Minute Mysteries*. Philadelphia: Running Press, 1989.

Appendix A

Contents (including short stories) in the Class Notes Packet 2007

— Edgar Allan Poe Facts
— "The Murders in the Rue Morgue" Edgar Allan Poe
— Sir Arthur Conan Doyle Facts
— "The Adventure of the Speckled Band" Arthur Conan Doyle
— Agatha Christie Facts
— Agatha Christie's Writing 1, 2 3
— "The Chocolate Box" Agatha Christie
— The American Hard-Boiled Genre 1 & 2
— Hard-Boiled Women
— "The House in Turk Street" Dashiell Hammett
— Similarities between Male Hard-Boiled and Female Soft-Boiled/Hard-Boiled
— Differences between Male Hard-Boiled and Female Soft-Boiled/Hard-Boiled 1 & 2
— 1980s Female Soft-Boiled Works
— Important Quotations: 1980s Female Soft-Boiled
— The Female Detective
— "A Poison That Leaves No Trace" Sue Grafton
— "The Maltese Cat" Sara Paretsky
— "Rounding Up Your Characters" Margaret Maron
— "Going Home" S.J. Rozan
— "Sadie When She Died" Ed McBain
— "Chee's Witch" Tony Hillerman
— "Dip in the Pool" Roald Dahl

Appendix B

Useful Collections of Short Crime Fiction Stories

Dahl, Roald. *Tales of the Unexpected*. New York: Vintage Books, 1990.
Duffy, Stella, and Lauren Henderson. *Tart Noir*. London: Pan Macmillan, 2002.
Hutchings, Janet, ed. *Simply the Best Mysteries*. New York: Carroll & Graf, 1998.
Mansfield-Kelley, Deane, and Lois A. Marchino, eds. *The Longman Anthology of Detective Fiction*. New York: Pearson Education, 2005.
Paretsky, Sara, ed. *Women on the Case*. New York: Dell, 1996.
Perry, Anne. *Malice Domestic*. New York: Pocket Books, 1997.
Wallace, Marilyn, ed. *The Best of Sisters in Crime*. New York: Berkley, 2000.
Weber, Ken. *Five Minute Mysteries*. Philadelphia: Running Press, 1989.

Adding Some Mystery
to Cultural Studies

STEVE HECOX

One of the functions of examining literature in the classroom is to bring students into contact with the lives and values of the people they read about. The best stories tell us about the culture of the people involved. They tell us what people care about, what they hold dear, and what they find both acceptable and unacceptable. This, it seems to me, is the reason for bringing mystery fiction into the classroom, for what tells us more about the values held by any society than what it considers to be crime and how vigorously and in what manner it pursues those who commit offenses against society?

Like any other good authors, mystery and detective fiction writers must make their characters believable. They need to put them in a time and place that is not only specific but realistic. As they do so, writers must be aware of their audiences and of the values that they share with them. They cannot deviate too far from the cultural norms or they will lose their readership. We can assume, therefore, that when popular authors write popular stories, their readers are in tune with those themes and those values that are expressed within them.

Certainly, there is not enough room here to explore this idea completely, so let us just look at a few ways that cultural studies can be explored in the context of a course in mystery fiction. We'll look at three examples: England at the turn of the nineteenth to the twentieth century, American society and its changes from the mid–twentieth century to the present, and the very different culture of the Navajo in the United States.

Surely, the greatest literary detective of all time is Sherlock Holmes, and he shows the Victorian world and its aspirations like no one else. When reading Holmes' stories, it is important to talk with students about the time in which he existed. It was the age in which the sun never set on the British Empire. It was an age in which the prevailing attitude was that one could accomplish anything if there was enough determination and concentration of the will. Of course, we do not see all of Victorian and Edwardian society in the stories. That would be impossible, but there is a good deal of that culture on display, as Holmes dives through the classes and examines the various strata of his society.

As students see Holmes and Watson, they not only see them interacting with others, but they also see the principal characters' own particular progressions through society. When they first meet, both are in financial straits. Holmes is trying to put together his own profession, which is only beginning to get on its feet. Watson is a newly returned, injured veteran of the Afghan war. They do not take rooms in Baker Street because they are friends. They have barely met, yet neither could afford suitable lodgings on his own. By the end of the saga, however, Holmes is quite wealthy, and Watson, who has had at least two wives in the interim, is financially stable as well, part of his income derived from the sale of his tales of his friend's adventures. Through these adventures, students can learn quite a bit about the British society of that time.

As stated before, it is a society which believes that whatever needs to be done can be done. Who more represents that ideal than Sherlock Holmes? His pursuit of facts and his ability to apply reason to them to solve the most complex problems epitomize more than anything else the can-do spirit of Victorian England.

Because of his fame, his reputation, and his disguises, Holmes finds himself in a variety of places that few other detectives ever would. Throughout the stories, students see people from cabinet-level ministers to members of the servant class. Holmes mingles with the grooms of the Serpentine Mews in "A Scandal in Bohemia." Disguised as an asthmatic old mariner, he visits the docks along the Thames in *The Sign of the Four*. On the other end of society, in "The Second Stain," he is visited by the Prime Minister, and in "The Bruce-Partington Plans," he is presented with an emerald tie pin by "a certain gracious lady" (Conan Doyle, "Bruce" 67).

There are three stories that I have found quite effective in describing some of the more interesting aspects of Victorian culture. "The Man with the Twisted Lip" opens with Holmes and Watson running into each other in an opium den. Both are there with good reason. Holmes is on a case and Watson is there to look for a friend at the request of his wife. It is a particularly interesting story, one that students have taken to for its irony alone. The tale revolves around Neville St. Clair, a journalist who has a nice middle-class home and family but leaves his profession to take up begging because he has discovered that if he puts up a good act, he can make more money on the sidewalk than he can by writing, something that English teachers can relate to. Students seem to enjoy talking about the idea as well.

In other stories, it is clear that Holmes has a low regard for the rich and the pompous oligarchs who pepper the upper levels of British society. We see this in a number of cases. For example, in "The Adventure of the Priory School," the child of the Duke of Holdernesse, a very wealthy and powerful man, has been kidnapped. Whenever he appears in the story, the Duke is shown to be pompous and arrogant. In the end, however, he hands Holmes the biggest check he ever receives. We see Holmes' attitude toward the self-righteous members of the upper classes at the end of the story as he pockets the Duke's check.

A third example is Holmes' relation to the characters in "The Problem of Thor Bridge." Here, we see again Holmes' contempt for the self-righteous but also his respect for the working woman, the latter being another theme that comes up often in the Holmesian canon. This story also brings up issues regarding the way that the British of the era viewed people of other lands. As he works to prove that Miss Grace Dunbar is innocent of killing the wife of J. Neil Gibson, the Gold King, we see Holmes' strong dislike of the former United States senator. Again, he scolds the high-and-mighty even as he solves their problems. We also see the attitude of the English toward Latin American women. Gibson's wife is Maria, a native of Brazil, who is described as "a creature of the Tropics.... Tropical by birth and tropical by nature. A child of the sun and of passion" (Conan Doyle, "Thor" 28). She is not only the dead woman in the story but the perpetrator of the frame of the genteel Miss Dunbar. A similar theme plays out in "The Adventure of the Sussex Vampire," in which the Peruvian-born Delores Ferguson is accused of vampirism. It would seem that the English of Holmes' time had a very rigid view of Latin American ladies. Nonetheless, "The Problem of Thor Bridge" gives students a chance to explore cultural biases, from the arrogant American to the fiery Latin-American woman, to the poor, innocent English woman, all within one short story.

American culture, of course, is more aptly explored through the adventures of the hard-boiled detective, and one of the most interesting things we, as teachers, can do is to help students examine the ways in which the values of this country have changed over the years. While there are countless hard-boiled characters to choose from, Raymond Chandler's Philip Marlowe (who appears in Chandler's fiction from the 1930s through the 1950s) is the most interesting detective in terms of examining the intricacies of the American culture of the time. First of all, he is a serial character; we see him in a number of works and in a number of different situations. Secondly, he has a literary child in the person of Spenser, the hard-boiled Boston detective created by Robert B. Parker, who was first introduced in 1973.

Marlowe represents the quintessential American hero. He is the one man who can stand up and defend those values that society holds dear. In that respect, he is the successor to the Western hero, the man who rides in on a white horse to save the town from those who would ravage it and destroy the social order. He takes a situation that is broken and makes it whole again. Obviously, this is a theme that can be discussed with great effect in class. I have found it helpful to supplement such discussions with Chandler's famous essay "The Simple Art of Murder" in which he describes the values that a chivalrous detective must have. It is an essay which helps students ground the role of the hero in twentieth-century American society. It provides the framework through which to discuss the vast majority of hard-boiled detectives.

Like the classic western hero, Marlowe is a loner. There is no serious love interest in any of the Chandler stories. While he does have some soft, romantic encounters with women, there is nothing that anyone would consider serious. He has only one consistent friend that we know about. Bernie Ohls is a police lieutenant that Marlowe knows from his days on the force. While they do not seem to be really close friends, they can trust each other, and in Marlowe's Los Angeles, that is significant.

Women in general are not treated well by Chandler. In fact, in all of his novels, the primary villains are women. In *The Big Sleep*, Carmen Sternwood is the cause of almost all of the trouble that ensues throughout the story. While not directly involved in all of it, everything, in one way or another, comes back to her. Following Carmen is a laundry list of female villains, the most notable of whom may be Velma Valento in *Farewell, My Lovely* and Eileen Wade in *The Long Goodbye*.

What this says about the culture of mid–twentieth century America I am not sure. It may say more about Mr. Chandler himself than about the society in which he lived. Certainly, it is an area worthy of exploration. What it does seem to say, though, is that Chandler's women are mysterious. They are creatures that are hard to understand, and they are capable of actions that no one would ever imagine. Chandler's villainous women stand out because they play against type. Females in college classes today were born with the expectation that they have the same opportunities as men. They did not in Chandler's day. Looking back to the past through such a lens is a way to get students, especially female students, to reflect upon the times when women were expected to stay in their place and to stay out of the public arena.

Chandler examines other social issues as well. The plot of *The Big Sleep*, for example, revolves around the rich and the gangsters doing whatever they want while the police are paid off to let them. Carmen poses for pornographic photos for Geiger, who sells them on Hollywood Boulevard with the full knowledge of the police. Eddie Mars runs a casino onshore and is never bothered because his local police are easily paid off. *The Big Sleep* is a story that is easy for students to digest, not only in terms of its literary qualities, but as a descriptor of the American culture of the time. The rich get to do what they want, and they are served by the legal system whether they are operating legally or not. The little people do not get a chance. It is always interesting to ask students if things have changed.

Five people are killed in *The Big Sleep*. Arthur Gwynn Geiger, the owner of the bookstore, is killed by Owen Taylor, the Sternwoods' chauffeur, who has a crush on Carmen. Joe Brody is killed by Carol Lundgren, Geiger's gay partner, who mistakenly believes that Brody killed his lover. Harry Jones is killed by Eddie Mars' hit man, Lash Cannino, who in turn is killed by Marlowe in a shootout. Finally, we have the death of the chauffeur himself, whose body was pulled from the water off the Lido pier. Who killed him? In a classroom setting, the list of the dead can be put on the board with the invitation to the students to fill in the perpetrator side. They will get most of them, but the one mystery they will have most trouble with is the question of who killed Owen Taylor. They will debate it. Most will say that it was Joe Brody, but no one will be sure. Who did kill Owen Taylor? Raymond Chandler was once asked that question and admitted that he did not know. That is the point. The death of a little man who sticks his face into the dealings of the rich and powerful does not mean anything in the culture of the time. Does it now? Students can spend some quality time thinking about that.

It is interesting to have students contrast Marlowe to Spenser, the hardboiled character created by Robert B. Parker, who has practically proclaimed himself to be Chandler's successor. When Chandler died in 1954, he had written two chapters of a novel called *Poodle Springs*. Parker took those two chapters and finished the novel himself, publishing it in 1990, a clear claim to succession. Perhaps names hold another clue. Students might want to guess if it is just a coincidence that Christopher Marlowe and Edmund Spenser were contemporary writers in late sixteenth-century England. Like Marlowe, Spenser is a tough, independent, and resourceful man. Like Marlowe, he had been on the police force, where he had problems taking orders from his superiors. When we meet him, he has his own office and his own apartment. He takes on the clients that come to him and is not afraid to get into trouble, and, like Marlowe, he ultimately finds a way to get out of it. There are, however, some significant differences between the two men, and examining those differences can become an interesting exercise.

The most significant difference between the two is their relationship with women. Unlike Marlowe, who, as stated earlier, is best viewed as a loner with no lasting romantic attachments, Spenser does have a significant other. His relationship with Susan Silverman is one of the central themes that run through the novels. She is the anchor of his relationship to the world outside the realm of crime, for she does understand what drives people to do what they do. Susan is a psychologist, a graduate of Harvard University who has her own practice. She is a self-contained, independent woman who needs neither Spenser nor any man to make her life complete. Still, she chooses Spenser, and he chooses her. That theme of choice runs throughout the stories. There are ups and downs in the relationship, but throughout the series, Susan is a driving force in Spenser's life. He depends on her for emotional support. He relies on her tender nature for his own well-being and upon her wisdom when he is trying to figure out why his clients and his adversaries are acting as they are. Most of all, he loves her. There are few things more evident in the Spenser novels than his feelings for Susan. While Marlowe could get by alone, Spenser cannot. He does not do well without Susan. She is the anchor of his emotional life, a kind of life we never see through Marlowe's eyes.

The two detectives also differ in their relationships to the African-American community. Marlowe has few dealings with it. In his Los Angeles, the communities seem to live, for the most part, separately, and they do not mix if avoidance is possible. The most notable interracial interaction in the Marlowe novels is likely the encounter that he and Moose Malloy have in *Farewell, My Lovely* at Florian's, the bar where Malloy's Velma used to work before he went to jail and which is now owned by African Americans. Malloy goes in, Marlowe follows him, and people end up dead.

Spenser's best friend, on the other hand, is black. Hawk, like Spenser, is a former boxer. He is also somewhat of a shadowy figure who often works as muscle on the wrong side of the law. He is fearless, flashy, reliable, and extremely effective. He is also quite intelligent, street smart, and quick with a good line. More than anything else, he is always there for his friend. Like Spenser, he is hard to dislike. This change in the way that race is depicted in these two series is something that students should consider as well.

They can also think about the status of homosexuality in Chandler's time and in Parker's. The issue arises in *The Big Sleep* with the relationship between Geiger and Carol Lundgren. Marlowe refers to them disparagingly as queens. Even after a fairly competitive fight with Lundgren, Marlowe claims that he knew he would eventually win because "a pansy has no iron in his bones" (61).

This is not something that would be heard from Spenser, who has no problem with anyone's sexual orientation. Another member of Spenser's inner circle is Paul Giacomin, a boy whom he rescued in *Early Autumn* and who has appeared in several other novels to date. Paul is a professional dancer. That alone, in Marlowe's world, would raise flags as to his orientation and would cause Marlowe to distance himself from him. That is never true for Spenser.

In *Hush Money*, these two themes of inclusion are explored specifically, as Spenser dives into the gay culture to exonerate an African-American professor who Hawk believes was wrongly denied tenure. It is not a case that would ever have come up in Marlowe's office. This is certainly one avenue that can be used with students as they confront the changing attitudes toward race and sexual orientation in our society. They can also discuss the possibility that some things in our larger culture have not changed at all. Perhaps only the heroes have.

Hard-boiled heroes today need not be loners, dependent on no one and reliant solely upon themselves. They can have significant others to whom they regularly express their love and devotion. Their tightest friends and partners can be of other races. They can be gentle and look after people even after their cases are over. They can be vulnerable. The change from Marlowe to Spenser reflects our society, and students can explore that change as they talk about who we are.

In the mystery classroom, we can also explore other cultures. Those of the American southwest are rich with possibility. Tony Hillerman is the author of nearly twenty novels featuring Joe Leaphorn and/or Jim Chee, two police investigators on the Navajo reservation in western New Mexico. Through Hillerman's novels and short stories, students get to see a pattern of life and a value to that life which, to most of them, is completely foreign. Leaphorn and Chee can be seen as representing two sides of Navajo world, the one that tries to abide by the norms of the larger society and the one that wants to return to the ways of the ancestors. Leaphorn is the more traditional policeman. He is methodical. He looks for small details. He follows procedures. Chee, on the other hand, tends to be more spiritual. He is concerned, in ways that Leaphorn is not, about the traditions of the Navajo way of life, about ceremony and spirituality.

Originally, the two were the lead players of two different series. According to Hillerman, it was only when a woman at a book signing seemed to think that his two main characters were one that he decided to put them together to highlight their differences. This anecdote itself tells us something about mainstream American culture, something that students should know. In some people's minds, when it comes to "the other" (whoever that might be in a given context), they all look alike. Hillerman has joined his two protagonists masterfully. Two novels that embody these themes and that students engage with well are *A Thief of Time* and *Skinwalkers*, the first two novels in which Langhorn and Chee are together.

One of the best qualities of Hillerman's works is that they give his readers a strong sense of place, of the vastness of the Navajo land in New Mexico and the importance of that land to their lives, of the spiritual nature of the culture, and of the sense of history that comes through in everyday Navajo life. Students love to see familiar places. When I first brought Hillerman into the classroom, I was in New Mexico and had Navajo students in class. Their presence led to discussions between students of different backgrounds that would not have happened otherwise. This principle can be applied anywhere. Now that I live in southern Virginia, my mystery students will never get away without exposure to Sharyn McCrumb, a wonderful writer who bases many of her tales in the Appalachian region. I cannot imagine students in Louisiana leaving a mystery class without an introduction to James Lee Burke and his detective, Dave Robicheaux, who explores the culture of New Orleans and the bayou region. And so it goes, and can go, everywhere.

There are countless works of fiction that provide students with insights into their own culture and that of others. Mystery fiction is an excellent vehicle, and it is not hard to figure out why. When students get exposed to any society, either domestic or foreign, it is usually through a process that goes from the top down. That is to say, textbooks generally look at the privileged and the gifted and explore what they do and the ways that they influence others. Mystery fiction, however, is often just the opposite. It goes from the bottom up. While there may be great murderers who lead countries (and we all can name a number of them), the way that any society works is through the people who live in it. These are the ordinary people, and if there is one thing that mystery fiction does very well, it is to examine the lives and passions of ordinary people.

All literature, however it is defined, explores the culture of the people who read it, write it, and are depicted in it, the latter often being the hardest to get right. While there are still those traditionalists who feel that mystery fiction has no place in the realm of literature, their ranks are diminishing year by year. One way to diminish them further is to examine the ways that mysteries explore the issues of how people live their lives and concern themselves with the values that they hold. Our students can find meaning in their society through an examination of its conflicts, and that is the heart and soul of mystery.

WORKS CITED

Chandler, Raymond. *The Big Sleep*. New York: Vintage, 1988.
Conan Doyle, Arthur. "The Bruce-Partington Plans." 1908. *His Last Bow*. Ed. Owen Dudley Edwards. Oxford: Oxford University Press, 1993. 37–67.
_____. "Thor Bridge." 1922. *The Case-Book of Sherlock Holmes*. Ed. W. W. Robson. Oxford: Oxford University Press, 1993. 23–49.

Teaching Detective Fiction
from a Feminist Perspective

Ellen F. Higgins

Teaching detective fiction from a feminist perspective means bringing female detectives into the classroom — in more than a token way. Once they are inside, these detectives, along with women writers, can be brought into the discussion of the paradigms of the genre, including its theory and history, as well as its definition of detective fiction and of the detective. Feminist criticism in literature studies has revealed that there are no "objective" or innocent readings; rather, critics and readers bring their own prejudices and expectations to the endeavor. One feminist approach to teaching detective fiction is to focus on the intersection of two strands in the tradition of mystery writers: women writers of detective fiction and women detectives in crime literature. Although there is no monolith of women's detective fiction, there are similarities in the way many women writers present the female detective and the process of detection in which other stories and other modes of seeing are valued. This is what a course from a feminist perspective would look like as detailed in Appendix A.

A good place to start is the short story "Crime Scene" (1989) by Carolyn Wheat, which is useful for reviewing literary terms and articulating generic conventions so that the class has a common vocabulary — an activity also valuable in introductory and advanced literature classes. Students often find the story clichéd, sentimental, and predictable. Surface characterizations contribute to this first impression. There is the crusty New York City detective, McCarthy; the young, innocent, female murder victim; and the young rookie cop, Toni Ramirez. With the use of a reading guide sheet (Appendix B) to identify the elements, such as imagery, setting, and characterization, students come to recognize Wheat's skillful construction. Wheat manipulates those clichés and conventions, as well as gender stereotypes. Toni, who graduated with honors from the Police Academy, stays controlled and objective when she comes upon her first crime scene — she takes it like a man or a good cop. It is the tough veteran, McCarthy, who teaches Toni a new way of seeing and detecting. He asks Toni to use her heart, to imaginatively identify with and feel for the victim in order to solve the crime. A classic binary opposition is presented: science/rational/masculine vs. imagination/emotional/feminine. However, McCarthy does not denigrate the crime scene technicians; rather he says people have to use all the equipment they were born with — hands and eyes and brains and heart. Further, Wheat, continuing to go against sex-role typing, does not present these skills as essentially feminine because she has McCarthy learn them from another man.

After this introduction, the course takes a largely chronological approach, beginning with stories from Poe and Conan Doyle to help reinforce many of the conventions of detective fiction, including locked-room mysteries, empirical and psychological analysis, and the characters of the super sleuth, the narrator/sidekick, and the bumbling police officers with their idée fixe. The unit also helps provide another model for the course — which challenges the ways authors and characters, especially female writers and detectives, have been traditionally represented — by showing how both can be misrepresented by popular and sometimes scholarly images; for example, Poe as a crazed, drug-and-alcohol-addicted madman/artist and Holmes as arrogant, isolated, and untouched by crime. This super-sleuth emphasis on ratiocination ignores Dupin's use of imagination, intuitive connections, and the irrational, as well as Holmes's characterization as supremely competent, but also human: emotional, musical, addicted to cocaine, and even bothered by failure. The works of Poe and Conan Doyle, however, do illustrate how female characters are often shadowy, colorless, and silenced in masculinist texts: The L'Esplanaye women are brutally murdered in "The Murders in the Rue Morgue"; the "Queen" in "The Purloined Letter" is the victim but never appears; and Elsie Cubitt in "The Dancing Men" is silenced even as men appropriate her story as they rush to protect her honor.

Next comes Susan Glaspell's "A Jury of Her Peers," which, along with Wheat's story and those of other women writers, not only shows that emotions do not interfere with deduction, but demonstrates that feelings are often necessary to solve a case. The emotional connection between Martha Hale and Mrs. Peters and between the women and Minnie, the suspect, is what brings about the solution. Because the official, male detectives enter the case with an idée fixe, or pre-existing notions, about what constitutes a crime and how to solve it, they do not see the clues right in front of them. Glaspell's story, or the play version, *Trifles*, is a classic in literature anthologies and argumentative writing texts. Either provides a rich occasion for exploring literary and historical contexts, especially with two critical articles, Judy Fetterley's "Reading about Reading" and Elaine Hedges's "Small Things Reconsidered," which highlight the isolation of women and their lack of political and legal recourse. A mock trial or debate, with the class dividing between the absolutist legal position of the prosecution and the relative position of the defense, can be effective in promoting discussion of Glaspell's political message about women's vulnerability under the law (no jury of their peers) and her argument, one of the earliest, for justifiable homicide.

Moreover, Glaspell's career, the course of her reception and reputation, also illustrates the different treatment of women in literature. Many women authors, like Glaspell, have experienced early critical acclaim, subsequent marginalization or erasure, and later revalorization. In fact, in the 1910s, Glaspell was often referred to as the Provincetown Players' preeminent playwright and, after Eugene O'Neill's work became popular, was considered one of the two leading dramatists of the period. Yet, unlike O'Neill, her work has languished until rediscovered by feminist scholars. For example, although as a one-act play, *Trifles*, continued to be performed in local and community theater groups, her play *Chains of Dew*, was produced for the first time since its original staging in 1922, meeting with critical acclaim for its freshness and relevance.

Confronting an ingrained bias or ignorance and providing historical contexts constitute part of the challenge of teaching the next works, stories featuring female detectives by Victorian women writers: Loveday Brooke by C. L. Pirkis; Florence Cusack by L. T. Meade and Robert Eustace; Lady Molly by Emmuska, Baroness Orczy; and Violet Strange by Anna Katharine Green, author of the nineteenth-century mystery bestseller *The Leavenworth Case* (see Appendix A). Many critics fail to acknowledge these writers and characters because of the masculinist model of detective fiction and the detective. In fact, some critics, such as Kathleen Gregory Klein, claim that though female detectives may be identified as the hero and may overtly claim professional competence, the successful pattern of crime solving is a male one which suddenly collapses when the detective is a woman. Small-group work is effective here: each group is assigned one of the four detectives and students enumerate their detective's characterization and style. By detailing the detectives and stories, the students are able to recognize that these four provide a powerful countervision because they all are professional detectives in their own right: Brooke and Strange work for agencies, Lady Molly is with the police, and Cusack is independent but assists the police. Moreover, all the detectives solve cases when others did not know the crime existed or were on the wrong track. The women also show extraordinary physical and moral courage by facing madmen and physical danger, or risking career, family, and even life to pursue their vision of justice.

Learning to see beyond stereotypes and preconceived notions is crucial in dealing with the work of Agatha Christie and Dorothy L. Sayers, too. These Golden Age authors, though sometimes denigrated, are both renowned for their generic innovations and their strong women characters. Christie's popularity has meant that her type of detective fiction is what most people think of when they think of mysteries. It has also meant that many writers have copied her plots, characters, and inventions so that her books when first encountered may seem clichéd. Miss Marple faces a similar perception problem because she is often dismissed by readers and other characters as a silly, nosy old woman. *The Body in the Library* (1942) is a good way to confront this prejudice since this is the novel in which Miss Marple first appears as a credible amateur detective and a recognized authority on crime instead of the snoopy spinster of the earlier works. Her investigative skill combines "womanly" knowledge about dresses and relationships with keen observation, shrewd psychology, and collection of physical evidence such as nail clippings and marriage records. Moreover, Christie challenges age and gender stereotypes by presenting an older woman who, without beauty or a husband, can still be fulfilled.

In *Gaudy Night* (1935), Dorothy L. Sayers shows through Harriet Vane what it means to be an intelligent and ambitious woman who must confront the either/or dilemma educated women faced at that time — either marriage and love or career and celibacy, never both. Set at a fictional women's college at Oxford University in the 1930s, this work can be enjoyed on many levels, not least as a mystery in which Harriet assists Peter Wimsey, Sayers's main detective. Sayers's goal was to combine detective fiction with the English novel in the tradition of Jane Austen, which can make this work challenging to teach because of its vocabulary, style, and length. However, it is worth the effort and can be used successfully in both introductory and advanced literature classes. Both the town and gown of Oxford and the remote interwar period, with the European turmoil and the rise of Hitler, can be made more real through film resources, such as the 1981 *Brideshead Revisited* adaptation, and through research projects on historical and cultural events. More advanced students can appreciate this consciously literary novel, filled with wordplay and allusions to a wide range of works, including quotations— mostly from sixteenth- and seventeenth-century British authors— that begin each chapter. An interesting project for these students is to investigate a quotation's author and source and then use this information as a gloss on what is happening in the chapter.

Although Harriet detects in the Wimsey-Vane novels, she is clearly an assistant, and this partner-in-crime role bridges the forty-year jump from *Gaudy Night* to the next work, *Dark Nantucket Noon*. There is a statistical drop in the number of female detectives appearing during this time, even though the numbers of women writers and new titles remain relatively constant. Also, many of the texts are unavailable because books by female writers more often go out of print than those by males. Women detectives become a regular and accepted part of the genre — as elderly and middle-aged snoops and as younger women and ingénues; but a common role is as part of a sleuthing couple — Nick and Nora Charles, Pam and Steve North, Perry Mason and Della Street — where women enter detection as partners in solving crimes.

Jane Langton's work is useful in illustrating this transitional period because, while her main detective, Homer Kelly, is male, he frequently gets assistance. In *Dark Nantucket Noon* (1975), for example, Homer is assisted by his wife and by Kitty Clark, his client. In superficial ways, Homer and Kitty fit the traditional male/female gender roles: Homer, a former police officer and district attorney, as the primary detective, and Kitty, a poet, as a naive, emotional "understudy." However, Homer is also a professor of American Romanticism, and his solutions often come from bursts of tremendous revelations. Moreover, he and Kitty work together to solve the crime, and the physical evidence Kitty discovers is crucial to the solution. Like Sayers, Langton uses literary allusions and quotations, primarily of Transcendental and New England writers, which can be a useful introduction for students to these American authors. In *Dark Nantucket Noon,* the works of Melville, whaling logs, and the island's early Quaker settlers amplify the novel's themes.

The author often credited with showing what could be done with a contemporary female private investigator is P. D. James with the publication of her novel *An Unsuitable Job for a Woman* (1972). Like many women writers before her, she creates a male as her main detective. Adam Dagliesh is the detective; however, in this book and a second, *The Skull Beneath the Skin* (1982), James also creates Cordelia Gray, a female private detective. As the title suggests, Gray, who inherits a detective agency at twenty-two, spends much of the book defending her right to such a career. Kathleen Gregory Klein and other critics like her make the same assertion about Gray as they do about Victorian detectives— she ultimately fails because she does not follow the male model of success. Students usually disagree, relating to Gray's age and achievement. She succeeds where others have not: she not only recognizes a crime as murder when the police believe it is suicide, but she solves that crime and prevents the police from discovering a retributive slaying of the original murderer. Moreover, she also holds her own against Dagliesh, who appears at the end, investigating the revenge murder. Furthermore, James presents Gray's method as a combination of the scientific (empirical observation and logic) and the empathic (emotional identification and compassion) as well as an example of individual, relative morality similar to what Glaspell depicts.

After James, there is plenty of opportunity for examining female characters in mysteries, especially professional detectives, because the late 1970s usher in what many critics consider the Second Golden Age of mystery writing. In the decade of the 1980s, the number of new mystery titles published by women nearly tripled, and the number of new series increased more than fivefold, a phenomenon scholars credit to feminism. In addition to the growth of the consciously feminist mystery, there is an increasing diversity of forms and a revising and blending of genres and types. Of particular importance are the female private eye and the deliberate reworking and appropriation of the hard-boiled subgenre, whose history and characteristics are covered in lectures and excerpts at this time.

Preeminent in rewriting the hard-boiled tradition is Sara Paretsky, who created V.I. Warshawski, the first truly sassy and sexual female. Paretsky combines her strong characterization with the social criticism of this subgenre, but with a feminist focus. She brings sexism and the condition of women to the forefront, highlighting issues from women's mobility and visibility in the workplace to their right to abortion and health care. *Bitter Medicine* (1987) takes on the issue of reproductive freedom and the world of corporate medicine, which values profits over human lives— issues still relevant today. Paretsky's fiction also promotes positive, powerful images of women in all levels of society, counteracting the misogyny of the subgenre. As a detective, V.I. Warshawski is tough but human, living by her wits and daring. Yet unlike the extreme individualism and emotional invulnerability of her male counterparts, she has a community of women and men for support.

Another reworking of the detective fiction genre is by lesbian feminist writers, who have produced many mysteries since the late 1970s. Despite this presence, lesbian mysteries are often overlooked in the dominant culture, in part because they were produced by small feminist publishing houses, such as Naiad Press, Seal Press, and The Crossing Press. Katherine V. Forrest, though she continues her work with these small presses, was picked up by a mainstream press midway in the series featuring Kate Delafield, a lesbian detective with the Los Angeles Police Department. Forrest's work participates in several traditions: the police procedural; feminist fiction, containing social and political analysis; and lesbian fiction, offering the lesbian bildungsroman or novel of development. Forrest uses her books to examine women's position and treatment in society, dealing especially with violent crimes against women, such as sexual assault, rape, child abuse, and incest. In *Murder by Tradition* (1991), she extends this portrayal to gay men, with the "tradition" in the title referring to gay-bashing. The identity of the murderer is known early in the novel, but he claims self-defense, asserting that he is the victim of an unwanted sexual advance. Kate must prove that the murder was a vicious, premeditated attack. Students, used to the *CSI* shows, appreciate the forensics of analyzing wounds and blood splatter, as well as the powerful courtroom scene, which can be compared to other courtrooms in literature and on television.

With her novel *Blanche on the Lam* (1992), Barbara Neely adds issues of race and class to those of gender and sexuality in detective fiction. Despite obvious contemporary clues, like a microwave, many students want to set the book in a much earlier time, so it serves for a good discussion of the continuing problem of racism as well as of sexism, heterosexism, and classism. The chapter "Black Women," from Frankie Y. Bailey's *Out of the Woodpile: Black Characters in Crime and Detective Fiction*, helps to enumerate the characters and stereotypes in the genre. Neely's detective is Blanche White, middle-aged, queen-sized, eggplant black, a single mother, and a domestic. Blanche is on the lam from an unfair jail sentence, and as she works to clear her name, she stumbles on a case of domestic malice — in this instance, greed and murder in the rich white family she keeps house for. Blanche uses her position as a housekeeper to detect. She eavesdrops, searches rooms, and makes use of her community networks and her spiritual connection to people and houses to solve the mystery. Though she has to literally fight for her life, Blanche, a survivor, both clears her name and eventually brings the guilty to justice, which means not just making people pay for crime but also improving the lives of those affected by the crime.

The women writers and their female detectives of this course have offered alternative models of detection and development for the genre. Though the detectives are often marginalized in society, they rely on the heart as well as the head, on their own resources as well as the resources of their community of family and friends. Teaching detective fiction from a feminist perspective opens the genre to allow consideration of works that are often excluded and counteracts the marginalization of women's detective fiction and other non-canonical writers. When we give equal weight to works traditionally excluded, there will be a paradigm shift in our conceptual understanding of literary movements and genres. This course brings women back into the syllabus, suggesting what the history, theory, and model of detective fiction might look like if women were given their fair due.

APPENDIX A

COURSE SYLLABUS
ENG 362L/WSS 362L — Ellen Higgins
WOMEN AND DETECTIVE FICTION

Course Description

This course uses a feminist critical perspective to examine women as characters and writers in the tradition of detective fiction. It takes into consideration such issues as genre development and classification, critical and generic trends, and social, historical, and cultural conditions. Though there is a special emphasis on contemporary authors and trends, it uses a chronological approach to acknowledge a hidden tradition of women mystery writers and female detectives.

Brief Course Outline

— Introduction to women and detective fiction
— Reading detective fiction: Carolyn Wheat — "Crime Scene" (McCarthy, Toni Ramirez)

— The Traditional Poetics and Canon
— Edgar Allan Poe — "The Murders in the Rue Morgue" and "The Purloined Letter" (Dupin)
— A. Conan Doyle — "The Adventure of the Dancing Men" (Holmes)

— Critical Strategies and Challenges to the Canon
— Susan Glaspell — "A Jury of Her Peers"
— Judith Fetterley — "Reading about Reading: 'A Jury of Her Peers,' 'The Murders in the Rue Morgue,' and 'The Yellow Wallpaper.'" *Gender and Reading: Essays on Readers, Texts, and Contexts.* Ed. Elizabeth A. Flynn and Patrocinio P. Schweikart. Baltimore: Johns Hopkins UP, 1986. 147–64.
— Elaine Hedges — "Small Things Reconsidered: Susan Glaspell's 'A Jury of Her Peers.'" *Women's Studies* 12 (1986): 89–110.

— The Female Detective: Victorian Age to the 1920s
— Short stories from Michele Slung's *Crime on Her Mind*
— C. L. Pirkis — "The Murder at Troyte's Hill" (Loveday Brooke)
— L. T. Meade and Robert Eustace — "Mr. Bovey's Unexpected Will" (Florence Cusack)
— Emmuska, Baroness Orczy — "The Fordwych Castle Mystery" (Lady Molly)
— Anna Katharine Green — "The Golden Slipper" (Violet Strange)

— The Golden Age of Detective Fiction
— Agatha Christie — *The Body in the Library* (Miss Marple)

— Feminism and the Detective Novel
— Dorothy L. Sayers — *Gaudy Night* (Peter Wimsey, Harriet Vane)

— "Partners in Crime": Bridge to the Second Golden Age
— Jane Langton — *Dark Nantucket Noon* (Homer Kelly, Kitty Clark)

— Contemporary Women Detectives
— P. D. James — *An Unsuitable Job for a Woman* (Cordelia Gray)

— Hard-boiled/soft-boiled and Alternative Detectives
— Sara Paretsky — *Bitter Medicine* (V.I. Warshawski)

— Lesbian Detectives and Police Procedurals
— Katherine V. Forrest — *Murder by Tradition* (Kate Delafield)

— Detectives of Color and Malice Domestic
— Barbara Neely — *Blanche on the Lam* (Blanche White)
— Frankie Y. Bailey — "Black Women." *Out of the Woodpile: Black Characters in Crime and Detective Fiction.* Westport: Greenwood Press, 1991. 101–16.

Appendix B

ENG 362L/WSS 362L — Ellen Higgins
Reading and Analyzing Detective Fiction
"Crime Scene" by Carolyn Wheat

1.Setting:
2.Characters:
    a. Toni Ramirez
    b. McCarthy
3.Plot:
4.Narration/Point of View:
5.Name 3 Images/Image Cluster:
    a.
    b.
    c.
6.What is the narrative surprise?
7.What is the central binary opposition?
8.What is the theme? (State it in a complete sentence.)

Fixing and Un-fixing Words

Nastiness, Fidelity, and Betrayal in Chandler's and Hawks's The Big Sleep

Alexander N. Howe

Barzun is famous for describing detective fiction as the "romance of rea-son" (250), a description that is valid, I would argue, only if we read this in terms of the "dark romance" practiced by Poe or Hawthorne. As the dark romance of the rationalism of the nineteenth and twentieth centuries, detec-tive fiction inevitably critiques the sinister side of the far-from-innocent dream of victorious Reason. Given the basic anti-epistemological gesture of detective fiction, I find it useful to teach whodunits in nearly all my courses in the English Department of the University of the District of Columbia. In this essay, I will outline a particularly successful unit of detective fiction used in my literature and film courses. Using Chandler and Hawks's versions of *The Big Sleep*, I invoke the critique of knowledge basic to all detective texts as a platform for reconsidering the issues of adaptation and translation between literature and film.

When teaching a literature and film course, regardless of focus, the first item that must be addressed is the issue of adaptation. "I liked the book better than the film" is a sentiment that is as common as it is misguided — and not just a little elitist. I have found a majority of my students to fall (more or less innocently) into this camp, which is not to say that they are without a genuine enthusiasm for film. Robert Stam suggests that this con-flict (i.e., film versus literature) might be bypassed by using the concept of "translation" rather than "adaptation." The latter term always suggests a hierarchy, a discourse of origin, and the measure of fidelity. If the film doesn't "get it right," it "gets it wrong." However, when moving from the page to the screen, this notion of remaining "true" to an original text is quite difficult to maintain. First and foremost, this is true given the change in signifying materials (Stam 56). Obviously, a film provides a concrete visual (and sonorous) representation of a linear, graphic text that was formerly experienced only in that shadowy, median space between the two-dimensional page and the reader's mind. In so doing, a film necessarily betrays the reader's imagination.

Now even the smattering of literary theory that students have had before arriving in my class should indicate that it is the height of presumption to assume that a reading screened in the space of their imagination (or in the space of their term papers) is a definitive presentation of a source text in its purity. However, I find it necessary each semester to remind them of this fact. Stam's deference to Bahktin's dialogism is helpful to these ends. Assuming that a text is a multivalent cultural construction made up of any number of prior (or even subsequent) texts, a translation becomes a rhetorical act of reading, one that might mobilize any number of intertextual references contained in the translated text — which can no longer be read as a straightforward wellspring. For example, a novel is not a single, discrete source that might be isolated from cultural or literary history. Rather, it is a relay in a larger chain that contains all texts whose vertiginous path vainly attempts to master the world. Acknowledging the complexity of this textual play, a film translation (of a literary text) becomes an opportunity to bring an infinite variety of textual strands and discursive practices into dialogue with one another.

This is not to say that the open-endedness of translation is without limits. Here, Stam gives the example of a fragmented, modernist text made linear for the accessibility of a larger audience. He describes this as an "ideologically driven failure of nerve" to deal with the challenges endemic to the text in question (75). My unit on Chandler is especially advantageous for analyzing this claim, as criticism frequently speaks of Hawks's film version of *The Big Sleep* (1946) in just these terms. From this perspective, the film needlessly imports a love story into a narrative that is, contrary to popular belief, without a good deal of romance. Further, the film famously covers over a number of holes in Chandler's original story through a radical revision of the ending. Reading *The Big Sleep* from page to screen, my goals are to analyze the applicability of this alleged "loss of nerve," and, through careful attention to the formal aspects of the film, reconsider the extent of Hawks's "betrayal."

Before beginning Chandler's *The Big Sleep* (1939), it is helpful to have students read another of the author's works that addresses the issues of origin, purity, and translation: "The Simple Art of Murder," the famous essay that first appeared in *The Atlantic Monthly* in 1944. Despite the fact that this document is taken as the founding manifesto of the realist charge of the hard-boiled detective, we know from correspondence that Chandler wrote it only grudgingly — as was his wont. Students are very quick to identify with Chandler's witty invective. This is not surprising given his skill at telling the story of an underdog, which is precisely what the hard-boiled narrative is for Chandler, in both theory and practice. In opposition to this upstart genre we find the well-known classical or "English formula," whose reliance on circuitous plots and arcane knowledge is remorselessly pilloried by Chandler.

In support of this discussion, it is useful to introduce Cawelti's notion of the "moral fantasy" at the base of genre fiction. Here the question is simply: What is the organizing vision of the world assumed in these texts? Including other genres in the discussion (e.g., romance, spy, adventure, horror) is profitable and necessary given Cawelti's reading of the hard-boiled in terms of adventure and romance (43). While the moral fantasy of the classical story, a world in which reason triumphs, is an easy pill to swallow for students, the reduction of the hard-boiled narrative to the victorious hero and enduring love is an open question that is worth taking up in light of Marlowe's knightly code—even as it is suggested in "The Simple Art."

Students find these distinctions appealing, but Cawelti's argument is quite different from Chandler's. Asking students to articulate this distinction will likely yield the response that Chandler is talking about the "real world," whereas Cawelti is describing a fantasy, or an escape from the real world. However, despite its compelling rhetoric, "The Simple Art" is not so straightforward. First and foremost, why does Chandler tell us that "honesty" is an art? This question will draw mixed responses, and students must be urged to look closely at Chandler's language. What metaphors does he use for this authenticity and the hero who defends it? (This tendentious phrasing cues attentive students to the difficulty in question.) When speaking of Dashiell Hammett, Chandler does not champion the author's stark honesty exactly. Rather, he claims that Hammett's subject matter had a "basis" in fact and suggests that it was "made up" of real things (16). The hard-boiled story depicts the (real) world we live in, but Chandler praises tough-minded, yet detached, writers who can "make very interesting and even amusing patterns out of it" (20). Detachment and artifice, and even a bit of irony, suddenly enter what was previously a deadly serious conversation.

The question remains: What is realism for Chandler? In her excellent essay on the history of Chandler's "Simple Art," Miranda Rickman concludes that Chandler's realism is in the end "an atmosphere, a way of handling character, and an attitude" (7). Art more readily enters the picture, but this art remains distinct from the artifice of the classical school of detective fiction. Writing in everyday language, the hard-boiled genre calls our attention to the schism at the heart of experience and the language we use to describe it. In this, Chandler wagers, we might find the elixir of beauty and the power of critique. The larger point to be taken from this discussion is that there is often a considerable gulf between what one assumes Chandler innocently says and what Chandler in fact writes. I gently encourage my students to mark this difference at every turn as we begin reading *The Big Sleep*.

Our initial discussion of the novel focuses on one apparently simple issue: Who is Marlowe? Asking this at the beginning of class results in a number of contradictory responses, the majority of which are mediated by Bogart's iconic portrayal of Marlowe in Hawks's film version of *The Big Sleep*. Students describe Marlowe as tough, cool, debonair, etc. It is likely impossible to teach Chandler's novel without encountering the mediation of Hawks's film, but such preconceptions are actually advantageous in a literature and film course focusing on translation and fidelity.

A second very straightforward question moves this initial discussion beyond such Bogartisms: What is Marlowe wearing as the novel begins? Although Chandler spends quite a few words on Marlowe's dress in the very spare introduction, students often skip over these details, no doubt on their way to ferreting out Bogart from the text. Yet, Marlowe's dress demands attention. Do "real men"— to recall Vivian's description of Rusty Regan — wear powder blue suits and socks with clocks on them? Male fashion has obviously changed considerably from the 1930s. However, it is safe to say, as Marlowe himself admits, that the detective looks a bit like a "stuffed shirt." He is willing to play a role of the "well-dressed detective," with all due self-irony, even if this is silly and uncomfortable (3). Marlowe's ease with self-parody instantly undercuts preconceptions of the detective as a suave lone wolf, just as his willingness to look the part when "calling on four million dollars" frustrates his working-class stance against the ruling elite (3).

Another aspect of Marlowe's character that requires a certain amount of "un-working" is the issue of chivalry. Duly interpellated by classic Hollywood concerning that time when "men were men" and honor was worth defending, students tend to gravitate toward the romance of Marlowe's knightly code. Of course, the famous stained-glass window above the entrance to the Sternwood mansion, a text that depicts a hapless knight in the process of rescuing a lady fair, is often taken as the defining figure of Marlowe's own chivalry. At first glance, the story is a familiar one: the hero gets the girl. However, upon closer inspection, we find the detective mocking the gaudy and futile romance inscribed there above the door. Naturally, neither the text nor the detective's mocking consideration should be taken at face value. Nevertheless, the courtly reference is quite distant from students' original expectations. Chivalry is always predicated upon impossible (courtly) love or prohibited contact with another and, thus, the world. As an artistic text— and there are many within the novel — the knight will remain frozen, incapable of action or embrace. (Naturally, these issues of art and (in)action must be taken up apropos of Marlowe at the completion of the novel.)

It is important to note that this is not the only stained-glass window Marlowe sees at the Sternwood mansion. The detective finds a second panel after he enters the home, but the details of this window are apparently of no importance. Marlowe glosses it merely as "another piece of stained glass romance" (4). These texts are so common and in keeping with the surroundings, which are frequently indicted for their artificiality, that they are not worth mentioning. Here one recalls Marlowe's turning over Carmen's photograph — a fantastic hard-boiled trope — looking for depth "underneath" or "behind" the text itself (58). Taking this "empty" second window as the "backside" of the first, neither window then possesses buried content or significant meaning. In this way, the empty text is actually a better figure for Marlowe's quest, a claim that finds evidence on nearly every page of the novel, as the detective calls attention to the artificial, yet always incomplete, nature of the texts he encounters. Suffice it to recall Marlowe's frequent description of Carmen Sternwood's face going "to pieces" (220).

In his famous essay on Chandler, Jameson speaks of this aspect of Marlowe's narration that "tends towards an automatization of ever smaller segments" (33). A strategy common to modernist art, this decomposition critiques the pretensions of knowledge construction and the orienting narratives that would defend the power of this knowledge — a critique that Chandler claimed fundamental to the hard-boiled in "The Simple Art." Students may balk at the suggestion that chivalry is not an operative "code" of the detective but merely another reference to the fragmentation of all narrative coherence within the space of *The Big Sleep*. However, it is short work to question Marlowe's chivalry and honor in discussing the conclusion of the novel. If he is honorable, why does Marlowe stand by and allow a murder to take place? Why does he allow a murderer and her accomplices to go free? Naturally, focusing on the famous line regarding "sleeping the big sleep" is an ideal way to broach these topics, as is Marlowe's suggestion that he is "part of the nastiness now" (Chandler 230).

On the way to addressing these larger questions, it is wise to identify a few of the more telling quirks in Marlowe's character. Acknowledging the power of Bogart's performance in Hawks's film, students should be asked if there is anything that Marlowe does in the novel that they find surprising. Without fail, the first or second example given will be that curious incident of Carmen Sternwood (in the nighttime). This is a jarring episode that is difficult to comprehend, so much so that "skimming" students may pass over it without contemplating its significance. Why is Marlowe so traumatized by this episode? Students often suggest that Marlowe tears the bed to pieces because he is torn between his desire for Carmen and his loyalty to the General. This is perhaps more correct of Vivian Regan, a case that is quickly made by comparing Marlowe's comments on the two sisters. (Admittedly, all women are "made animal" in the course of the sleuth's narration, but this occurs to a lesser extent with Vivian.) This is an apt moment to discuss Marlowe's admiration for General Sternwood, as well as the apparent homosocial characteristics of the detective's narration, which seem to suggest a filial bond that is threatened by the very presence of a woman.

The greater difficulty found here is why the search for knowledge, the detective's basic charge, must take this detour through sex. This obviously has everything to do with the failure of reason and its sanctioning paternal agency, failings that result in the radical embodiment of a detective who is no longer free to solve abstract problems in the drawing room. To these ends, a historical detour through the early work of the hard-boiled genre during the 1920s is helpful, and naturally the nineteenth amendment to the Constitution is no small reference in this genealogy. The point to be taken is that the hard-boiled detective emerges historically at a time when masculine authority is under great duress. The successes of woman's suffrage and the malaise of the Depression years—along with later developments, such as changing gender roles during the Second World War and post-war economic prosperity that results in the "company man"—are significant experiences that rearticulate the roles of men in their public and private spheres. Masculine authority no longer goes without saying, or goes unchallenged. While the narrative space of the classical tale was safely delimited by the detective's eloquence, in the hard-boiled world, words no longer guarantee power; rather, words now guarantee (bodily) struggle. Clearly, the hard-boiled detective's concise narration and strict moral code serve to re-entrench this contested power. However, the genre convention that requires the detective to be the victim of violence betrays the dubiousness of this enterprise.

As is well known, the great test of the now embodied detective is the *femme fatale.* It is critical commonplace to read the relation between the detective and this lethal woman as a clear binary representing what must be forbidden if white male authority is to be re-entrenched in the hard-boiled narrative. However, I find it more persuasive to read the *femme fatale* as an embodiment of the anxiety, and thus ambiguity, of masculinity as it is represented in the genre. This reconsideration of conventionally scripted gender roles is certainly present in Chandler's work, proceeding as it does by sentimental narration, homosocial bonding, and the relentless hystericization of the detective, Marlowe.

Of course, this reading is a matter of debate that must be brought before the class. The compulsive distance Marlowe keeps from the women of the novel, and the fact that the detective repeatedly assures the reader that he finds them repugnant, is perhaps a strong argument for the prosaic binary of male power and female transgression. Regardless of one's perspective on the matter, in the midst of this discussion another significant quirk in Marlowe's character must be acknowledged, that is, his hysterical laughter. The first example in the novel occurs in Joe Brody's apartment after the armed Carmen Sternwood has come to retrieve her pictures from Brody. After the group (Agnes, Brody, Carmen, and Marlowe) wrestle for guns and exchange blows, Brody pleads with Marlowe to not let Carmen kill him. At this point, for some odd reason, Marlowe tells us, "I began to laugh. I laughed like an idiot without control" (87). I ask my students to consider the significance of this apparent breakdown and also direct their attention to the uneasiness of Marlowe's narration throughout this scene. In a very Marlowe-esque reflection, the detective tries to describe Agnes as they wrestle on the couch during the altercation. The reader is told that the "blond" is strong with the "madness of love or fear, or a mixture of both, or maybe she was just strong" (87). This passage is significant, as Marlowe is (again) overpowered, both in body and in the body of his narrative, by a woman. (Attentive students will note the fact that Agnes escapes from the circuit of the text only through the demise of Harry Jones, a "small" character with whom Marlowe identifies on a number of telling occasions.)

In the second instance, Marlowe "laughs like a loon" after killing Lash Canino, Eddie Mars' hired gunman (202). This outburst follows the well-known Silver Wig (i.e., Mona Mars) episode, a strange sequence in the novel where the captive Marlowe oddly falls in love with Mona Mars. (Not so incidentally, Mars is hiding out in a house outside the small town of *Realito*. This is adjacent to Art Huck's Garage, a felicitous name that immediately questions the veracity of Marlowe's own art.) Elevating Mars to the status of courtly lady at this moment of life and death underscores the threat of Marlowe's relation with the predatory women of the text and offers him some sort of imagined protection. Students may be tempted to read this as just another instance of Marlowe's (i.e., Bogart's) "way with women," but such a reading is complicated in light of his hysterical laughter, as well as the awkward silence he remembers sharing with Mars on the drive back to Los Angeles (207).

If nothing else, this episode goes a long way toward revealing the way Marlowe's narration of masculinity, like all the stories he tells, is shaky at best. As is the case throughout the novel, the language of his narration amplifies the failure of his words. For example, when first describing the platinum beauty, Marlowe notes Mona's "smooth silvery voice that matched her hair. It had a tiny tinkle in it, like bells in a doll's house. I thought that was silly as soon as I thought of it" (191). Clearly, there are more than just a few things wrong with this passage. Marlowe is taken with the voice and beauty of Mars and the symmetry between these two items. Unfortunately, it is not possible for Mars' voice to match her hair in an "authentic" fashion, as the wig is artificial and part of an elaborate ruse that is ultimately meant to cover over the murder of Rusty Regan. In a brilliant moment of narrative futility, Marlowe offers a tortured simile that falls flat the moment that he thinks it, as he suggests. In other words, Marlowe's attempt to "grasp" hold of Mona through narration fails from the outset.

Christianson's study of hard-boiled language, and what he terms "hard-boiled conceit" (i.e., hard-boiled metaphors and similes), is very helpful here. The critic's most basic claim is something that students have already sensed, that is, hard-boiled language is "a linguistic assertion of power over experience" (153). However, like Jameson, Christianson finally links hard-boiled language with the modernist project that produces a "multivalence of meaning" that actually resists verbalization and visualization (158–59). Thus the hard-boiled project, and Chandler's *The Big Sleep* in particular, witnesses to the contemporary "struggle to make meaning" (160). As such, contrary to students' initial perceptions, Marlowe's narrative incessantly calls into question the position of its own utterance, at the same contesting definitive statements of knowledge, power, and gender.

Beginning Hawks's *The Big Sleep* after reading the novel in this way allows the instructor to now focus on the stakes of the film translation. Naturally, discussion must begin with the obvious question: How does the novel differ from the film? And why does it differ so drastically? Many critics see the indeterminacies in Marlowe's narration passed over in favor of the love story between Humphrey Bogart and Lauren Bacall. It is well known that the studio desired to capitalize on the chemistry between the two actors, which was freshly minted in *To Have and Have Not* just two years prior in 1944. This "romance" certainly dominates Hawks's film, and the potential threat of Vivian is safely contained, as typified in the character's comment that there is "nothing wrong" with her that Marlowe "can't fix." Abbott makes the excellent point that it is not simply the *femme fatale* who is thus reduced, but also the unfettered man (i.e., Marlowe) who formerly roamed freely beyond convention (141). Ending with the promise of a predictable love affair, Chandler's criticism of masculinity seems lost. This containment is all the more apparent with the scapegoating of Eddie Mars, who becomes Regan's murderer in the film. A very conventional Hollywood narrative, there are good guys, bad guys, and women in need of fixing.

One does not need to look very far for the cause of this "ideological loss of nerve," as Stam would have it. The moral standards of the Hays Production code, in place from 1930 through 1967, prohibited illicit sexuality and adultery as well as unpunished and sympathetic criminals. The lack of explicit reference to Geiger's homosexuality and the above mentioned changes to the story clearly represent a deference to these ideological imperatives, which were made all the more rigid during wartime. At first glance, then, Hawks's *The Big Sleep* seems to fail at translating the more challenging aspects of Chandler's novel.

As compelling as such a reading may be, I ask my students to consider the possibility of the covert subversion of visual and moral norms in Hawks's film. This practice is, of course, the hallmark of film noir. Abbott describes this practice as "smuggling" — a term borrowed from Scorsese — that, in spite of conservative film conventions, allows for the inclusion of a "stylistic or visual twist that shakes the film out of its slick, orderly narrative, that suggests hidden fetishes and tensions at work in its evocation of hardboiled masculinity" (134). For example, Abbott reads Bogart's odd practice of rubbing his earlobe as symptomatically marking the embodied, and thus vulnerable, detective. Covertly, thinking becomes physical and therefore pleasurable, as well as fallible (152). There are many instances of smuggling in Hawks's exceptionally complex film, and students inevitably find this tack productive. Asking who killed Owen Taylor — a question that Chandler could not answer for Hawks — at a pointed moment in this conversation is an excellent method for revealing the seams of the film narrative. Students become increasingly sympathetic to the possibility that these gaps and inconsistencies do not "ruin" the film but serve to tell a second story quite apart from the primary narrative.

Before concluding, I would like to call attention to what I take to be another brilliant instance of smuggling at work in the film, the inclusion of numerous graphic texts throughout Marlowe's quest. Many of these instances occur from the first-person perspective, presumably depicting Marlowe's own reading. Importantly, this method for portraying the act of reading was common in films of the 1930s and 1940s that addressed women issues— such as domestic life, motherhood, romance — a broad group of works often called "weepies" or "tear-jerkers" (Doane 206). From the first shot of the film focusing on the name "Sternwood" emblazoned on the mansion's front door, to Marlowe's research at the Hollywood Public Library that has him reading a book on collecting books, these shots disrupt the filmic narration by confronting the viewer with written text. These texts inevitably suggest dissimulation, even when referencing something as simple as a name on a door or mailbox. Hawks shrewdly punctuates this "gray" distinction among male characters by including a horse (or knight) statuette on the desk of every office that appears in the film. A dominant example of this practice is the name "A.G. Geiger" painted on the deceased pornographer's mailbox. This proper name is shot each time the film returns to the Geiger home, a site that is as orientalized as it is in the novel, and therefore marked with sexual deviance, despite the fact that Geiger's sexuality is not spoken of directly. This haunting signifier, which appears far more frequently than the live Geiger, marks Marlowe's own fragmentary reading. On this note, it is no accident that Marlowe's glib, two-minute concluding "explanation" of the case (i.e., Mars did it) occurs in Geiger's home. In the surplus of this locale, the pat Hollywood ending rings hollow, leaving, appropriately, a vast gulf between what Marlowe says and what Hawks's film shows the viewer.

Naturally, this is but one reading among many. But I find that this framing of Chandler's and Hawks's versions of *The Big Sleep* effectively brings students to reconsider the moral fantasy of the hard-boiled detective story and explore the ways in which Chandler's lamentation on the limits of language might be applied to the question of "fidelity" in adaptation and translation. As Chandler tirelessly shows— Bogart's Marlowe notwithstanding — remaining true never kept anyone from the nastiness.

WORKS CITED

Abbott, Megan. *The Street Was Mine: White Masculinity in Hardboiled Fiction and Film Noir.* New York: Palgrave Macmillian, 2002.

Barzun, Jacques. "Detection and the Literary Art." *The Mystery Writer's Art.* Ed. Francis Nevins, Jr. Bowling Green, OH: Bowling Green University Popular Press, 1970. 248–62.

The Big Sleep. Dir. Howard Hawks. Perf. Humphrey Bogart and Lauren Bacall. Warner Brothers, 1946.

Cawelti, John G. *Adventure, Mystery, and Romance: Formula Stories as Art and Popular Culture.* Chicago: University of Chicago Press, 1976.

Chandler, Raymond. *The Big Sleep.* First Vintage Crime Edition. New York: Vintage Crime, 1992.

_____. "The Simple Art of Murder." *The Simple Art of Murder.* New York: Ballantine, 1950. 1–22.

Christianson, Scott. "Tough Talk and Wisecracks: Language as Power in American Detective Fiction." *Journal of Popular Culture* 23:2 (Fall 1989): 151–62.

Doane, Mary Ann. "The Clinical Eye: Medical Discourses in the 'Woman's Film' of the 1940s." *Poetics Today* 6:1/1 (1985): 205–27.

Jameson, Fredric. "The Syntotic Chander." *Shades of Noir.* Ed. Joan Copjec. New York Verso, 1993. 33–56.

Rickman, Miranda B. "Introduction: The Complex History of a 'Simple Art.'" *Studies in the Novel* 35:3 (Fall 2003): 285–304.

Stam, Robert. "Beyond Fidelity: The Dialogics of Adaptation." *Film Adaptation.* Ed. James Naremore. New Brunswick, NJ: Rutgers University Press, 2000. 54–78.

Historical Mysteries in the
Literature Classroom

ROSEMARY JOHNSEN

This essay describes some of the ways I have used historical crime fiction in literature courses as a way of getting students actively involved in exploring historical context. My essay is based on English Department courses in which I have incorporated historical crime fiction; these were not courses in crime fiction (although I have taught a course on crime fiction under the general heading of "genres and themes"), but literature courses in which I used crime fiction to introduce relevant historical context through the accessible, appealing form of the mystery plot. There are many contemporary writers of crime fiction who produce historical mysteries that are grounded in careful research and that offer readers leads for pursuing their own research afterwards. Students have responded positively to the inclusion of these "history-mysteries" on course reading lists, and many became motivated to seek out more of the historical context for the other course readings. The historical mysteries gave students useful historical information but also a new understanding of the significance of the cultural context in which our literary texts were produced.

My first experience of using detective fiction was in three sections of Women and Literature at Michigan State University where I was a Visiting Assistant Professor in 2000–01. I chose examples of historical crime novels, or history-mystery, to include among the readings of classic novels, contemporary poetry, accessible feminist theory, and other texts. The first semester I taught the course, I included two history-mysteries: Miriam Grace Monfredo's *Seneca Falls Inheritance* and Laurie R. King's *A Monstrous Regiment of Women*. I did so with some trepidation, fearing that students might complain about reading mysteries in a serious literature course. As it turned out, however, for some students those books were the highlight of our reading, and for all students they served to generate an interest in historical context.

Before describing some of the specific outcomes of using history-mystery in this class, let me give some background information on the course. MSU's Women and Literature is a 300-level course that serves primarily

English majors but also some majors from outside the College of Arts and Letters. The course is listed in a group of courses from which students must select one to fulfill a requirement in "diversity literature." This requirement affects not only traditional English majors but also those in English secondary education and English elementary education. There are also a few other majors, such as advertising, which offer students a similar list of diversity-related courses in the English Department and require them to select one. The result of this requirement is a very broad spectrum of interest among students in the course, which is capped at forty and usually runs close to that maximum. Some of the English majors are excited about reading women's literature and take an interest in feminist approaches to literature (which is mentioned in the official catalogue description). At the other end of the spectrum are those who resent taking a diversity requirement and have chosen Women and Literature not because of any interest in the subject matter but because it seems less objectionable to them than the alternatives. The variation in student ability is also fairly broad, from advanced students of literature late in their academic program to non–English majors "getting it out of the way" as soon as possible.

The history-mysteries we read offered benefits to students across the spectrum, and they allowed the course to engage cultural context in meaningful ways. For some students, literary works such as Edith Wharton's *The House of Mirth* or Eavan Boland's *Object Lessons*, a memoir and reflection on women's place in Irish literature, were perceived as too difficult, too tedious, or too remote from their own situations. Obviously, class discussions and other activities were designed to show the value and interest of these readings, but pockets of resistance remained. For those students, the history-mysteries were a more pleasant read, and as they followed the mystery plot they developed their awareness of women's historical circumstances. More broadly, the history-mysteries provided the class as a whole an accessible way to learn about women's history and to find ways to learn more about it.

For many literature courses, one of the central objectives is to read the literature in ways that are sensitive to the context which produced it, and this is particularly important in the case of a course such as Women and Literature. In some circumstances, the professor simply delivers relevant historical and cultural information to the students through lectures or handouts. A more active process of engagement than that is obviously preferable, and the history-mysteries included in Women and Literature opened up a space for the students to see the importance of context to the literature, and to women's lives more generally. I would characterize some of the ways this process developed as following.

First, while literary texts written during a remote time period offer indications of cultural context, the process of recognizing them can be difficult for readers lacking knowledge of the period. That is, first they have to recognize that something is a clue to cultural context, then decode what it signifies to the reader. This is often where the professor needs to step in and explain that no, divorce was not legally possible for this character, or that yes, people could be imprisoned for debt. Subtler restrictions placed on groups of people need even more interpretive reading than that to see their presence in the text. These history-mysteries offered students a mediated window into history because while they are set in the past, they are written for contemporary readers. This may seem like an obvious point, but it plays out in the classroom in significant ways. Mid-nineteenth-century political realities that would have been taken for granted in a novel of the period are explained by Monfredo as the mystery develops. Students learned about property law, about the originators of the United States women's suffrage campaign being trained by their work in the abolition and temperance movements, and about how some then-contemporary literature might have been considered unsuitable for library patrons—especially female library patrons—to read.

In the first section of Women and Literature I taught, some of these themes connected to King's consideration of women's activism in post World War I-England and led naturally to a discussion of how voting rights for women were won in the two countries and how voting related to a whole constellation of issues. Margery Childe's New Temple, a space where Childe leads religious services along with a host of other activities, provides a vehicle for King to take up naturally a variety of issues in 1920–21 England; as Childe explains to Mary Russell, "Our goal, simply stated, is to touch everything concerned with the lives of women.... We have four areas we're concentrating on at the moment: literacy, health, safety, and political reform" (50). These history-mysteries provided a different approach to some of the themes broached by Virginia Woolf in *A Room of One's Own* about women's financial, educational, and civic status. In the subsequent section of Women and Literature, I substituted Charlotte Brontë's *Jane Eyre* for one of the novels included the first time: this is one of the contemporary novels that Glynis Tryon's library board chairman thinks is immoral and unsuitable in *Seneca Falls Inheritance*. These are just some examples of how the history-mystery authors' direct address to contemporary readers allowed students to understand the historical context of other course readings in a more three-dimensional way.

The mystery plots also inspired student interest in historical context. One of the particular strengths of Monfredo's first Glynis Tryon mystery, and one reason I included it every time I taught Women and Literature, is how she builds the crime plot carefully around the historical circumstances of

1848. The central mystery and its attendant complications embody the consequences of social and legal codes that denigrate women. The backdrop to the mystery is Elizabeth Cady Stanton's planning of the Woman's Rights Convention, held in Seneca Falls, New York, in July 1848, and the impetus for the first murder is New York State's Married Women's Property Act, enacted in April 1848. Monfredo's fictional victim, Rose Walker, would have been one of the first beneficiaries of the Married Women's Property Act, but her husband, unwilling to give up the financial resources to which he has become accustomed, murders her before she can take steps to remove her assets from his control. Walker had made the trip to Seneca Falls to speak with Elizabeth Cady Stanton, who played a role in passage of the Act and seemed like someone who could advise Walker; seeking information about Cady Stanton's whereabouts, she ends up at the library run by Monfredo's sleuth, Glynis Tryon, before her husband catches up with her. This very brief plot summary is offered to indicate how historical information and feminist analysis are integral to Monfredo's crime plots, not supplemental to them. Hans Bertens and Theo D'haen's study, *Contemporary American Crime Fiction*, cites this aspect of the book as one of its strengths: "One of the strong points of *Seneca Falls Inheritance* is how the Woman's Rights Convention, and the historical conditions of women in the mid–nineteenth century, meaningfully inform the crime plot" (156). Monfredo's series, and especially this first book, looks explicitly at how the framework provided by the legislative and judicial codes of mid–nineteenth century America impacted women. What this meant in the classroom was that students who became engrossed in the mystery itself were learning important historical context even if they disliked the characters or minimized the significance of the commentary.

Furthermore, history-mystery writers use a variety of means to offer information to the reader Monfredo's book puts a lot of information directly in front of readers and provides clear paths to further information. The Author's Note that precedes the novel provides an overview of the historical context, names some of the historical figures included, and identifies two late-nineteenth-century books as key sources. (Her long list of research libraries and archives in the Acknowledgments identifies resources that my MSU students were unable to access during our course; what a field trip that would have been!) After the novel, Monfredo's Historical Notes cover a range of subjects from individual historical figures either present in the text or alluded to by characters (Elizabeth Blackwell, Frederick Douglass), important events (the outbreak of Genesee Fever), concepts (the cult of single blessedness), landmarks (the Wesleyan Chapel that was the site of the 1848 convention), and institutions (libraries). These examples, plus the many other entries, provide starting points for interested readers to learn more. During the semester, students also sought out Monfredo's website, and several used the e-mail link to send comments or ask questions.

King's *A Monstrous Regiment of Women* is the second book in her series about Mary Russell, the young, female investigative partner she created for Sherlock Holmes. (Unlike Watson, Russell becomes an equal partner to the famous detective.) Partly as a consequence of her narrative frame — that she is the editor of manuscripts that are delivered to her house — King does not provide a contextualizing author's note or other fact-based direct address to the reader as Monfredo does.

This lack of direct, authoritative address to the reader does not mean that her book did not inspire students to look beyond the pages of her text to investigate the issues she raises Class discussion of the relation between epigraph and chapter content developed students' ability to read critically, but some students followed up on the epigraphs outside of class. These students would bring to class information about who some of the sources were and in what context they had written the quoted words. Her use of Holmes got students thinking about the social beliefs that may have been mirrored by Conan Doyle's late Victorian stories. Student interest led me to bring in the Sherlock Holmes story "A Scandal in Bohemia" as a way to compare the original Holmes figure — and some of the beliefs he and Watson express — with King's representation of him. Even something as erudite as Russell's explanation to Childe after hearing her sermon concerning the ways in which "'an entire vocabulary of imagery relating to the maternal side of God has been deliberately obscured'" (57) prompted some voluntary outside research. A question about King's qualifications for making these claims and their accuracy led some students to read the M.A. thesis King wrote at the Graduate Theological Union, Berkeley, on "The Feminine Dimension of Yahweh."

It is also significant that these "clues" offered students considerable incentive for learning more. Some students were motivated by curiosity: why did John Knox use the phrase "monstrous regiment of women?" Others were responding to implications that challenged their beliefs, or even offended them: where does a mystery writer get off talking about problems in Biblical translation? A third group, and the one that I suspect corresponds most closely to the general readership enjoyed by history-mystery writers, was inspired by the feminist voice in the books to seek out more information. Students who chose to write about the history-mystery, as a primary focus or as part of a broader topic, approached the gathering of secondary sources differently than is the norm in English classes. They often found leads for those sources within the primary texts, and the sources ranged impressively: from King's M.A. thesis to personal e-mails from Monfredo; from biographies of real historical figures to facts about the fate of the shell-shocked after World War I; from reviews of the book to narratology.

Finally, as I suggested above, the interest created by the history-mysteries made it natural for the class to talk about these kinds of issues as they relate to the other course readings. Students began to see places where they could ask questions and seek information about historical context for older texts, and for contemporary authors who are drawing on historical information. Beyond our class discussions, the final exam questions for my second offering of Women and Literature suggest some of the areas into which we delved. The closed-book portion of the exam was comprised of several types of questions: short-answers or identifications, identification of speeches by characters in the fiction we read, and paragraph-length discussions of key topics. The short-answer section, taken as a whole, is weighted toward the important contextual elements of our reading, though traditional literary analysis is also present:

1. Most of the women who took up the cause of women's rights in the mid–nineteenth century got their start in politics in one of two movements. Identify those movements.
2. Identify two of the real people who appear during the events of *Seneca Falls Inheritance*.
3. Identify the Freedmen's Bureau and name some of its responsibilities.
4. Why is the women's home in *Paradise* called "the Convent?"
5. Whose wedding does Edna refuse to attend in *The Awakening*?
6. Which of our authors won the Nobel Prize for Literature?

Of these questions, 4 and 5 ask students to remember specific information from course readings, while 1 and 2 focus on historical information presented directly by Monfredo's crime novel. Question 3 asks about historical context related to Toni Morrison's novel, *Paradise*; this information was not included in the novel but came up through class questioning and investigation. Question 6 refers to Morrison and again relies on outside information, although this fact was presented to the whole class on the cover of our book; it was included as a way of emphasizing the fact that women writers are increasingly accorded a position far from the margins.

The essay topics given for the in-class essay portion of the final also capitalized on how the class had really engaged the context for the literature we read. Here are those topics:

1. *Tradition & inheritance*

In *A Room of One's Own*, Woolf proposes the importance of tradition, or inheritance, for all writers: any individual book, she writes, continues a series of other books. Consider 3 of our course texts as part of the tradition of women's writing: In what ways do they continue their predecessors and provide inspiration or models for their successors? How are they linked thematically, structurally, stylistically?

2. *History*

Many of our course texts address history — both individual/personal history and collective/public history — as part of their project. Analyze how history is represented by 3 (or more) of the course writers.

3. *Fiction and reality*

In *A Room of One's Own*, Virginia Woolf writes that "fiction ... is not dropped like a pebble upon the ground, as science may be; fiction is like a spider's web, attached ever so lightly perhaps, but still attached to life at all four corners." How and where are our course novels clearly "attached to life" in this way? Use at least 3 different writers in your answer.

Many students chose to incorporate history-mystery as part of their final-exam essays, even — to my surprise — on the question concerning tradition and inheritance.

The Women and Literature course at MSU was the first course to which I added history-mystery. Based on its success there, I also found room on the syllabus for historical crime fiction in a 200-level early English literature survey course at Grand Valley State University, and most recently in a graduate course in Women's Literature at Governors State University. When I was a Visiting Assistant Professor at Grand Valley State University, the two-semester English Literature survey sequence was split earlier than usual, so that English Literature I included only volumes 1A (The Middle Ages) and 1B (The Sixteenth Century / The Early Seventeenth Century) of the standard anthologies. In some sections of the course, I used Sharan Newman's history-mystery set in medieval England, *Cursed in the Blood*, as a transition between the two volumes. Following the success of history-mystery at Michigan State University, I wanted to test its potential to involve students in relevant historical context that was much farther from our own time. Part of the learning — and fun — of including Newman's book developed from the students' growing interest in what was real and what was not. In class, students would volunteer that they had looked up Godric of Finchale, Aelred of Riveaulx, or St. Serf, all included in Newman's epigraphs. Students really wanted to know who was a historical figure and who was a fictional creation of Newman's. As they went beyond what was required by the professor, and beyond what the book put in front of them, they were truly expanding their grasp of early English literature. When they came across texts in Newman that we had read in our anthology — the *Battle of Maldon*, the writings of Geoffrey of Monmouth — they felt corroborated in what they had already learned, and they began to make connections among the ancient literature and real people. As Newman's epigraphs set the stage for her fictional tale, students enjoyed the awareness of their own knowledge and profited by seeing it re-enacted in a form to which they could relate.

Most recently, I included a history-mystery novel in a graduate-level course at Governors State University. This was a course I designed and offered for the first time in fall 2007. The course focus was on women's historical fiction, and I included one mystery book, Candace Robb's *The Apothecary Rose*. Her book, with the oldest historical setting on the syllabus (the four-teenth century), was the first piece of fiction we took up, and it served as a useful model as we moved forward into more literary fiction. Students found the book a congenial introduction to historical fiction, and its afterlife illus-trates one of the extra-classroom benefits of using history-mystery in the lit-erature classroom. One student's father was hospitalized late in the semester; she looked over her books and sent him Robb's. He liked it, so she sent him later titles in the series. Another student told me he had put books from two class authors on his Christmas list; one of the authors was Robb. These com-ments reminded me of an experience I had in the summer at MSU, more than a year after I had first added history-mystery to the Women and Liter-ature course. I ran into a student from that first course on one of the bridges over the Red Cedar River, and she was happy to see me. She wanted to tell me that while she generally never read anything that was not assigned for a class, she had so enjoyed the Monfredo books that she had independently read all the others in the series. My doubts about including history-mystery had been dispelled by that point, but her story seemed like a final blessing on the enterprise. Not only had Monfredo's crime novel helped this student understand important aspects of women's history in the United States, it had inspired her to do unassigned additional reading.

In conclusion, I would like to note that my initial decision to include historical crime fiction came out of my own research. My story of putting detectives in the classroom is one instance of how our scholarship can inform our teaching while our teaching energizes our scholarship In the years imme-diately preceding my decision to put history-mystery on the syllabus, I was pursuing analysis of these works as part of my scholarly endeavors. I presented on the subject at conferences including the Hystorical Fictions conference at the University of Swansea, Wales, the Colloquium on Violence and Religion, and multiple presentations at the Medieval Congress in Kalamazoo. One of my Medieval Congress presentations was part of a roundtable with authors and scholars, entitled "Sleuths on the Syllabus," at which I spoke about my use of Newman's *Cursed in the Blood* in the survey course. Initially, I considered these conference presentations as isolated papers, a chance to present on work that I thought had a broad appeal, but not part of a larger project. It was the enthusiastic response of my students when I put some of these books on the syllabus that convinced me to develop this work into a book: the result was *Contemporary Feminist Historical Crime Fiction*, published by Palgrave Macmillan in 2006, in which I acknowledge the role of my students. While the book is not focused on teaching, the preface — on a community service project I did with young readers — and some of the discussion of specific authors do suggest additional ways to bring history-mystery into the classroom.

WORKS CITED

Bertens, Hans, and Theo D'haen. *Contemporary American Crime Fiction*. New York: Palgrave, 2001.

Boland, Eavan. *Object Lessons*. 1995. New York: Vintage, 1996.

Brontë, Charlotte. *Jane Eyre*. 1847. New York: Signet, 1997.

Conan Doyle, Arthur. *Sherlock Holmes: The Complete Novels and Stories*. New York: Bantam, 1986.

Johnsen, Rosemary Erickson. *Contemporary Feminist Historical Crime Fiction*. New York: Palgrave Macmillan, 2006.

King, Laurie R. "The Feminine Dimension of Yahweh." M.A. thesis Graduate Theological Union, Berkeley, 1984.

_____. *A Monstrous Regiment of Women*. New York: St. Martin's, 1995.

Monfredo, Miriam Grace. *Seneca Falls Inheritance*. 1992. New York: Berkley, 1995.

Morrison, Toni. *Paradise*. New York: Plume, 1999.

Newman, Sharan. *Cursed in the Blood*. New York: Tom Doherty Associates, 1998.

Robb, Candace. *The Apothecary Rose*. New York: St. Martin's, 1994.

Wharton, Edith. *The House of Mirth*. 1905. New York: W. W. Norton, 1990.

Woolf, Virginia. *A Room of One's Own*. 1929. New York: Harcourt Brace, 1989.

African Crime/Mystery Stories
Triggering Provocative Classroom Topics

Virginia Macdonald

Although enjoyable for their own sakes, African crime/mystery stories are highly effective in high school and college for providing distanced contexts through which to explore ethnic, gender, and family concerns that many students may find touching so closely on issues in their own lives (such as racial attitudes and parent-child relationships) that they are uncomfortable discussing them directly. Chinua Achebe's *Things Fall Apart* (1958), Alan Paton's *Cry, the Beloved Country* (1948), and James McClure's *The Steam Pig* (1971), singly, in pairs, or as a set explored in this order, make for exciting learning experiences. The last two confirm Achebe's premise that white colonialism began a pattern of disintegration still at work in Africa today. Achebe pits tribal concepts of justice against the brutality of British imperialism; Paton mourns the loss of tribal ways and the family breakdown leading to urban crime and Apartheid, while McClure shows apartheid at its worst in the 1970s, with the natives so oppressed and marginalized that the whites' greatest fear is to be reclassified black. Depending on time limitations, one could end this sequence with John Le Carré's *The Constant Gardener* (2001) to bring students into the twenty-first century and the continued exploitation of Africans, in this case by multinational conglomerates. Given the geographically challenged nature of the modern student, providing a precolonial map of Africa or the modern Peters Projection World Map (<http://www.petersmap.com>) demonstrating the enormity of Africa compared to Europe is essential.

Chinua Achebe's Things Fall Apart

While not a traditional crime story, Chinua Achebe's *Things Fall Apart*, a clear, simple, easy-to-follow psychological story, raises significant questions about crime and how different cultures define and deal with crime. At its heart lies genocide, an ethnocentric crime evident in the Sudan today, so its assertions about historical colonialism can lead to modern applications (the documentary film *Lost Boys of the Sudan*, 2006, or the massacre scene in *The Constant Gardener*, the 2005 film based on Le Carré's novel, are good follow-up experiences). *Things Fall Apart* effectively makes students consider points of view different from their own. Achebe's central theme is the loss of a viable tribal system that would have changed and developed over time (as did the European systems) but that was absolutely destroyed by the British substitution of foreign ways for local ways.

Achebe suggests that the Igbo's tribal system of rewards and punishments worked effectively through most of the nineteenth century. Community service merited titles publicly declaring worth. Wife-beaters ordered to desist faced community scorn, a fine, or enforced divorce. Crimes were punished by degree of classification. An accidental murder called for confiscation of possessions and exile to one's mother's land for seven years. An outsider murdering a tribe member necessitated negotiation, with the choice of intertribal war or replacement of the dead (a murdered wife replaced by a younger woman) and a sacrificial victim (executed as blood revenge). Other acts defined as criminal within our culture (leaving twins to die in the Evil Forest) were accepted as normal, but clearly the society was open to change.

However, the tribe had never experienced genocide as a method of punishment until they encounter the British. The British annihilate the village of Abame, killing everyone as punishment for a tribe member killing a British representative. When the angered warrior Okonkwo kills a British spokesman, his act pales beside what Okonkwo realizes will be the British response: the utter destruction of his tribe. To appease these invaders and thus save his people, Okonkwo commits suicide, thereby losing his place in his people's history: his name becomes taboo. Through Okonkwo's sacrifice, Achebe shows readers the major crime of the novel: the British destruction of the Igbo way of life (their religion, justice system, governmental system, sense of family and community), leaving in its place a chaos that can only end in senseless deaths.

Classroom Quizzes, Activities, Assignments

Students may at first dislike this story if it is their first introduction to a different culture and way of thinking, but usually by midnovel they are engrossed in the story and by the end are outraged that a man who cannot even speak Igbo (the District Commissioner) could dismiss Okonkwo with a paragraph (his intention in a book he plans to write) when Achebe has written a whole book exploring his complicated nature and worth. To assure reading and to engage students in thinking about the differences in expectations between the Igbo of the story and their own lives one could assign the following:

1. Categorize and list the types of dangers the Igbo faced on a regular basis. Be specific. Provide examples from your book.

Example:

category: disease *example*: leprosy

2. Categorize and list noncrimes that occur in the village that would be considered crimes in a modern culture.

Useful too might be a selected reading from any of the British boy's books about Africa that Achebe found so aggravatingly racist, such as Joyce Cary's *Mister Johnson,* or a selection from Joseph Conrad's *Heart of Darkness* describing the cruelty with which nineteenth-century Europeans treated Africans. When students are midway into the book, a longer brainstorming assignment to promote class discussion could follow:

Brainstorm about the following with a classmate.

1. (a) What is the narrator's attitude toward his ancestral culture? Characterize his mixed views in a half dozen or so descriptive words (e.g., *respectful, contemptuous,* etc.).

   (b) What 2–3 scenes best encapsulate these attitudes? Name particular scenes.

2. (a) Characterize the narrator's attitudes toward African colonialism in 2–3 descriptive words.

   (b) What scene (or scenes) best encapsulates these attitudes? Name particular scenes.

3. Describe the author's narrative technique. How does he convey information?

   Perhaps looking at the structure of a single chapter will help make this clear: How does a typical chapter begin? What follows? What happens at the end of the chapter?

4. What is African about the way the story is told? Be specific. Illustrate.

5. What types of mixed feelings does Achebe wish to give his Igbo audience? How do you know?

6. What types of mixed feelings does Achebe wish to give his Western audience? How do you know?

7. How much of the book is devoted to the Igbo people? How much is devoted to the British? Why do you think this is? What is Achebe's intention here?

8. What evidence does Achebe provide that the Igbo had a functioning tribal system to promote community harmony?

Such brainstorming compels closer observation of the text than a normal student reading might produce and also compels student involvement in the discussion that follows.

A quiz asking about Okonkwo's flaws, his conflict with his son (reasons? effects?), or the significance of the title (Cf. Yeats's poem "The Second Coming") can lead to paper topics on (1) Okonkwo as a tragic hero, (2) A psychological study of what personal demons drive Okonkwo, (3) Achebe's representation of the fate of the entire tribe through one family, or (4) proof things fall apart in Igbo society with the coming of the British. A discussion of how to approach each topic would help students delve deeply and perform well. For instance, topic (1) calls for applying the tragic pattern of the rise and fall of a great man to Okonkwo by first proving his greatness— those virtues and accomplishments which distinguish him in his culture — then his character flaws (as with Shakespeare's Coriolanus, Okonkwo's strengths are his weaknesses) and the negative acts such flaws produce, and finally his heroism, revealed in his final actions sacrificing his life and reputation for the survival community. Achebe's irony is the Christlike end of this Igbo warrior, who is as subject to psychoanalysis as any European.

Making Connections

Cry, the Beloved Country works well in combination with Chinua Achebe's *Things Fall Apart*, as a before-and-after sequence, with Achebe presenting the prototypical African village before the arrival of whites, thus framing the South African story. Both novels give a sense of loss, as the village society is decimated while the destroyers provide no moral foundation or viable code to enable social coherence. Both tell a crime story that goes beyond the one-on-one crime they describe to suggest a social offence, with the individual crime a minor sample of the colonial destruction of a way of life, including the livelihood of a people and their loss of tribal authority and values.

Alan Paton's Cry, the Beloved Country

The crime/social protest novel Alan Paton's *Cry, the Beloved Country* is highly suitable for the high school and college classroom: its story simple and clear, its vocabulary and syntax accessible to those age groups. Its message is clearcut, its main character endearing, its application of a single crime story to an entire society compelling. The story of a youth, Absalom Kumalo, far from the village that would have watched his behavior and chided him for straying and from a caring father whose gentleness, strength, and strong moral principles would have kept him in line, is clearly tragic. It is a story credible in any culture: a county boy, far from home, strongly influenced by his city cousin, whose father is too busy with politics to keep track of the trouble the cousins get into. The youths start their criminal careers with minor thefts, and, after a stint in the local reformatory where they learn additional criminal strategies from more hardened criminals, move up to burglary. When the city cousin places a gun in the hand of his inexperienced and fearful country cousin, the stage is set for disaster, and it comes in a form familiar to urbanites worldwide: a frightened youth with a weapon in his hand, caught in a criminal act, terrified, and shooting automatically, without thought. This is a situation students can relate to their own local headlines.

Absalom Kumalo has the ill fortune to hit and kill his target. Inevitably captured, tried, convicted, and sentenced to be hanged, he has no strategies for self-defense; his father, an honest man, and his lawyer, working *pro bono*, advise confession and reliance on the mercy of the court. But there is no mercy. His cousin and another accomplice are released because of the lack of evidence in their case, and their lawyer undermines Absalom's implication of them in his confession.

Broader Applications

What makes Paton's novel so effective in the classroom, however, is not the question of whether justice was done in this single criminal case. There is no question about whether Absalom committed the crime, and yet his Biblical name, carrying with it the implication of a sacrificial victim, compels readers to look more deeply. Paton makes sure they do through numerous passages introducing readers to that time period between the colonial break-up of the villages and the beginnings of apartheid to make clear that the tragedy of one family is the tragedy of the community, as its sons and daughters, hungry and without means of support, journey to Johannesburg to find the means to survive or to search for loved ones who have disappeared into that city, only to be caught up themselves in its demands and temptations.

Questions that will help students see the broader nature of the crime, the white community's assault on the black community, could begin with explorations of the title's connotations and its repetition throughout the story, and then examine the contrast between the opening passage focused on the beauty of South Africa and later passages focused on the ugliness and loss brought on by mining and other destructive "modern" activities. Questions should prompt discussion of passages in which multiple voices carry the cries of the title as shantytowns grow up overnight and "Pass" and "Compound" laws force the native population out of the city at night. The bus strike against raising the fare is an effective focal point, given student understanding of how much transportation costs figure in their own ability to get an education. Student research on apartheid in South Africa and why our own country and many others cut relations with South Africa in that period promotes student interest.

Paton raises important questions for our time about the responsibility of the community for the plight of its poorest and its disenfranchised, and about the dangers of segregating groups into separate enclaves, whether by law or economics. Since murdered and murderer come from the same village and the murdered man has done much to help the plight of the South African natives, the stunning conclusion students must reach is that if young Kumalo had ever had an opportunity to meet young Jarvis, he would never have killed him. They would have recognized each other; Absalom would not have been afraid, and the ending would have been very different. However, even though they were from the same village, white and black never met, never talked, never had a chance to form a friendship, so in the fateful moment that determined both their destinies, they were strangers, and black fear of white reaction took precedence.

Films

Two good films of the same title as the book bring this story to life for students: the 1951 black-and-white version starring Sidney Poitier and the 1995 version starring James Earl Jones (filmed in Capetown). Both involve students in the story and make them return to the text. Both cut characters and scenes to focus the story more tightly. That make makes it easy for teachers to test whether the students have read the book or simply seen the film. Asking students to compare and contrast the two films, to list those events/characters/actions that appear in the book but not in the film, or to contrast their mental image of a scene or character from the book with that of the film are effective ways to hone students' ability to observe details but also a means to check whether or not they really read the book. The mental imagery discussion invites exploration of a highly sophisticated topic — what happens when we read against what our reaction is to a supplied visual image — through a discussion grounded nicely in particulars.

Classroom Quizzes, Activities, Assignments

Quizzes are not only means to check reading but also to promote discussion, with questions like "Why does Stephen Kumalo come to Johannesburg?" "What frightens him about the city?" "In his village he was treated with respect and care. What personal encounter in the city makes him wary of others?" "What has happened to his sister?" "Do you think she could ever go back to the village? Why or why not?" The specialized vocabulary of apartheid merits discussion as well: "What are the Pass Laws?" "What are the Compounds?" Asking about vocabulary might be the bridge to discussing how Paton makes a single story reflect the story of a nation: "What does Paton do to show that what happens to his one family is happening to all South African native families?" "How does Paton capture white voices?" or "Who bears moral responsibility for such crimes? Why?"

An effective way of bringing students into the discussion is to assign short, three-to-five-minute oral reports. Having two of the best students start the reports sets a standard others will try to meet. The following questions can be a launching point for expanded discussion, but the key is to control responses to some degree in order not to steal the thunder from later speakers.

> Brainstorm in pairs about your assigned topic. Prepare to explore the topic in class; class discussion will follow your lead. (Division of topic assignments depends on class size.)
>
> 1. How does Paton show us the breakdown of cultural ways? What are some situations, characters or incidents that confirm the idea that things are falling apart on every level: in the family, the village, the city, and the country as a whole?
> 2. The man of God, the prostitute, and the labor leader — two brothers and a sister — provide their own comment on how much African tribal culture changed from the village society of the past; so too do the two cousins and the daughter-in-law. How do these relatives represent the directions taken by the tribe when the tribe fell apart: The man of God? The prostitute? The labor leader? The labor leader's son? The man of God's son? The murderer's pregnant girlfriend/wife?
> 3. How does the title fit with the idea of tribal life having fallen apart?
> 4. What is the countryside/country village like?
> 5. How does it contrast with Johannesburg? What is the big city like?
> 6. What is the function of the city priest who shows the rural priest around? How is he different from the country priest? Why is he different?
> 7. What physical contrasts exist between the living conditions of whites and blacks in the story?
> 8. What negative examples of white treatment of blacks does Paton provide to upset his audience?
> 9. What positive examples of white treatment of blacks does Paton provide to balance his portrait?
> 10. What does Paton do with the two fathers, the father of the murder victim, the father of the murderer?
>   a. What is their relationship at the beginning?
>   b. What happens at their first urban meeting?
>   c. How do these two men change over the process of the story?
>   d. What hope comes from their relationship that makes two senseless deaths have value? How does Jarvis surprise everyone?
> 11. Despite the crime story ending in execution, the human story continues, with the two fathers speaking together in ways previously impossible and with real hope for the future, a hope that was not realized historically. What happened historically in South Africa after 1948?

Follow-up questions on an exam might take a slightly different form, for instance:

1. Stephen Kumalo and his brother, John, have very different personalities and very different views of their country and its future. List sets of differences between them.

   The minister (Stephen)   The labor leader/politician (John)

2. How do these differences carry Paton's argument about the kind of person who can help change South Africa? Which of the two does he think has a better chance? Why?

A major paper assignment might ask students to list all of the parent-child relationships in the story and categorize them, explaining which parents are good and which are bad parents, why, and how; what parents endure for the sake of these children, how parents affect children and how children change parents. It might ask them to contrast those changes which are destructive in the novel (for whom and how) and those changes which are creative (for whom and how), or it might ask students to sum up the debate about crime in the story, from the point of view of the natives and from the point of view of the European immigrants.

James McClure's The Steam Pig

Although James McClure's *The Steam Pig* and the other South African mysteries in the Tromp Kramer/Zondi detective series were not reissued in the 1980s because they had served their author's purpose of combating and helping end apartheid in South Africa, they were reprinted in the mid–1990s and are available through Amazon.com. *The Steam Pig* depicts South African society approximately twenty-five years after *Cry, the Beloved Country*, with all the fears that Paton expressed having come true: a nightmare society segregated by race and ruled by fear. When introducing the novel, teachers must clearly establish McClure's audience, for he is not writing to South African liberals who will agree with his attack on apartheid, but to South African racists who approve of apartheid. Thus, he seeks to capture and deconstruct their racist biases through his central detective figure, Tromp Kramer, an Afrikaaner proud of his roots, disdainful of liberals and Brits and even cities like Durban that lack the pristine racial separation of Johannesburg. African-American students will find Kramer offensive, and they should. Kramer uses torture to wring information out of witnesses, jokes about the ineptitude of native officers, and in public maintains the image of full-fledged Boer racist. Yet personal events in his life have gradually changed his attitudes: the loss of a childhood friend whose family was reclassified black and moved into a native area; the camaraderie that develops with his Bantu partner, Zondi, whose close observation and sharp mind have won Kramer's respect. Kramer is McClure's lever to dislodge his audience's racist certainties.

Classroom Quizzes, Activities, Assignments

A quiz on this book should check to see if students have puzzled out the mystery, recognized the genuine clues and the red herrings, and understood the nature of the detection. Questions might be about the implications of the murder weapon (a bicycle spoke); the importance of a piece of burnt tape, the song "Greensleeves," and the blue contact lens; the role of the city council members in the mystery; the detective strategies of Tromp Kramer versus the detective strategies of Zondi; and the role of racial division in crime solutions. As with *Cry, the Beloved Country*, group presentations are an effective way to launch students into discussion of the story:

Class Presentations

Break into pairs. Complete one of the following as assigned. Be sure to (a) create a handout for the class, a list of important quotations or information on your topic for me to photocopy for your class; (b) write all the names of group members so you all get credit! No more than 3 members per group.

Group I: Characterize Zondi, the Bantu detective. What kind of person is he? Provide some incidents to illustrate his character and skills. How is Zondi different from the other detectives we learn about? How does he negotiate his problem of race and power? Provide examples of deference and "cheekiness."

Group II: Characterize Kramer, the Boer detective. What kind of person is he? Provide some incidents to illustrate his character and skills. How is Kramer different from the other white detectives we learn about? How does he balance acceptance by his peers with treating Zondi humanely?

Group III: Give at least 4 or 5 examples of South African treatment of the native peoples, the Zulu and Bantu. How do the rules of apartheid separate people?

Group IV: What characteristics of the detective story are at work in this novel? Who does the detection and of what does it consist? What kinds of detective procedures do the investigators use? What kind of barriers do they run into?

Group V: How does the detective genre reveal cultural and racial realities in South Africa? How does the genre allow social protest and even promote reform, as McClure does throughout his South African detective series? In what ways does *The Steam Pig* create contradictory sympathies that entrap readers who believe in apartheid or racial segregation?

Group VI: List at least 3 examples of how strict "one-drop" Apartheid regulations destroy lives. Briefly explain.

Group VII: Find examples of and references to torture. Who uses it and for what purposes?

Group VIII: In Achebe and Paton we saw the breakdown of families corresponding to the breakdown of culture. Does McClure follow this pattern? How?

Group IX: McClure finds the South African whites puritanical and hypocritical about sex. Provide examples of puritanical ideas and behavior as well as of hypocrisy in the story.

Group X: List elements in the novel that are *not* racial, but rather universal, applicable to people of all races.

Group XI: How difficult would it be to keep the general story but change the setting to another continent? Explain. For example, would this story work using different ethnic groups instead of different racial groups? Is it transferable to an American context, modern or historical?

Later exam questions could grow out of these discussions, with short questions like "What qualities do Zondi and Kramer share that helps cement their friendship?" or longer questions like "Both Alan Paton and James McClure think that laws separating races and punishing violators (laws that both describe in South Africa) are dangerous and counterproductive. What examples of separation do they provide? What dangers do they warn against? What long-term negative effects do they anticipate? Be specific." The crime in this story often leads to discussions of race relations under segregation in the American South, and the attempts of African Americans to pass for white (some students will have seen *The Human Stain*, a 2003 film based on Philip Roth's novel). The question of how to recognize, confront, and overcome unjust laws is essential to any discussion of this work.

Overview Applications

These three novels together can lead to very interesting discussions and paper topics. Essay topics for longer papers exploring the connections among the three novels discussed above might focus on the following:

1. Achebe demonstrated the destructive nature of change, and yet change is a value we Americans hold dear and think has positive virtues. First, discuss some of the destructive changes portrayed by Achebe, Paton, and McClure. Then contrast these with the positive changes they provide. Link the evolution of the characters, for instance, Stephen Kumalo and James Jarvis changing for the better as a defense against changes for the worse in their society (as demonstrated through Kumalo's brother, John, and sister, Gertrude).

2. What does Africa mean to the following authors and characters: Chinua Achebe, Okonokwo, Alan Paton, Jarvis, The Kumalo family, Zondi, Kramer, James McClure? Provide a brief answer and then write a short essay.

3. List all of the parent-child relationships mentioned in the Achebe, Paton and McClure novels, and say something about each one. Which parents are good parents and which are bad? Why? How so? What do the par-

ents endure for the sake of these children? Are parenthood issues the same the world over? Where possible explain how the parents affect the children and how the children change the parents. Do not retell plot. Focus instead on parenthood.

4. Conrad's very powerful image of a "heart of darkness" applies to the three works we have read. What is the heart of darkness in *Things Fall Apart*, in *Cry, the Beloved Country*, and in *The Steam Pig*?

These work well as final examination essay topics, with students possibly offered the option of making informative charts to cover them instead of writing full essays.

An overview consideration for a final discussion (or even a classroom debate, organized formally) is whether or not modernism has been worth the sacrifice of family, tribe, community, religion, tradition, ecology, and even language, as well as a sense of belonging and a community-centered lifestyle. Related, of course, is whether the technological advances Westerners touted as justification for replacing "primitive" ways with "civilized" really ever reached large numbers of those whose way of life was utterly destroyed.

Conclusion

If one has less time to spend on African crime stories, short stories such as Ray Bradbury's science fiction murder story "The Veldt" (1951), which employs Africa as a symbolic projection of the psychotic obsessions of spoiled youngsters who kill their parents, or Bessie Head's "Looking for a Rain God" (1992), which shows Africans in times of extremity returning to their ancient practices (blood sacrifice of their children to bring rain) and facing the punishment modern courts demand, can be exciting studies. While a number of outsiders like Bradbury and Le Carré certainly write worthwhile mysteries set in Africa, those works by insiders— including Achebe, Head, Paton, and McClure — who mine the possibilities inherent in colonialism and postcolonial exploitation are often the most effective pieces to choose for the classroom. They distance issues important in the United States and Great Britain as well as assert the rightness of opposing unjust systems that methodically destroy tribal ways and undercut the worth of whole races. They provide students new perspectives, make them see with new eyes, and raise their consciousness about issues that will continue to affect their adult lives.

Murder in the Classroom
Teaching Detective Fiction at the Graduate Level

LOIS A. MARCHINO *and*
DEANE MANSFIELD-KELLEY

Although at one time or another some students might feel like "doing away" with a professor or vice versa, that is not what we teach in our graduate mystery courses at the University of Texas at El Paso. Instead, we present the rich, extensive world of detective fiction, an area of literature that in recent years has been drawing much critical examination and acclaim. Graduate students generally approach the class with a very positive attitude, assuming it will be an interesting change from their other graduate readings, which is true. They may also assume it might be "easier," with less research and writing, which is not true. The fact that students are not quite sure what to expect is often an advantage to the professor, and the required readings sell themselves. Ask any teachers who use detective fiction in their classes: students read it, if only to find out whodunit. And because they have read it, students are generally eager to discuss the works in class.

It is worth mentioning that few undergraduate or graduate students have a wide literary background in detective fiction. As the semester continues and students broaden their knowledge, they share their favorites and suggest other readings, but neither students nor professors should fall into the trap of saying, "What, you haven't read ___?"

The goals are those of any literature course: to read extensively, think critically, explore in depth a variety of works, and learn basic information about the history and importance of the genre and its relationship to other literature, to social consciousness, and to one's own life. Much of the best contemporary writing is in the area of crime fiction, and students should — and almost inevitably do — learn to appreciate the works read. The long-standing belief in literature as both entertaining and educational holds quite obviously true with detective fiction.

The general approach to the course is to examine the three basic categories of detective fiction: the amateur detective (one who is not connected with law enforcement professions), the P. I. (the private investigator who works for hire on various cases), and police (law enforcement professionals in any category). There are infinite possibilities within the three basic categories, and at times they overlap, such as an ordinary citizen (amateur) solving a case along with a sheriff (police).

We organize our courses around these three major categories. We start with the amateur detectives, since that was the first detective fiction. Edgar Allan Poe is generally considered "the father of detective fiction" with his short story "The Murders in the Rue Morgue" (1841) and detective C. Auguste Dupin. Poe introduced many of the enduring characteristics of the genre: an emphasis on what he called "ratiocination," a combination of logic and creative thinking; the search for truth ending in detecting the criminal; the "armchair" detective who solves cases primarily by information provided by others; the "locked room" mysteries in which the crime seems impossible because the room is locked from the inside; psychological understanding of the criminal mind in order to detect the criminal; and a disdain for the police, who are unable to solve the crime. Poe even created the detective fiction series, with three other stories featuring C. Auguste Dupin. The amateur sleuth remains the most popular category, perhaps in part because it suggests that potentially anyone could be the sleuth.

By the early 1920s, cases that involved private investigators became popular. The writers most remembered from the period leading up to and after World War II are Dashiell Hammett and Raymond Chandler. They and others created an enduring image of the tough, "hard-boiled," often hard-drinking and hard-living loner with his own code of ethics and, as Chandler says in his essay "The Simple Art of Murder" (1944), must go down the "mean streets" and solve crime however he can, whatever the cost to himself. That image of the hard-boiled P. I. was dramatically enlarged in the early 1980s when writers such as Marcia Muller, Sara Paretsky, and Sue Grafton began to popularize the tough female P. I., who walked equally "mean streets" in her process of detection, and was especially aware of the social issues related to the crimes. The P.I. category remains one that readers find alluring and heroic.

The third category was the last to be developed in the genre, the police, or more formally the police procedural, in which a group of professionals work together to solve the crime. Although there had been some stories featuring a police officer before the late 1940s and the 1950s, it was during that era that the police procedural began to achieve considerable popularity. It also is a very popular category now, not only because it depicts those who actually solve most of the real crimes that are solved, but because the police or other law enforcement agents in these stories make use of a vast array of new forensic techniques and recently developed innovations, such as DNA testing, which readers find informative and fascinating.

Within each of the three categories, we generally prefer to proceed chronologically. This helps students to see the changes and developments in the genre and to learn more about literary history. It is likewise interesting to consider how what was going on in society influenced the types of characters and ideas of justice, and, vice versa, how the popularity of detective fiction changes individual and social attitudes and actions.

As a genre, detective fiction, with its emphasis on character and plot, also offers a clear basis for examining the elements of fiction. From television and film, students already know the genre, although they may need to be reminded of what they know: there must be a crime, a victim, and someone to identify the perpetrator. Throughout the course students become aware of the malleability of the genre and the ways it is constantly being modified and expanded.

In our graduate courses, students are also required to write their own original short detective story toward the end of the semester. They usually do this without complaint, often even with considerable enthusiasm, and it is always amazing to see how well they do. Time is allowed during a class period for them to share, if not by reading the entire story, at least through a synopsis and account of how they developed their ideas.

The students in the graduate course we team-teach submit their stories in time to have all the stories bound into a booklet, complete with a title they choose. The "book" is distributed to them at the beginning of the final exam. As part of the exam, they read one of the stories by another student and then write an analytical review of it, with emphasis on the degree to which the story fits the category of amateur, P.I., or police. It is a treat to read their stories and their papers about their classmates' stories.

We were fortunate that during one semester of the course the Left Coast Crime conference was held in El Paso. The majority of those who attend this conference are writers, although many fans also attend. Students were assigned to attend at least one panel session or speech and to interview one author, with preconference arrangements for the interview made by e-mail. Reports on the sessions and the interviews were read or discussed in class. Some of the students continued to correspond with their authors after the conference. Although seldom is a crime conference so handy, it is still possible for students to interview authors over the Internet. Most authors now include their websites on the jackets of their books.

The conference also provided an opportunity to learn about the detective fiction "culture," with its major conferences, awards and how they are selected, on-line discussion list-serves such as *DorothyL*, and information about detective fiction magazines, such as *Ellery Queen Mystery Magazine*, *Alfred Hitchcock Mystery Magazine*, and *The Strand*. Students discovered where they might be able to send their own stories. We also told students about the Popular Culture Association conferences, which have numerous panels on detective fiction, providing professors and graduate students alike an opportunity to present critical papers on the works of their favorite authors.

Other resources students use include fan magazines, chat rooms, numerous mystery websites in addition to author websites and blogs, and general reference books and bibliographies such as *The Mystery Story* (1976), edited by John Ball; *An Introduction to the Detective Story* (1987), by LeRoy Lad Panek; *Reference Guide to Mystery and Detective Fiction* (2004), by Richard J. Bleiler; and *The Cambridge Companion to Crime Fiction* (2006), edited by Martin Priestman. There are many other fine sources available on detective fiction in general and on individual writers.

In some detective fiction courses we have used additional strategies to expand student interest and information. Classes have included having a local P. I., police detective, or local detective fiction author come to class as a guest speaker, which always generates high interest with students asking almost endless questions. One graduate class together as a group saw the film *The Departed* at a nearby theater, and this led to considerable discussion as well as an increased sense of camaraderie.

At least one film is included in most of our mystery courses, sometimes related to an assigned reading, such as Walter Mosley's *Devil in a Blue Dress* (1995, with Denzel Washington as Easy Rawlings), or the outstanding 1958 film of Agatha Christie's *Witness for the Prosecution* (with its additional surprise ending after the surprise ending of the story). These serve well to critique the differences between print and film versions. Other films also work well, including vintage films like one of the comic Charlie Chan movies, or classics such as *The Maltese Falcon* (1941, with Humphrey Bogart as Sam Spade; one class even saw the two earlier film versions based on Dashiell Hammett's novel as well). Students find it interesting to discuss these period films and to contrast them with approaches in current films.

In one course, students watched three different film versions of Agatha Christie's *4:50 to Paddington* (its first U.S. release titled *What Mrs. McGillicuddy Saw*) outside of the regular class period. Seeing Miss Marple played by Joan Hicks, Geraldine McEwan, and Margaret Rutherford (in the film based on the same novel but titled *Murder, She Said*) certainly made the point that different interpretations of detective fiction characters are possible. The same phenomenon is dramatically clear in the endlessly changing image of Nancy Drew on television and in film.

The novels assigned in the graduate course in detective fiction class vary from semester to semester, since there are so many excellent ones available, which is another advantage for the professor. We often wish we could immediately teach the most recent novels that we are excited about in our own reading, but we wait until they appear in less costly paperbacks.

In addition to graduate detective fiction courses, we have also taught general undergraduate detective fiction courses and several special topics courses. A few of these, with sample readings, are as follows.

Detective Fiction by Women Writers: This course concentrates on women writers who have contributed widely to the genre, particularly authors featuring women protagonists. In addition to such classic writers as Agatha Christie, Dorothy L. Sayers, Josephine Tey, and Dorothy Gilman, it looks particularly at contemporary feminist women writers.

Books

Sara Paretsky, ed., *Sisters on the Case: Twenty Years of Sisters in Crime*
Nevada Barr, *Track of the Cat*
Patricia Cornwall, *Cruel and Unusual*
Katherine V. Forrest, *Murder by Tradition*
Sue Grafton, *"L" Is for Lawless*
Laurie R. King, *A Grave Talent*
Margaret Maron, *Bootlegger's Daughter*
Allana Martin, *Death of a Healing Woman*
Marcia Muller, *The Broken Promise Land*
Carol O'Connell, *Find Me*
Sara Paretsky, *Bitter Medicine*
Barbara Paul, *The Fourth Wall*
Elizabeth Peters, *The Hippopotamus Pool*
Mary Willis Walker, *Under the Beetle's Cellar*

There are almost endless choices, including several anthologies of mystery short stories by women authors and many book-length critical works about detective fiction by women.

The Literary Detective: This course examines detective fiction novels in which real literary figures serve as detectives or characters. Emphasis is placed on the real lives and the important literary contributions of these authors as well as on how they are depicted as fictional characters.

Books

Matthew Pearl, *The Dante Club* (Longfellow, Lowell, Holmes)
Frederick Busch, *The Night Inspector* (Melville)
John MacLachlan Gray, *Not Quite Dead* (Dickens, Poe)
Louis Bayard, *The Pale Blue Eye* (Poe)
Anna Maclean, *Louisa and the Missing Heiress* (Louisa May Alcott)
Peter King, *The Jewel of the North* (Jack London)
Harold Schechter, *The Tell-Tale Corpse* (Poe, Alcott, Thoreau)

There are also mysteries that feature Wilkie Collins, Jane Austen, Mark Twain, Benjamin Franklin, Bram Stoker, Emily Dickinson, and others.

International Detective Fiction: This course studies detective fiction written in various countries around the world. It may also examine the legal systems of each country.

Books

Arthur W. Upfield, *The Bone Is Pointed* (Australia)
Garry Disher, *The Dragon Man* (Australia)
Louise Penny, *Still Life* (Canada)
William Marshall, *Yellowthread Street* (China)
P. D. James, *Original Sin* (England)
Reginald Hill, *Bones and Silence* (England)
Georges Simenon, *Maigret and the Madwomen* (France)
Vikram Chanora, *Sacred Games* (India)
Bartholomew Gill, *The Death of a Joyce Scholar* (Ireland)
Donna Leon, *A Venetian Reckoning* (Italy)
Janwillem van de Wetering, *Tumbleweed* (The Netherlands)
Stuart MacBride, *Cold Granite* (Scotland)
Ian Rankin, *The Naming of the Dead* (Scotland)
Craig Johnson, *A Cold Dish* (United States)
James Lee Burke, *Burning Angel* (United States)

There are numerous other good choices available, as more writers from many countries are increasingly visible and notable contributors to the detective fiction genre.

The students in our graduate detective fiction classes are usually predominantly literature majors, plus several in Creative Writing and a few from other programs, such as Education or the Masters in Interdisciplinary Studies. This mix makes it readily clear to all of them that detective fiction is relevant to a wide variety of disciplines and interests. We encourage those who are going into teaching to consider including detective fiction when they have some control over curriculum, just as we encourage colleagues in the English department to do so, including the composition teachers. Teachers of the Entering Student seminars have done so with success as well.

A favorite example of using detective fiction in courses outside the English department is a Social Work professor who recently used Margaret Maron's *Bootlegger's Daughter* and Carol O'Connell's *Crime School* in her graduate class that focuses on learning how to write psychosocial assessments. Students found most of the information they needed from the novels, and they also interviewed each other, with one role-playing the relevant character.

We enjoy teaching detective fiction and are pleased that our English department curriculum includes both undergraduate and graduate detective fiction courses among the degree options. We hope other teachers will feel the same way when they teach detective fiction, either in a full course or as part of another course, in whatever department.

The syllabus included here is the one we used when we team-taught the general graduate course in detective fiction. It shows a preference for short writing assignments for almost every class period, which also aids in class discussion. The longer papers required student research in secondary sources, at least some of which had to be from critical works other than information available on-line. Information gathered on-line needed to be cross-checked with one or more other sources, on-line or off. The syllabus is based on a fifteen-week plus final-exam-week semester. The course met twice a week, on Tuesdays and Thursdays. Course policies, dates, details about office hours, etc., have been eliminated here, but we include our e-mail addresses if anyone wants to contact us. At the end of the syllabus is a handout of further information about writing assignments and a sample quiz on James Lee Burke's *Purple Cane Road*.

Student evaluations have commented on the sustained interest in the readings and the high degree of learning from the challenging courses, but they also comment on the more relaxed atmosphere that the detective fiction seminar encourages. As professors, we are consistently impressed and supported by the enthusiasm of the students, who continue to explore the detective fiction genre.

WORKS CITED

(also see reading lists in the essay
and the appended syllabus)

Ball, John, ed. *The Mystery Story*. San Diego: University Extension, University of California, 1976.

Bleiler, Richard. *Reference Guide to Mystery and Detective Fiction*. Englewood, CO: Libraries Unlimited, 1999.

Chandler, Raymond. "The Simple Act of Murder." *The Simple Act of Murder*. New York: Vintage, 1988. Cited in *Death by Pen: The Longman Anthology of Detective Fiction from Poe to Paretsky*. Ed. Deane Mansfield-Kelley and Lois A. Marchino. New York: Pearson Longman, 2007. 219.

Panek, LeRoy. *An Introduction to the Detective Story*. Bowling Green, OH: Bowling Green State University Press, 1987.

Priestman, Martin, ed. *The Cambridge Companion to Crime Fiction*. New York: Cambridge University Press, 2003.

APPENDIX

Course Syllabus

English 5350 Detective Fiction Syllabus
Marchino — Mansfield-Kelley
lmarchin@utep.edu;deane@utep.edu

Textbooks

Deane Mansfield-Kelley and Lois A. Marchino, eds., *Death by Pen: The Longman Anthology of Detective Fiction from Poe to Paretsky*
Max Collins, Th*e London Blitz Murders*
Margaret Maron, *Bootlegger's Daughter*
Harlan Coben, *Fade Away*
Patricia Cornwell, *Cruel and Unusual*
Rex Stout, *The Doorbell Rang*
Sara Paretsky, *Killing Orders*
Robert Parker, *Small Vices*
S.J. Rozan, *Reflecting the Sky*
P.D. James, *Original Sin*
James Lee Burke, *Purple Cane Road*
Reginald Hill, *Pictures of Perfection*
Carol O'Connell, *Shell Game*

Note: All writing assignments are due at the beginning of class on the day listed. All are to be typed, double spaced. Have all works read before class on the day listed and be prepared to discuss them. Enjoy! "Come, Watson, come. The game is afoot!"

WEEK 1:   T   Introduction to Course.

Basic elements of detective fiction.

Tr   "Introduction" in *Death by Pen*, 1–10;

Ball, "Murder at Large," 11–24; "The Amateur Detective," 25–28; Poe, "The Murders in the Rue Morgue," 54–81. Note: All readings other than the novels are from the *Death by Pen* anthology.

WEEK 2:   T   Maida and Spornick, from "The Puzzle Game," 29–38; Conan Doyle,"Silver Blaze," 81–101; Christie, "The Witness for the Prosecution," 101–118. Writing assignment: Discuss elements of "puzzle game" in both stories. How helpful do you find this as an approach to these works? What would be another approach that would fit both stories? Length: 1–2 typed double-spaced pages (approximately 250–500 words). All writing assignments are due on the day listed.

Tr   Collins, *The London Blitz Murders*. Writing assignment: How do you think you would have felt differently about the novel if it had not featured Agatha Christie as a central character? Length: 1 page.

WEEK 3: T Sayers, "The Haunted Policeman," 118–134; Carr, "The House in Goblin Wood," 134–151; Queen, "'My Queer Dean,'" 151–156; Maron, "Deborah's Judgment," 156–172.

          Tr Maron, *Bootlegger's Daughter.*

Writing assignment: Discuss the ending of the novel in terms of Deborah Knott's sense of justice, and compare it to the ending of "Deborah's Judgment." What do you see as Maron's primary narrative strategy in leading you to your conclusion? Length: 2–3 pages.

WEEK 4: T Talburt and Young, "The Many Guises of the Contemporary Amateur Detective," 39–53; McCrumb, "Nine Lives to Live," 172–185; Davidson, "Cold Turkey," 185–198; Burke, "Revised Endings," 199–204.

Writing assignment: In what ways can "Revised Endings" (or one of the other stories) be used to summarize the elements associated with the amateur detective mystery? Length:1–2 pages.

          Tr Coban, *Fade Away.*

Writing assignment: Write a potential scene to follow the end of the novel. Length: 1–3 pages.

WEEK 5: T Cornwell, *Cruel and Unusual.*

          Tr Amateur mystery paper due. Critical analysis of one or more of the assigned works with reference to other critical works. Cite 4 or 5 sources. The essay should discuss one or two aspects of the mystery genre, e.g., plot development, characterization, concepts of justice, social consciousness, etc. What do your reference sources say about the topic, and how do these commentaries apply to your primary source? Bring at least one book or article cited to class. Length: 4–5 pages. In class: develop template for interview with an author at Left Coast Crime Conference. (By now you should have decided on one or two authors to contact.)

WEEK 6: T "The Private Investigator," 205–207 Chandler, "The Simple Art of Murder," 208–219; Hammett, "The Gutting of Couffignal," 229–253.

          Tr Chandler, "Trouble Is My Business," 253–294; Haywood, "And Pray Nobody Sees you," 319–331.

Writing assignment:Discuss how the Private Investigators in Hammett, Chandler, and Haywood illustrate the characteristics of the "hard-boiled" detective. Length: 1–2 pages.

WEEK 7: T Stout, *The Doorbell Rang.*

Writing assignment: Write a scene for the novel that features a conversation/confrontation between Nero Wolfe and J. Edgar Hoover. 1–3 pages.

          Tr No class. Left Coast Crime Conference.

WEEK 8:	T	Reports on Left Coast Crime Conference. Written interviews due.
	Tr	Kaufman and Kay, From "Grafton's Place in the Development of the Detective Novel," 219–228; Grafton, "The Parker Shotgun," 295–308.
WEEK 9:	T	Paretsky, *Killing Orders.* Writing assignment: Discuss the portrayal of women in the P.I. fiction you have read. Length: 2–4 pages.
	Tr	Paretsky, "Skin Deep," 308–319; Rozan, "Going Home," 331–335. Writing Assignment: Topic of your choice. Length: 1–2 pages.
WEEK 10:	T	Parker, *Small Vices.*
	Tr	Rozan, *Reflecting the Sky.* Writing assignment: Discuss the impact of "place" in the four P.I. novels you have read. 2–4 pages.
WEEK 11:	T	"The Police," 337–340; Panek, "From 'The Police Novel,'" 341–357.
	Tr	Cesar Chavez Day — No Classes
WEEK 12:	T	Crofts, "The Hunt Ball," 364–373; McBain, "The 87th Precinct," 358–363; McBain, "Sadie When She Died," 383–411.
	Tr	P.D. James, *Original Sin.* Writing assignment: Discuss many of the implications of the title of this novel as the plot evolves. Length: 2–4 pages.
WEEK 13:	T	Rankin, "The Dean Curse," 419–437; Robinson, "Missing in Action," 457–473. Writing assignment: Discuss how war affects the concept of crime as illustrated in these stories.
	Tr	Burke, *Purple Cane Road.* Quiz over the novel.
WEEK 14:	T	Detective fiction story due. In class discussion of students' detective characters.
	Tr	Hill, *Pictures of Perfection.* Writing assignment: Topic of your choice. Length: 1–2 pages.
WEEK 15:	T	O'Connell, *Shell Game.* Writing assignment: Consider the issues of conscience, duty, and moral judgment. Is Mallory moral or immoral, a hero or an anti-hero? Length: 1–2 pages.
	Tr	Hillerman, "Chee's Witch," 411–419. Howard, "Under Suspicion," 437–457. Police paper due.
FINALS	Tr	FINAL EXAM Comprehensive. Short answer and essay questions.

English 5350 Instructions for Major Writing Assignments

Week 5—Critical analysis paper due for amateur detective section. Use MLA format for Works Cited page. Be sure to have a clear thesis, or central argument, and use quotations and examples from the relevant works to support your thesis. Topics are to be cleared with the professor. Bring to class one of the books you used for reference. It is also at this time that the class will discuss specific questions to be asked in all interviews, as well as other topics depending on the individual author. Format for the written presentation of the interview will be included.

Week 8—Written interview due with the detective fiction writer from the Left Coast Crime Conference that you interviewed and your summary and commentary on at least one of the sessions you attended.

Week 14—Your original detective fiction short story is due. It may feature an amateur detective, a private investigator, or a police officer or officers. Length: Depends on your story, but approximately 6–20 pages. Be especially careful in proofreading your work.

Week 15—Critical analysis paper due for police section. Length: 4–6 pages. Include at least two critical references.

Quiz Over Purple Cane Road

1. Name three of the people Johnny Remeta kills.
2. What makes Remeta such a distinctive (unique) hit man?
3. How does Dave Robicheaux know about the switch made by Letty and Passion Labiche?
4. What is the connection between the title and the plot of the novel?
5. Briefly summarize any one of the numerous memorable scenes in the novel, explaining where it took place, who was there, and what happened.
6. Make up your own question about the novel. (You do not need to know the answer.)

Introducing Literature
Through Detective Fiction
An Approach to Teaching Online

Meg Matheny

Enticing students to take literature courses is often a challenge for many community colleges, as it is at my institution, Jefferson Community and Technical College Southwest in Louisville, Kentucky. When most students are not planning to major in the humanities and need only one or two courses to satisfy the humanities requirement, it is often difficult for a standard literature survey to compete against courses such as History of Rock & Roll. Formulating a literature course along a particular theme can spark students' interest, and offering the course online can increase the student audience. This essay discusses the benefits of using detective fiction to introduce students to the elements of fiction and strategies for using a course management system such as Blackboard to deliver the course to a broad student audience.

Currently, there are few collections of detective stories designed for use as a course textbook. One of the better selections is *The Longman Anthology of Detective Fiction* (1st edition), which includes short stories and a few critical essays in the genre. This book divides the stories into the three main types of detectives in fiction — the amateur detective, the private investigator, and the police — making it easy to separate the course into distinct units. Critical essays are also included in the anthology, allowing students to read a different type of literature (essay) and to evaluate others' insights into detective fiction.

While *The Longman Anthology* does not include any poetry or drama, supplemental materials can be required without adding a lot of expense for the students. Amazon.com and other booksellers offer reasonably priced collections of Agatha Christie's plays, for example, that include *The Mousetrap, Ten Little Indians, Witness for the Prosecution,* and other classics. Online sources are also available; for example, Lazy Bee Scripts provides script texts online for two comedic murder mystery plays: Stuart Ardern's *Death in Character* (one act) and Matthew Lynch's *The Murder of Arthur Bennington* (full length). While fully readable scripts must be purchased, reading the one-act play online is not especially taxing and can give students a sense of how detective fiction is treated dramatically.

Considering the online format, setting up the course on a weekly schedule allows flexibility for students and time to address their questions about the text. As shown on the sample schedule at the end of this essay, most of the weekly assignments involve reading a story and/or critical essay, completing an online quiz, and posting at least one message to the discussion boards. In other weeks the writing assignment may be longer, such as a reader-response paper or report. At the end of each unit, students have one week to complete an open-book essay exam.

Through the reading assignments, students are introduced to the traditional elements of fiction: character, narration, setting, plot, theme, and writing style. Weekly lectures posted online highlight these elements and guide students in making connections and understanding how each element works in the story as a whole. For example, detective fiction gives us a good opportunity to distinguish between fully developed "round" characters and less developed "flat" characters. While the detective is usually the most round character in a story, there are exceptions: in "The Hunt Ball," Inspector French does not appear until shortly before the end of the tale, and in "The Haunted Policeman," Police Constable Alfred Burt reveals almost as much of himself as Lord Peter Wimsey does. Students tend to prefer stories in which the detective's personal life is exposed; Ed McBain's Steve Carella is a favorite, as are Kinsey Millhone (Sue Grafton) and V.I. Warshawski (Sara Paretsky).

The stories also introduce students to various types of narration: first person, third person singular, and third person omniscient. (A fourth type, the self-conscious narrator, is also introduced but does not appear in any of the stories we read for the course.) Since most of the stories are told by a first person narrator (as in Poe's "The Murders in the Rue Morgue," the Sherlock Holmes tales, and Sue Grafton's stories) or a third person singular narrator (as in Tony Hillerman's "Chee's Witch"), students become accustomed to receiving the details of the story from the perspective of a single character. When a story using a third person omniscient narrator, such as "The Hunt Ball," comes along, students often react negatively to this type of narration; they do not like knowing who the killer is that far before the detective does, and they prefer to follow along with the detective in solving the mystery. These different narrator types give us a chance to question the authors' choices and examine the trustworthiness of the different narrators.

Detective stories take place in a wide variety of settings, from the mansions and moors of amateur detective fiction to the gritty urban streets frequented by the private eye. Ed McBain's comment about his *87th Precinct* stories that "the city is a character in these books" (361) can be used to show students the importance of setting and how it affects the characters. For my students in Kentucky, the most unique setting in the stories of *The Longman Anthology* is the Navajo reservation in Tony Hillerman's "Chee's Witch." Students are fascinated by Hillerman's descriptions of "miles of half-graded gravel and unmarked wagon tracks of the Arizona-Utah-New Mexico border country" that the detective, Jimmy Chee, must traverse to get to and from the crime scene (412). Student reactions to the plots in detective stories vary depending on their previous experience with the genre. At first students who are unfamiliar with detective fiction are somewhat dismayed that in many of these tales, the crime (usually murder) has already taken place by the time the story begins. As the detective goes through his investigation — examining the scene, talking to suspects and witnesses, etc. — the students begin to understand that in this type of story, the real action is not the crime but the solving of it. Students come to expect that the detective always will "get his man," so a plot twist is sometimes met with resentment. The fact that Leonard Vole gets away with murder in "The Witness for the Prosecution" usually does not sit well with students, but including the play version as well (which ends with the murder of Leonard) can spark interesting discussion about how writers adapt their work for different audiences.

While most detective fiction stories usually follow the general theme of "justice wins out in the end," certain stories do not give us the satisfaction of seeing the culprit thrown in jail. Poe's "The Murders in the Rue Morgue" sometimes leaves students disappointed that a lower animal commits the brutal crimes and cannot be "forced to the gallows" as one student put it. Other stories allow students to question their own concepts of justice and whether justice can be satisfied outside the law. For example, Sue Grafton's detective, Kinsey Millhone, ends "The Parker Shotgun" by giving the stolen firearm to the widow of the murder victim instead of turning this key piece of evidence over to the police: "I'd talk to Lieutenant Dolan," Millhone says, "but I wasn't going to tell him everything. Sometimes justice is served in other ways" (Parker 308).

Other stories show the students that detective fiction is not always dark and dreary. The spoonerism wordplay in Ellery Queen's "'My Queer Dean!'" is lighthearted while providing important clues (the title itself is a spoonerism), and students enjoy relaying found spoonerisms and discovering that their own slips of the tongue actually have a name.

A variety of online activities can be used to help students develop their understanding of these elements of fiction in detective stories. Since we do not have the benefit of spontaneous classroom discussion in an online format, discussion boards provide an opportunity to gauge student perceptions of what they read. These forums serve two primary purposes: 1) to get students in the habit of writing about the readings, and 2) to offer a way for students to know what their classmates think about these works. Usually I assign a question or two for response, but often the more successful discussion boards invite general comments about a particular reading. I tend to avoid interjecting any comments until the week's work is over to allow students free reign in the discussion. When I add my own comment at the end of the week, it is usually just to remark on particularly insightful observations or to correct any factual errors.

While there is nothing like the experience of a lively classroom discussion, the online discussion boards are not a bad substitute, and the results are often as good as what happens in the classroom. For example, when I first taught this course online, a group of students noticed the nuances of the title "Skin Deep," Sara Paretsky's tale of murder and racism, before I had a chance to bring it up. Watching that discussion develop online (without instructor interference) was quite rewarding.

As in any online course, discussion boards also should be set up for general student questions about the syllabus and instructions for exams and other assignments. This public forum allows other students with similar questions to see the instructor's answers, helping to prevent a series of e-mails to the instructor about the same concern.

One problem with discussion boards is that students who may not be reading or thinking about the material very carefully can sometimes make it appear that they are by entering the discussion late and just agreeing with whatever has been said previously. Therefore, online quizzes are given to ensure that each student is grasping the key aspects of the readings. Blackboard makes it easy to create quizzes with objective questions (true/false, multiple choice, and multiple answer), as well as short-answer and fill-in-the-blank types of questions. The online quizzes are not overly complex but nearly always ask students to identify the victim, perpetrator, and means of the crime as well as what type of narrator tells the story. For an introductory course, students could be given the quiz questions in advance to help them know what to look for as they read.

To give students another way to write about the readings, short papers can be assigned. These assignments could range from reader response to more traditional literary study, such as character analysis, within the realm of detective fiction. The sample assignments at the end of this essay require students to read closely and focus their discussion, skills that are needed in any course of study, and may require work with more than one reading selection. For example, the assignment on Christie's "The Witness for the Prosecution" requires students to provide evidence from one of the critical essays in the textbook as well as from the story itself.

The exams at the end of each unit are further opportunities for students to delve into particular stories and make connections between the readings. My online exams are very similar to those I would give in a face-to-face class but require more depth in the responses since the online exams are open book, and students have about one week to complete them. Each exam is divided into four sections: Identification, Definition, Short Answer, and Short Essay.

The Identification and Definition sections require very short responses. In Identification, students must identify particular characters by explaining their role in the particular story, or particular authors by explaining their contributions to the detective fiction genre. In Definition, students must define several terms and give an example from one of the stories. For example, the exam on amateur detectives includes terms such as "protagonist" and "narrator," which apply to fiction generally, and "fair play rule," which applies to detective fiction in particular.

The Short Answer and Short Essay sections require more writing. For the Short Answers, students are instructed to compose one or two fully developed paragraphs in response to three of five questions. These questions do not reiterate what students have already done on the quizzes and discussion boards but ask them to make additional connections. For example, the exam on the police includes a short-answer question that asks students to explain why realism is so important to the police category of detective fiction.

For the Short Essay, students are asked to compose a one-page (double-spaced) essay-style response that begins with a clear thesis and refers to specific examples from the stories to support that thesis. Often the essay questions make reference to an idea in one of the critical essays and ask students to apply this idea to the stories, as in the following example from the private investigator exam: Using examples from two stories, explain what elements of the private investigator category of detective fiction appeal to an audience "with a sharp, aggressive attitude to life" (Chandler 216).

In addition to traditional methods of evaluation such as quizzes and exams, projects that allow students to apply what they learn make the course more interesting and more interactive, and students usually respond positively to these activities. Because detective fiction is so ingrained in American popular culture, students usually are happy to embark on a project that explores this connection between literature and life. There are many options for such a project: comparing an original detective film to its remake (such as *The Pink Panther* starring Peter Sellers and its remake starring Steve Martin), examining a particular television show to determine how well it meets the criteria of its type of detective fiction (*Law & Order* and *Monk* have been popular choices), or surveying a bookstore and the Internet to gauge the popularity of a favorite author. The *Internet Movie Database* is an excellent starting point for learning about detective movies and television shows. Students then write about their findings in an evaluative term report or paper that can be made available to other students in the class through the Groups feature of Blackboard or a similar feature that allows file sharing among the members of the class.

Teaching literature online can be as rewarding as teaching it in the classroom if the topic is interesting and the students are inspired to share their ideas. Detective fiction meets both of these requirements and provides a rich, satisfying course for instructors and students alike.

WORKS CITED

Ardern, Stuart. *Death in Character. Lazy Bee Scripts.* n.d. October 15, 2007. <www.lazy beescripts.co.uk/OneActPlays/Death_in_Character.htm>.

Chandler, Raymond. "The Simple Art of Murder." 1988. Mansfield-Kelley and Marchino 208–19.

Christie, Agatha. *The Mousetrap and Other Plays.* New York: Dodd, Mead & Company, 1978.

_____. "The Witness for the Prosecution." 1933. Mansfield-Kelley and Marchino 102–18.

Crofts, Freeman Wills. "The Hunt Ball." 1943. Mansfield-Kelley and Marchino 364–73.

Grafton, Sue. "The Parker Shotgun." 1986. Mansfield-Kelley and Marchino 295–308.

Hillerman, Tony. "Chee's Witch." 1986. Mansfield-Kelley and Marchino 412–19.

The Internet Movie Database. <www.imdb.com>.

Law & Order. NBC. Wolf Films, 1990-present.

Lynch, Matthew. *The Murder of Arthur Bennington. Lazy Bee Scripts.* n.d. October 15, 2007. <www.lazybeescrits.co.uk/FullLengthPlays/The_Murder_Of_Arthur_Ben nington.htm>.

Mansfield-Kelley, Deane, and Lois A. Marchino. *The Longman Anthology of Detective Fiction.* New York: Pearson Longman, 2005.

McBain, Ed. "The 87th Precinct." 1979. Mansfield-Kelley and Marchino 358–63.

_____. "Sadie When She Died." 1972. Mansfield-Kelley and Marchino 384–411.

Monk. USA. Mandeville Films, 2002–present.

Paretsky, Sara. "Skin Deep." 1987. Mansfield-Kelley and Marchino 309–19.

The Pink Panther. Dir. Blake Edwards. Perf. Peter Sellers. Geoffrey Productions, 1963.

The Pink Panther. Dir. Shawn Levy. Perf. Steve Martin. Metro-Goldwyn-Mayer, 2006.

Poe, Edgar Allan. "The Murders in the Rue Morgue." 1841. Mansfield-Kelley and Marchino 55–81.

Queen, Ellery. "'My Queer Dean!'" 1955. Mansfield-Kelley and Marchino 152–56.

Sayers, Dorothy. "The Haunted Policeman." 1938. Mansfield-Kelley and Marchino 119–34.

APPENDIX

Course Syllabus
ENG 230 Online
Fall 2007
Matheny

Weekly Schedule of Assignments

INTRODUCTION

WEEK 1: Introduction to course. Read syllabus and introductory lecture. First discussion board (DB) response and Quiz #1 due.

WEEK 2: Read "Introduction," pp. 1–10, and the Week 2 Lecture.

UNIT I: THE AMATEUR DETECTIVE

WEEK 3: Conan Doyle, "Silver Blaze," pp. 81–101; DB response and Quiz #2 due.

WEEK 4: Poe, "Murders in the Rue Morgue," pp. 54–81; DB response and Quiz #3 due.

WEEK 5: Christie, "Witness for the Prosecution," pp. 101–18, and Maida and Spornick essay, "The Puzzle Game," pp. 29–38; Reader response (RR) #1 due.

WEEK 6: Sayers, "The Haunted Policeman," pp. 118–34, and Queen, "'My Queer Dean,'" pp. 151–56; DB response and Quiz #4 due.

WEEK 7: EXAM I due. (See Week 7 Lecture for help with review.)

UNIT II: THE PRIVATE INVESTIGATOR

WEEK 8: Hammett, "The Gutting of Couffignal," pp. 229–53; DB response, Quiz #5, and topic for term report due.

WEEK 9: Chandler essay, "The Simple Art of Murder," pp. 208–19, and Paretsky, "Skin Deep," pp. 308–19; DB response and Quiz #6 due.

WEEK 10: Grafton, "The Parker Shotgun," pp. 294–308, and Kaufman and Kay essay, "Grafton's Place in the Development of the Detective Novel," pp. 219–28; RR #2 due.

WEEK 11: EXAM II due. (See Week 11 Lecture for help with review.)

WEEK 12: As a substitute for DB response and Quiz #7, a status report on your term project is due (worth 20 points). See the Week 12 Lecture for guidelines.

UNIT III: THE POLICE

WEEK 13: Crofts, "The Hunt Ball," pp. 364–73, and Panek essay, "The Police Novel," pp. 341–57; DB response and Quiz #8 due.

WEEK 14: Simenon, "Inspector Maigret Deduces," pp. 373–83, and Hillerman, "Chee's Witch," pp. 411–19; DB response and Quiz #9 due.

WEEK 15: McBain, "Sadie When She Died," pp. 383–411, and McBain essay, "The 87th Precinct," pp. 358–63; DB response and Quiz #10 due.

WEEK 16: Term report due. (See Week 16 Lecture for help with preparing the report for evaluation.)

FINALS: EXAM III due. (See Final Lecture for help with review.)

Assignment for Reader Response #1

Christie's "Witness for the Prosecution" and "The Puzzle Game" essay (50 points)

Choose one of the characters listed below and write an analysis of that character's role in the puzzle-game presented in "Witness for the Prosecution." Your paper should address the main issue — How important to the story is this character? — by answering the following questions: What is this character's function in this story? How does he or she fit into the puzzle game? How would the story be different without this character? Use evidence from both the story and the essay to develop your response.

Character choices: Mr. Mayherne, Leonard Vole, Romaine Heilger, Janet Mackenzie.

Assignment for Reader Response #2

Grafton's "The Parker Shotgun" and the Kaufman and Kay essay (50 points)

With reference to *both* the story and the essay, discuss how Grafton's use of a female detective affects the traditional hard-boiled detective character type. Consider the standard description of the hard-boiled private eye discussed in the Unit II lectures: The detective is a loner with few social ties and no family. He is physically strong, willing and able to fight, and always armed, usually with a gun. Until recently, the private eye was almost always male, which makes for interesting study of the role of female characters in these stories. The private investigator usually distrusts women, and he absolutely does not trust the police.

Mysteries of Oʻahu

Local Detective Fiction in the Composition Classroom

STANLEY D. ORR

The question of appropriate subject matter has always vexed composition instruction. Even as many have argued for the transformative power of reading literary texts in the writing classroom, critics warn that such material may dominate the course and impair the focus on basic skills. Still others champion mass and popular culture as the best way to engage student writers; as Marjorie Smelstor and Carol Weiher have it, "There is no shortage of discussion or complaints that 'I don't know what to write about' when popular culture is the vehicle for teaching composition" (42). Smelstor and Weiher suggest attention to popular genres such as the detective story, as do other commentators such as Veleda Boyd and Marilyn Robitaille. At least one instructor, Robert Georgalas, describes a composition course that revolves entirely "around authors such as Edgar Allan Poe, Arthur Conan Doyle, Agatha Christie, Dashiell Hammett and others." In teaching several sections of the "Writing Skills" course at the University of Hawaiʻi, West Oʻahu, I find that a tandem emphasis upon mystery and local setting successfully engages composition students in a variety of majors. Heeding the caveat that literary and/or mass cultural subject matter may "take over the course" (Tate 305), I seek to provide a learning experience directed to writing skills that traverse a range of academic disciplines.

A historically upper-division institution, UH West Oʻahu has for some years organized its writing curriculum around "Writing Intensive" courses that span the disciplines. These courses require twenty pages of formal academic writing including a drafting component that may take the form of peer-editing or instructor review. Enrollment in these courses is contingent upon a placement essay exam by which students may be either placed in or exempted from "Humanities 310: Writing Skills": a cross-curricular writing course that emphasizes the basic conventions of college research and writing. While some students are eager to take the preparatory "Writing Skills" course, many more are reticent. This is not surprising, given that most of these folks struggle with college writing and have now been given another reminder of their difficulties. Such disappointment is compounded by the fact that the enrollee has already passed one or two lower-division writing courses at another institution. A recent internal assessment project reveals that UHWO students on the whole understand and appreciate the need for a review course prior to upper-level Writing Intensive courses. But this hindsight has little to do with the dejection that often attends a negative score on the placement exam and the prospect of sixteen weeks in a difficult course only indirectly related to one's major field of study. In this respect, UHWO's composition course distills the almost mythic predicament in which instructors and students find themselves: how to animate the complicated and sometimes arduous process of teaching and learning academic writing.

Integrating the mystery genre with local setting dramatically extends this course's appeal, affording students a broader range of topics for discussion, research, and writing. Beginning with relevant secondary texts, we survey "mysteries of O'ahu" written throughout the twentieth century. Students must write five thesis-oriented essays: an article review, two short critical essays, a research paper, and an in-class final exam. While instructor guidance plays a major role in organizing discussion and generating paper topics, students have also demonstrated a great deal of initiative in bringing their diverse interests and knowledge to the texts at hand. Our first reading assignments involve essays that establish the course's focus. With recourse to relevant chapters from Michael Harvey's *The Nuts and Bolts of College Writing*, we discuss the basics of the college essay genre: thesis, structure, exposition of evidence, mechanics, and documentation. Students then read one or two web-based encyclopedia entries on the history of mystery fiction before reviewing a critical essay about twentieth-century cultural imaginations of Hawai'i. Available online via Findarticles.com, Chris Routledge's entry on "Detective Fiction" in *The St. James Encyclopedia of Popular Culture* provides not only a helpful overview of the genre but also an exemplum of academic writing conventions that students are expected to adopt and emulate. George Lewis's 1996 article "Beyond the Reef: Cultural Constructions of Hawaii in Mainland America, Australia and Japan," on the other hand, speaks to the ways in which the islands have been narrated as a setting for Euroamerican love and leisure. Published in the *Journal of Popular Culture*, this piece is available to students via UHWO's online research databases. These secondary texts, drawn from the adjacent disciplines of literary studies and cultural history, respectively, enable discussion of formal issues such as voice, structure, evidence, and documentation. We compare the respective merits of the essays and reflect upon revisions that might lend to clarity and persuasiveness. Students enjoy the opportunity to react and respond to published academic writing, recognizing the fact that even accomplished writers may benefit from revision. Our first writing assignment asks students to compose a brief thesis-oriented summary of one of these pieces, an overview that confines personal response or critique to the conclusion. This summary may be revisited as students draft successive papers that invoke these secondary texts. I cannot overstate the importance of assigning secondary texts to serve as models for student writing; drawn from a variety of disciplines, such inclusions help to maintain a general emphasis upon academic writing rather than literary criticism alone.

After clarifying distinctions between primary and secondary texts, we move from critical essays to fiction and film. This phase of the course broadly conforms to Routledge's historical survey of twentieth-century mystery fiction: a treatment of the Golden Age "cozy" followed by encounters with hard-boiled fiction, the police procedural, and late twentieth-century revisionist or "anti-detective" stories. With respect to O'ahu mysteries, the Charlie Chan novels of Earl Derr Biggers make for an effective historical starting point: I have assigned *The House Without a Key* (1925) and *The Black Camel* (1929) with good results. I generally make the latter available via library reserve. After visiting Waikiki as a tourist, Biggers published *The House Without a Key* in serial installments for *The Saturday Evening Post*; this first Charlie Chan novel inaugurated a six-book series that concluded with *The Keeper of the Keys* (1932). While *The House Without a Key* subordinates detective fiction to the coming-of-age adventure of its hero, priggish Bostonian John Quincy Winterslip, *The Black Camel* reflects the growing popularity of Honolulu Police Inspector Charlie Chan. Recalling our recent discussions of literary and historical scholarship, I encourage students to compose papers that generically and historically situate Biggers' fiction:

> With recourse to Chris Routledge's article "Detective Fiction" discuss the ways in which writer Earl Derr Biggers uses various mystery subgenres in *The House Without a Key*. Is this novel a Golden Age mystery, a hard-boiled fiction, a police procedural, or a combination of these various formulae?
>
> Digest George Lewis's article "Beyond the Reef" and use this piece to interpret the treatment of Hawai'i tourism in *The House Without a Key*. You may wish to consider issues such as cultural tourism, descriptions of the setting, and romance/sexuality.

While these prompts seem most appropriate to literary and cultural history, the Charlie Chan novels also sustain critiques more relevant for students in the Social Sciences. As with later assignments, a student may research and deploy relevant clinical resources in order to analyze a literary character:

"Describe the psycho-emotional growth of John Quincy Winterslip in *The House Without a Key*. Consider the extent to which John Quincy's Hawaiian sojourn contributes to his 'psychic' transformation. Feel free to use any relevant secondary sources." Although this topic appears a variation on literary criticism, I have known psychology instructors to assign papers in which students must exercise their diagnostic abilities upon subjects drawn from fiction and film.

The foregoing topics elide the controversies surrounding Charlie Chan novels and films, but these debates likewise enable writing projects. Beginning in the 1960s, critics such as Frank Chin, William F. Wu, and Sheng-mei Ma have condemned the Honolulu policeman as a racist caricature that dominates perceptions of Asian-Americans. Jessica Hagedorn, for example, decries Charlie Chan as "our most famous fake 'Asian' pop icon—known for his obsequious manner, fractured English, and dainty walk" (xxi). I suggest that interested students familiarize themselves with this response to Charlie Chan and compose an essay about the extent to which *The House Without a Key* or *The Black Camel* contributes to racist stereotypes of Chinese-Americans and Asian-Americans in general.

Even as Biggers integrated romantic, touristic visions of Hawai'i with the pastoralism of the Golden Age cozy, other writers found in the islands material for hard-boiled fiction and film noir. We begin this phase of the course with one of O'ahu's historical mysteries: the catastrophic episode known as the "Massie Affair." In 1931, Thalia Massie, the wife of a naval officer, accused five local teenagers of sexual assault. These youths, all working class Hawaiians and Asian Americans, were subject to police misconduct and victimized by servicemen outraged at the affront to white womanhood. This vigilantism peaked when Thalia's husband, along with her mother, Grace Fortescue, and two sailors, kidnapped one of the suspects, Joseph Kahahawai, and shot him to death while attempting to coerce a confession. Although Kahahawai and his friends were never convicted of the crime, the vigilantes were found guilty of manslaughter and sentenced to ten years in prison. Yielding to political pressure exerted by high-ranking naval officers, Territorial Governor Lawrence M. Judd commuted the killers' sentence to one hour. Prefiguring the Sleepy Lagoon incident that transpired in Los Angeles some ten years later, the Massie case exposes the racism and brutality that has marred Hawai'i's recent history. In "Writing Skills," we screen Mark Zwonitzer's film *The Massie Affair* (2005) and discuss various implications of the case. Useful resources for this *American Experience* film, including a full transcript, are available via the PBS website. Students may then respond to one of several prompts that generally recall assignments in a history or political science course:

With respect to the Massie case, describe the role of either business, politics, or journalism.

Review George Lewis's article "Beyond the Reef: Cultural Constructions of Hawaii in Mainland America, Australia, and Japan." What are the basic themes that inform "hapa haole" (Euroamerican) representations of Hawai'i? Is this vision of Hawai'i supported or contradicted by the events described in *The Massie Affair*?

Describe the extent to which the Massie case reflects race and class tensions present in Territorial Hawai'i.

I have consistently assigned *The Massie Affair* throughout my several sections of "Writing Skills"; invariably responding with deep interest, students have composed some of their best papers on this engaging documentary. In my experience, incorporating a "true crime" text into the course offsets its literary nature and provides a natural segue into adjacent disciplines.

Following discussions of *The Massie Affair*, we turn our attention to hard-boiled crime stories. Although Routledge's survey of the mystery story here again proves useful, this commentator has also written discrete entries on hard-boiled detective fiction and film noir. I have variously led discussions of these materials at the outset of the "unit" and set them aside as resources for individual writing prompts. With Routledge's remarks in mind, we consider William Campbell Gault's 1947 short story "Hibiscus and Homicide." Originally published in *Thrilling Detective* magazine, this story has been collected in Maxim Jakubowski's *The Mammoth Book of Pulp Fiction*, which, with Biggers' novel, I place on library reserve. This unusual story revolves around a hard-drinking Honolulu private investigator named Sandy McKane. A Filipino boxer hires this cynical dick to find his missing girlfriend, Waikiki torch singer Dolly Valdez. Throughout the course of his investigation, McKane ranges about O'ahu, rubbing shoulders with criminals and cops, working folk and Honolulu's elite. Here again, detective fiction evokes a spectrum of disciplinary responses:

Using Stevenson's article or another relevant secondary source, discuss William Campbell Gault's "Hibiscus and Homicide" as an example of hard-boiled detective fiction.

After consulting appropriate secondary sources of your own choosing, offer a psychological analysis of protagonist Sandy McKane. Direct particular attention to McKane's alcohol use and his relationship with various authority figures.

Armed with Routledge's definition of the hard-boiled formula, students find in "Hibiscus and Homicide" a local reiteration of conventions most often associated with Dashiell Hammett and Raymond Chandler. But literary history offers only one of many avenues into this piece: even as psychology students enjoy analyzing McKane's alcohol abuse, business students find in the private detective an exemplum of the entrepreneur.

Midcentury examples of film noir set in Hawai'i are quite as scarce as hard-boiled fictions, and yet at least one example may be found in John H. Auer's 1954 *Hell's Half Acre*. Written by Steve Fisher (who penned the roman noir *I Wake Up Screaming*, published in 1941), *Hell's Half Acre* is a convoluted melodrama about a woman seeking her MIA husband in Honolulu. This melodramatic B film turns upon nicely expressionistic sequences shot on location in the titular neighborhood of downtown Honolulu. Moreover, it is a rare example of film noir that foregrounds a female protagonist. We have enjoyed many productive discussions about the ways in which Fisher and Auer juxtapose gritty urbanism with touristic images that hearken back to the 1920's "hapa haole" era discussed by George Lewis.

As Routledge suggests, hard-boiled realism prepared the way for the semi-documentary techniques of the police procedural, which "has become the dominant form of detective fiction":

> Police-procedurals adapt readily for TV and film, and come in many forms, adopting elements of the classical and hard-boiled forms in the police setting.... What all of these variations have in common, however, is that the detectives are backed up by state organization and power; they are clever, unusual, inspiring characters, but they cannot operate as detectives alone in the way that Sherlock Holmes and Philip Marlowe can [Routledge].

In "Writing Skills," we treat a series of O'ahu procedurals, including *Hawaii Five-0*, arguably the most famous police story of all time. With their emphasis upon civil service, such texts prove especially relevant for the many Public Administration students who take this course. In one instance, I assigned early chapters of John Jardine and Edward Rohrbaugh's *Detective Jardine: Crimes in Honolulu*, a memoir of O'ahu police work during the 1920s through the 1940s. At least one student found herself so intrigued with *Crimes in Honolulu* that she procured and read her own copy of this out-of-print book. Born and raised on O'ahu, Jardine offers a local's perspective of the interplay between civil authority and lived experience: he is a dedicated policeman who yet bends and even violates established procedures. I therefore ask students to consider writing a paper that treats *Crimes in Honolulu* within the context of public administration theory and practice. Edward Ludwig's Red Scare adventure *Big Jim McLain* (1952), on the other hand, returns to the conventional Hollywood take on Hawai'i: John Wayne and James Arness play FBI agents bent on rooting out an incipient communist cell in the islands. During the investigation, Mal Baxter (Arness) struggles to maintain his cool while Wayne's McLain finds true love with a secretary (Nancy Olsen). These developments enable students to broach the question of professional ethics, along with other topics:

> With recourse to George Lewis's "Beyond the Reef," describe the portrayal of tourism in *Big Jim McLain*. To what extent does the film function as a travelogue that acquaints viewers with island attractions? What kinds of tourism are reflected and reinforced within the film?

> With characters such as Willie Namaka in mind, discuss the uses of psychology in *Big Jim McLain*. In what ways does the film conflate neurosis or deviant behavior with communist activity? What is the effect of such associations?

> John Wayne is often considered a paragon of American masculinity. What does *Big Jim McLain* have to say about gender roles? How does the film encourage distinct behaviors and divisions of labor for men and women?

Many writers have productively approached this film via issues and contexts drawn from earlier discussions; in an exemplary paper, one student argued that Ludwig skillfully integrated tourist attractions into the film in ways that are aesthetically appealing and also culturally important to Oahu residents. I advise those who investigate *Big Jim McLain* to peruse secondary sources such as Emily Soares's online piece "A Heavy-Handed Message of Patriotism in 'Big Jim McLain'" and Rob Wilson's brief commentary on the film in *Reimagining the American Pacific: From* South Pacific *to* Bamboo Ridge *and Beyond*.

Rivaled only by Biggers's Charlie Chan fictions, *Hawaii Five-0* (1968–80) is the most famous police story set in the islands. Not surprisingly, this television series sparks energetic classroom discussions and writing projects. I have experimented with various episodes, including the program's pilot "Cocoon" (1968) and "Sweet Terror" (1969). Pitting hero Steve McGarrett (Jack Lord) against his Red Chinese nemesis, Wo Fat (Khigh Dheigh), these episodes persist with the Hawai'i Cold War drama inaugurated by *Big Jim McLain*. On one hand, students may write on administrative issues that arise from *Hawaii Five-0*: "Compare and contrast Jim McLain and Mal Baxter with Steve McGarrett as public servants. Consider whether these law enforcement officers embody professionalism, abuse of power, or some mixture of both attributes." But students have also discerned the social and political implications of *Hawaii Five-0*'s frame narrative, which, as critics such as Wilson point out, reiterates the colonialist hierarchies of twentieth-century Hawai'i. Answering directly to "the Governor" (Richard Denning), Steve McGarrett and his lieutenant, Danny "Dano" Williams (James MacArthur), in this respect deploy Hawaiian and Asian-American labor in the service of U.S. power in the Pacific. In one recent section of "Writing Skills," we screened episode 23, "The Big Kahuna" (1969), in which McGarrett and the team rescue native

Hawaiian Sam Kalakua (John Morley) from unscrupulous relatives who exploit his religious fervor for financial gain. Many students recognized in this episode a paternalistic dismissal of indigenous beliefs and a subtle argument for "haole" (non–Hawaiian) administration in the islands. And yet this seemingly monolithic series exemplifies the porous nature of television programs, which emerge from the intersection of many distinctive and even contending creative visions. Written by celebrated Samoan-American dramatist John Kneubuhl, "Strangers in Our Own Land" (1969), the second episode of *Hawaii Five-0*, scripts a tragic feud between Native Hawaiians with opposing visions of progress and assimilation. In addition to returning to questions about the police procedural and professional ethics, students may also offer an interpretation of the frame narrative of *Hawaii Five-0* or explore Kneubuhl's dissonant contribution to the series: "Review John Kneubuhl's *Hawaii Five-0* episode 'Strangers in Our Own Land.' With attention to specific moments in the text, describe the extent to which the character Benny Kalua (Simon Oakland) emerges as a hero or a villain. What does this ambiguous figure suggest about Kneubuhl's view of Hawaiian history and society?"

With *Hawaii Five-0*, we conclude our survey of conventional O'ahu mysteries—that is, fictions and films drawn from the subgenres of the Golden Age cozy, hard-boiled fiction, and the police procedural. Composing a research paper, writers may either return to an earlier draft or pursue a new project on any of the texts or issues treated in the course. Preparations for this assignment include an annotated outline that holds a working introduction, a topic sentence for each point or section of the paper, and a working bibliography.

Even as students develop the conclusive research essay, we turn our attention to a final exam that treats one or two short mystery texts of the later twentieth century. *Magnum PI* (1980–88) and *Dog: The Bounty Hunter* (2004) furnish useful focal texts for this exam; students may compare and contrast these two unusual TV detectives or write about the way in which one of the programs represents Hawai'i and its peoples. More often than not, however, I conclude "Writing Skills" with Gary Pak's "The Valley of the Dead Air," a 1992 short story in which a mysterious stink or "hauna" descends upon the residents of a small windward O'ahu farming village. Throughout the course of the story, rational investigations fail to discover the source of the smell and the villagers must ultimately submit themselves to an ethical, supernatural resolution. In this respect, "The Valley of the Dead Air" may be discussed in terms of anti-detective fiction, which for Routledge "provides an interesting view of detection, and a comment on the futility of trying to understand the universe." While Pak's story may not recall the postmodernist anti-detective fictions of Jorge Luis Borges or Paul Auster, this tale does question the Enlightenment epistemologies that have historically governed the mystery story. As these exemplary questions suggest, I make every attempt to pursue the cross-curricular nature of the course into the final exam:

> Compare and contrast Gary Pak's "The Valley of the Dead Air" with another O'ahu mystery. Describe the vision of Hawai'i that emerges from each text.

> Analyze portraits of business that emerge from "The Valley of the Dead Air." Which characters may be said to be "businessmen" and what are the ethical implications of their business practices? In other words, what is Pak saying about business?

> Analyze the government official in "The Valley of the Dead Air." How does this figure relate to the residents of Kanawai? What lessons does this character hold for students of public administration?

> How might "The Valley of the Dead Air" be interpreted as a story that symbolizes various peoples and events in Hawaiian history? Consider the ways in which each character (or character groupings) represents larger communities such as kanaka maoli (native Hawaiians), immigrants, and settlers. What might Pak tell us about the history of the islands and what might he prescribe as a response for problems that face Hawai'i today?

After appropriate discussion, I provide an assignment description and a set of writing prompts; students must compose a five-to-seven paragraph argumentative essay in response to one of the questions. Although use of secondary materials is optional, the response must include direct references and quotations to the primary texts. After preparing an outline, students write the essay in class during the two-hour final exam period. Citing the convenience of working from a written text, students consistently favor "The Valley of the Dead Air" over the aforementioned television programs.

The student response to "Mysteries of O'ahu" has been overwhelmingly positive. With respect to course evaluations, respondents affirm this course an effective workshop for learning and improving academic writing. Some few students underscore the advantages of focusing on local detective fictions; while one commentator deems the course material an "interesting and relevant vehicle to teach writing skills," another recommends, "Essay questions were thought provoking. The course has allowed me to give more thought to books I read." Only a few students in a single section of the course noted a feeling of confinement and a desire to move beyond the subject matter of detective fiction. I am pleased to report that most students direct their comments to writing instruction. "I really needed help with writing basics and I feel more confident with writing assignments now," suggests one reviewer: "I even find myself analyzing how other pieces are written and applying that to my own style."

Yet more persuasive are the many original writing projects engendered
by the course. Although most of my students work within the various assigned
topics, many writers take advantage of the prompts as an opportunity to
develop compelling original essays. For example, in an outstanding comparative paper, an English major points out that John H. Auer's *Hell's Half Acre*
(1954), while not as acclaimed as Carol Reed's film noir classic *The Third
Man* (1949), contains many of the same elements as the earlier film. Attention to texts beyond the syllabus constitutes one way in which students interpret course assignments; others bring new and unexpected paradigms to the
narratives discussed in class. Even as one enterprising business major applies
Stephen Covey's *The Seven Habits of Highly Effective People* (1989) to the protagonist of *The House Without a Key*, another uses the SWOT analysis
(Strengths, Weaknesses, Opportunities, Threats) to assess the business of PI
Sandy McKane in "Hibiscus and Homicide." A number of psychology students, on the other hand, interpret McKane via the *Diagnostic and Statistical
Manual of Mental Disorders*, probing this detective figure for the symptoms
of alcoholism. In my view, writing projects such as these evince the way in
which the "Mysteries of O'ahu" course encourages students to develop writing skills within their respective disciplines.

However valuable in terms of course content, the detective story also
allows us to reflect upon our own teaching practices. Whether reviewing secondary literature or experiencing the composition classroom firsthand, we
might be tempted to deem writing instruction itself a great academic mystery. I would like to think that we could approach this conundrum with the
best traits of fictional detectives: the rationality and erudition of the Victorian amateur, the gentility and good humor of the Golden Age sleuth, the
tenacity and resolve of the hard-boiled dick, and the patient professionalism
dramatized in the police procedural. And yet each of these detective subgenres also encourages a drive for certainty and finality that is inimical to good
pedagogy. As Robert Davis and Mark Shadle suggest, mystery is not an enemy
to be vanquished, but rather "a source of inquiry, research, and writing": "A
collective appreciation of mystery can also be a basis for revising the academy, making it truly a place of free inquiry, where the unknown is approached
from many directions, using a variety of ways of thinking, writing, and making" (446). We would therefore do well to temper our investigations of writing instruction with the open-endedness common to anti-detective fiction.
In my own experiments with writing instruction, I have found detective
fiction an effective way to energize a difficult and intimidating course. And
yet the attractive subject matter of the detective must not be regarded a
definitive "solution to the mystery" nor allowed to become the sole focus of
the course. Given the pervasiveness of the detective story, virtually all geo-

graphical regions have been treated in mystery fiction, film, and television. Keeping an open and creative mind, each of us may discover a rich archive of local mysteries that will enliven the writing classroom.

WORKS CITED

Big Jim McLain. Dir. Edward Ludwig. Warner Home Video, 1991.

Biggers, Earl Derr. *The Black Camel*. Indianapolis: Bobbs-Merrill, 1929.

_____. *The House Without a Key*. New York: Buccaneer Books, 1975.

Boyd, Veleda, and Marilyn Robitaille. "Composition and Popular Culture: From Mindless Consumers to Critical Writers," *English Journal* 76.1 (1987): 51–53.

Covey, Stephen. *The Seven Habits of Highly Effective People*. New York: Simon and Schuster, 1989.

Davis, Robert, and Mark Shadle. "'Building a Mystery': Alternative Research Writing and the Academic Act of Seeking." *CCC* 51.3 (2000): 417–46.

Diagnostic and Statistical Manual of Mental Disorders. Washington, D.C.: American Psychiatric Association, 1980.

Gault, William Campbell. "Hibiscus and Homicide." In *The Mammoth Book of Pulp Fiction*. Ed. Maxim Jakubowski. New York: Carroll & Graf Publishers, 1996.

Georgalas, Robert, et al. "What the English Faculty Say About Teaching Composition." *Welcome to English and Composition*. College of DuPage. 05 Dec. 2007 <http://www.cod.edu/academic/acadprog/tranprog/engl_com/engcomp.htm.>.

Hagedorn, Jessica. Introduction. *Charlie Chan Is Dead: An Anthology of Contemporary Asian American Fiction*. New York: Penguin, 1993. xxi-xxx.

Hao-Tamon, Shelly. "Tourism in Edward Ludwig's *Big Jim McLain*." Pearl City, HI. Unpublished essay, 2007.

Harvey, Michael. *The Nuts and Bolts of College Writing*. Indianapolis: Hackett, 2003.

Hell's Half Acre. Dir. John H. Auer. Republic Pictures, 1954

Jardine, John, Edward Rohrbough, and Bob Krauss. *Detective Jardine: Crimes in Honolulu*. Honolulu: University of Hawaii Press, 1984.

Kneubuhl, John, Herman Groves, and Herschel Daugherty. "Strangers in Our Own Land." *Hawaii Five-0. The First Season*. Hollywood, CA: Paramount Home Entertainment, 2007.

Lewis, George H. "Beyond the Reef: Cultural Constructions of Hawaii in Mainland America, Australia and Japan." *The Journal of Popular Culture* 30.2 (1996): 123–35.

The Massie Affair. Dir. Mark Awonitzer. PBS Home Video, 2005.

Pak, Gary. *The Watcher of Waipuna and Other Stories*. Honolulu: Bamboo Ridge Press, 1992.

Rose, Lili Marlene. "Into the Shadows, A Comparison of: *The Third Man* and *Hell's Half Acre*." Pearl City, HI. Unpublished essay, 2007.

Routledge, Chris. "Detective Fiction." *St. James Encyclopedia of Popular Culture*. 2002. Gale Group. 15 Dec. 2007 <http://findarticles.com/p/articles/mi_glepc/is_tov/ai_2419100335>.

Smelstor, Majorie, and Carol Weiher. "Using Popular Culture to Teach Composition." *The English Journal* (March 1976): 41–46.

Soares, Emily. "A Heavy-Handed Message of Patriotism in 'Big Jim McLain.'" Cold War

Experience. *CNN Interactive*. <http://www.cnn.com/SPECIALS/cold.war/experi
ence/culture/movie.club/big.jim.mclain>.

Tate, Gary. "Notes on the Dying of a Conversation." *College Composition and Communication* 7 (March, 1995): 306–08.

The Third Man. Dir. Carol Reed. London Film Productions, 1949.

Wilson, Rob. *Reimagining the American Pacific: From* South Pacific *to* Bamboo Ridge
and Beyond. Durham, NC: Duke University Press, 2000.

1930s–1940s Hard-Boiled Detective Fiction and 1940s–1950s Detective Noir

Christine Photinos

This essay describes an approach to teaching American hard-boiled detective fiction of the 1930s–1940s, as well as 1940s–1950s screen adaptations of these stories that have been categorized as film noir. Students examine hard-boiled detective stories and their film noir adaptations both in terms of how they can be understood to break with "classical" predecessors (hard-boiled detective fiction with classical detective fiction, and detective noir with classical Hollywood cinema), and in terms of how they can be viewed as continuous with these traditions.

Teaching 1930s–1940s Hard-Boiled Detective Fiction

Hard-boiled detective fiction is generally defined in opposition to the detective fiction that preceded it. The detective story, broadly understood, can be traced far back into literary history (for example, to *Oedipus Rex*, or to *Hamlet*), but the modern form of the detective story is considered by most to have first appeared in Edgar Allan Poe's 1840s Inspector Dupin stories. It was popularized in the turn-of-the-century Sherlock Holmes stories of Sir Arthur Conan Doyle, and the number of its practitioners greatly expanded in the 1920s–1930s — detective fiction's so-called "Golden Age." In laying a foundation for the study of hard-boiled detective fiction, Conan Doyle's 1892 short story "The Adventure of the Speckled Band" provides a fairly representative example of Holmes and his methods. For an example of a "golden age" detective, and to set up a point of comparison for the study of detective noir, students might watch *The Kennel Murder Case* (1933; dir. Michael Curtiz) — either the entire film or just the final 12 minutes in which detective Philo Vance solves the mystery ("Gentlemen, I think I can fit the pieces of this jigsaw puzzle together...."). Both the Sherlock Holmes story and the Philo Vance film illustrate character types and plot patterns generally associated with the "classical" detective story: the figure of the genteel amateur detective, the ratiocinative approach to detection, the search for clues in a bound setting (e.g., a locked room), and the restoration of order in the story's conclusion.

The hard-boiled detective story deviates from the classical model in a number of ways. To get at some of the key differences between the two, students can examine the above-mentioned literary and filmic texts alongside one or both of the best-known 1930s hard-boiled detective novels: Dashiell Hammett's *The Maltese Falcon* (1930) and Raymond Chandler's *The Big Sleep* (1939). Teaching novels generally requires distributing reading assignments across two or more class meetings. To mitigate students' potential resistance to discussing a detective story before reaching the end, it is helpful to point out that *The Maltese Falcon* was originally serialized, appearing in five parts in the pulp magazine *Black Mask* between September 1929 and January 1930; and that Chandler expressly sought to write hard-boiled detective fiction that would hold interest beyond its plot and final resolution: "It is implicit in my theory of mystery story writing that the mystery and the solution of the mystery are only what I call 'the olive in the martini,' and the really good mystery is one you would read even if you knew somebody had torn out the last chapter" ("Letter" 130). However, if time is limited, short stories that can be approached along essentially the same lines as the novels are Hammett's 1932 "Too Many Have Lived," one of three short stories featuring detective Sam Spade; and Chandler's 1935 "The Killer in the Rain," the plot and characters of which Chandler later incorporated into *The Big Sleep*.

A simple heuristic such as the one below will help students begin thinking comparatively about "classical" and "hard-boiled" detective fiction:

What kind of person is the detective?

Students will observe that the classical detective is a gentlemanly figure whose investigations are primarily motivated by intellectual curiosity. In "The Speckled Band," Watson explains that Holmes detects "for the love of his art rather than the acquirement of wealth." His profession is "its own reward" (216). Spade and Marlowe, on the other hand, are explicitly defined as working detectives engaged in earning a living. They are not members of genteel society. Rather, they are loners working out of rented office space whose few acquaintances tend to be associated in some way with the criminal milieu (e.g., law-enforcement officers, hotel detectives, bootleggers). Their relations with women also lack the polite gentility of the detective's interactions with female characters in "The Speckled Band" or *The Kennel Murder Case*: Spade bullies his secretary and sleeps with his partner's wife; Marlowe slaps women.

What methods of detection are emphasized in the story?

Students will note the "street smarts" of the hard-boiled detective in contrast to the detached, scientific reasoning of the classical detective. In "The Speckled Band," Holmes ponders the case and forms a hypothesis before stepping foot outside his Baker Street residence. Philo Vance explicitly compares his own case to a "jigsaw puzzle." In conducting his investigation, he studies miniature building replicas and draws upon his knowledge of Chinese porcelain. In Hammett's and Chandler's stories, the detective conducts his investigation by directly intruding upon — often at great personal risk — the activities and interactions of various suspects. Spade says to Brigid, "My way of learning is to heave a wild and unpredictable monkey-wrench into the machinery" (86).

What is the resolution of each story?

Students will rightly point out that in all of the stories a wide field of suspects is narrowed to one or two, their guilt exposed in the story's final pages. What is to be noted, then, is the lingering disorder and diffused guilt of the hard-boiled stories: *The Maltese Falcon* ends on a desultory note as Spade's conflicts with his partner's widow resume. In *The Big Sleep*, a gangster strolls out of the police station cleared of all charges.

Hard-boiled detective fiction is thought to have brought to the mystery genre a greater "realism"—a critical category that opposes itself to both the "classical" and the "romantic." A quick review of the qualities associated with the "classical" might note the term's association with established models and standards, clarity, ideals, and order. "Romanticism" is understood to reject classical constraints. Of particular importance in considering the history of crime fiction is the Gothic romance. Students might explore the Resources area of *www.litgothic.com* and then work in groups to synthesize their findings and produce lists of common elements— e.g., the exotic and the sensational, melodramatically drawn heroes and heroines, and atmospheric settings. They can then identify some of these elements in Conan Doyle's "The Speckled Band."

Realist claims for the hard-boiled can be found in both the stories themselves (e.g., "I'm not Sherlock Holmes or Philo Vance," Marlowe asserts in *The Big Sleep*. "I don't expect to go over ground the police have covered and pick up a broken pen point and build a case from it" [213]) and in Chandler's and Hammett's nonfictional writings. Hammett wrote a series of mystery-novel review essays for *The Saturday Review of Literature* in the late 1920s, including one that ruthlessly details plot implausibilities in a Philo Vance mystery; and Chandler wrote a 1944 article for *The Atlantic Monthly* (titled "The Simple Art of Murder") in which he explicitly critiques the classical detective story and ranks it beneath the hard-boiled detective story on the grounds that only the latter deals with "real things" (14). Students can be asked to read these texts and identify the authors' central ideas and shared concerns. They should also be encouraged to consider what the authors present (implicitly or explicitly) as the significance of their arguments, and how these arguments are carried out. For example, students might discuss the rhetorical means by which artificiality is coded as feminine and realism as masculine. Finally, they should discuss the point on which Chandler parts with Hammett specifically and the realist project more generally in his essay's conclusion. What kind of detective does Chandler advocate for here, and how are his ideas realized in the character of Marlowe?

The above question can be used to initiate a broader conversation about aspects of hard-boiled detective fiction that move beyond the confines of realism. For example, in what ways might each of the detectives considered thus far (Holmes, Vance, Spade, and Marlowe) be viewed as a larger-than-life figure? Also of interest is recurring evidence that the hard-boiled detective is ultimately indifferent to money: Marlowe, for example, is paid off by the General but continues his investigation. How does the presentation of the hard-boiled detective's down-scale way of life as self-chosen suggest similarities with the classical detective? Also noteworthy is the deeply romantic conclusion of *The Big Sleep*, which finds Marlowe alone in a bar thinking about "Silver-Wig," the woman whose life he has saved and whom he will never see again.

With a little prodding, students can also begin to identify in both *The Maltese Falcon* and *The Big Sleep* Gothic imagery that serves each story's mysterious and foreboding atmosphere. The falcon, for example, invokes a long, exotic history. It is sought by an international gang of criminals, including a "Levantine." Spade himself possesses some dark-romantic traits: In the novel's first paragraph he is likened to a "blond satan." He has "yellowish" eyes that "glint" and "glow," and he flies into powerful rages. In *The Big Sleep*, Marlowe travels along glistening, rain-slicked streets, crossing back and forth between the baroque Sternwood mansion and Arthur Geiger's house, where Geiger lies murdered beside a plush Chinese rug, surrounded by Chinese strips of embroidery and ornate jade-green lamps. Geiger's house is presented as a space of otherness, full of foreign objects and occupied by sexually deviant men and women (the homosexual villain and the femme fatale). Non-Western cultures, homosexuality, and female sexuality are all implicitly interdefined and made to serve as signifiers of mystery, corruption, and danger.

In selecting additional writers to study, a strong case can be made for Leigh Brackett, who is best known for her science fiction but who authored roughly the same number of crime novels as Chandler and Hammett over the course of her career, and who co-scripted the 1946 screen adaptation of *The Big Sleep*. Although she herself dismissed her first crime novel as "Raymond-Chandler-and-well-water" ("From *The Big Sleep*" 137), her hard-boiled detective stories represent a departure from both Hammett and Chandler in their deepening of the protagonist's history and injuries. One of her finest stories is "I Feel Bad Killing You" (1944), in which a former police detective who has been brutally driven out of town returns to investigate and avenge the murder of his brother. Genre critic John Cawelti has argued that genre fiction allows readers to "experience in a carefully controlled way" fearful or anxiety-producing conditions (35). Brackett's story can be examined in comparison with the Conan Doyle, Hammett, and Chandler stories in terms of the greater demands it makes upon readers in this regard. Brackett's hard-boiled prose also helps disrupt understandings of the "tough-guy" style as the "natural" literary mode for tough-guy writers describing social reality — a view that suppresses attention to the hard-boiled as itself a style.

Mickey Spillane's first Mike Hammer novel, *I, the Jury*, appeared in 1947 and was a runaway bestseller. The first chapter of this novel can be used to introduce students to the author whose work would achieve such enormous popularity in the decade to follow when six of the ten bestselling novels of the 1950s were Mike Hammer novels (Whitfield 34–35), and to establish the main characteristics of Spillane's detective hero: e.g., "I do my own leg work, and there are a lot of guys who will tell me what I want to know because they know what I'll do to them if they don't" (10). A second text students might examine is a "playlet" Spillane wrote and then filmed with his friend Jack Stang playing the part of Hammer (Spillane's hope — unrealized — was that Stang would be offered the part of Hammer in the film adaptation of Spillane's 1952 novel *Kiss Me, Deadly*). This text, published as "The Screen Test of Mike Hammer," concludes with Hammer's trademark violent elimination of a treacherous woman. To establish the centrality of this moment in the Hammer series, students might also read the final passages of *I, the Jury*; *The Big Kill*; and *Kiss Me, Deadly*.

As a historical note, students might be interested to know that Spillane's Hammer, rather than marking a departure from the hard-boiled tradition, harkens back to its origins and closely resembles pulp writer Carroll John Daly's detective, Race Williams. The first two paragraphs of Daly's 1927 novel *The Snarl of the Beast* offer a succinct presentation of this early hard-boiled detective and Spillane influence: e.g., "I stand on my own legs and I'll shoot it out with any gun in the city — any time, any place" (2).

A different view of the vengeance-seeking, judge-jury-executioner figure can be found in Cornell Woolrich's 1937 "Deadly Night Call." In this story, a man's sister is driven to suicide by a tormentor she refuses to identify before her death, and who is known to her brother only through the pattern of his phone calls: "Five times, then quit, then call back again" (36). Working with the few clues his sister has left behind, the brother goes in pursuit of the man for the express purpose of personally ensuring that his punishment is death, and nothing less: "This was a sentence from which there was no appeal. Because somebody had killed her — by calling her on the phone. The law mightn't see it that way, but I did" (35). He follows the clues and carries out the execution. Upon returning home, the phone rings five times, stops, and starts again. Although the protagonist of the story is, technically, not a detective, the story (which is quite short — only 5 pages) can serve as a thought-provoking counterpoint to the Spillane reading.

Woolrich also provides a good transition into discussion of 1940s–1950s film noir, as his stories capture many of the elements that are most closely associated with this cycle of films.

Teaching 1940s–1950s Detective Noir

Just as hard-boiled detective fiction was initially defined in opposition to classical detective fiction, "film noir" was first defined in opposition to "classical" Hollywood studio fare. In thinking about the claims made for film noir, it is helpful for students to be familiar with a few aspects of classical Hollywood cinema that film noir has been said to challenge in some way. Thus, they should understand that classical Hollywood cinema emphasizes omniscient narration and narrative clarity. Viewers know what they are seeing and what is happening. They know what kind of people the characters are and what motivates them to do what they do. Questions raised during the film are answered by its conclusion. Style is subservient to storytelling and adheres to established conventions which render it invisible.

It is also helpful for students to know the kinds of content most closely associated with Hollywood cinema in the years preceding and coinciding with the film noir era, among them idealized portrayals (e.g., attractive and nobly intentioned heroes and heroines), romantic plots (of the one hundred films included in Bordwell, Staiger, and Thompson's random sample in *The Classical Hollywood Cinema*, eighty-five present heterosexual romance as "the principal line of action" [16]), and happy, undisturbing endings. While any number of exceptions might be listed here, films of Hollywood's "golden age" tend to be understood as depicting a bright world of bright and beautiful people who overcome difficulties and look forward to bright futures.

The term "film noir" came into existence to name a perceived break with the above. In the first book-length study of film noir, Raymond Borde and

Etienne Chaumeton's 1955 *A Panorama of American Film Noir, 1941–1953*, the authors describe the 1946 arrival in Paris of ten American films—four of them adaptations of hard-boiled detective novels—that impressed French critics with the idea that Americans were making a "new type" of film. Nino Frank is credited with inaugurating film noir criticism in his August 1946 essay "The Crime Adventure Story: A New Kind of Detective Film." Students can consider Frank's essay and chapter two of Borde and Chaumeton's study ("Towards a Definition of Film Noir") alongside the 1941 adaptation of *The Maltese Falcon* (dir. John Huston), a film commonly identified as the first film noir.

In discussing the French critical writings, students might consider questions such as: How does Frank's comparison of S.S. Van Dine (author of the Philo Vance stories) and Dashiell Hammett relate to his comparison of different kinds of Hollywood films? What qualities does he find in the new detective movies that he does not find in the old (and vice versa)? According to which criteria does Frank privilege the "new kind" of detective films over the old? In what ways do his criteria correspond with the criteria implied and stated in Hammett's and Chandler's writings on detective fiction? What does Frank's essay have in common with the definitional chapter from Borde and Chaumeton's study? What are Borde and Chaumeton's specific contributions? What do they see as the particular significance of the figure of the hard-boiled detective? Of the casting choice of Humphrey Bogart? What changes do they find in the portrayal of screen violence? On what basis do they describe the atmosphere of film noir as "dreamlike" (11)? What elements of these films serve to "disorient the spectators" (12), and what, in their view, is the source of film noir's essential "incoherence" (11)? In what way do all of these qualities break with the classical drama to which "the cinema public was habituated" (12)? It should be pointed out to students that many of the qualities these critics single out for praise are associated with modernist thematic and stylistic emphases.

A viewing of *The Maltese Falcon* will help illustrate the elements that were of particular interest to the French critics: for example, character ambiguity, the use of shadowy, "criminal" lighting for the film's hero-protagonist, and the linking of criminality and eroticism. Since the film adheres closely to the novel, it is possible, if time is limited, to watch specific scenes in isolation from the film as a whole. These might include: Sergeant Tom Polhaus and Lieutenant Dundy's visit to Spade's apartment to confront Spade about Thursby's murder; Spade and Brigid's late-night romantic interlude in his office, during which a lone gunman (shown in long shot) watches Spade's apartment from a shadowy doorway across the street; Spade's speech to Brigid at the end of the film, delivered in a deeply restrained but subtly maniacal manner; and the final shot of Brigid, her face obscured behind the bars of an elevator gate as she is taken away to prison.

To begin a discussion about how generic categorizations shape reception, a particularly good film to use is the 1946 adaptation of *The Big Sleep* (dir. Howard Hawks). The key idea to get at with a viewing of this film is that the category of "film noir," once in place, encourages viewers to emphasize certain traits over others in films that have been thus categorized. In other words, if we are aware that we are watching a "film noir," then we are especially attentive to aspects of *The Big Sleep* that lend it to this categorization: character ambiguity, high-contrast lighting, fragmentary and confusing plotting, etc. But if the film is presented to us as golden-age Hollywood cinema, then we are likely to pay more notice to stars, comic dialogue, romance, glamour lighting, and Bacall's musical number.

With *The Big Sleep* established as a point of reference, students will better understand the enormous enthusiasm among film noir critics for *Kiss Me Deadly* (1955; dir. Robert Aldrich). Here, all of the thematic and stylistic elements that initially attracted the attention of the French seem to come together in one film, with its disorienting visuals (beginning with its backward-scrolling opening credits), its skewed camera angles and subjective point-of-view shots, its intertwining of sex and violence, its desolate and alienating urban landscape, its sneeringly arrogant detective protagonist, and its audacious ending. Some students will express that they do not "like" the film. This provides an excellent starting point for discussion. Why not? What expectations do we bring to detective narratives that are not met, or violated, here?

While there will be a temptation in teaching detective fiction and film noir to provide students with some sort of textbook overview, it is often better to allow students to dig into the literature, films, and early critical works on their own, thereby encouraging and authorizing them to think carefully and independently about their objects of analysis. Working as a group, the class can complicate some of the critical oppositions that have been painted in broad strokes—oppositions that continue to shape reception within and beyond the detective genre.

WORKS CITED

The Big Sleep. Dir. Howard Hawks. Warner Brothers, 1946.

Borde, Raymond, and Etienne Chaumeton. *A Panorama of American Film Noir, 1941–1953*. 1955. Trans. Paul Hammond. San Francisco: City Lights, 2002.

Bordwell, David, Janet Staiger, and Kristin Thompson. *The Classical Hollywood Cinema: Film Style & Mode of Production to 1960*. New York: Columbia University Press, 1985.

Brackett, Leigh. "From *The Big Sleep* to *The Long Goodbye*." *The Big Book of Noir*. Ed.

Ed Gorman, Lee Server, and Martin H. Greenberg. New York: Carroll & Graf, 1998. 137–41.

_____. "I Feel Bad Killing You." 1944. *A Century of Noir: Thirty-Two Classic Crime Stories*. Ed. Mickey Spillane and Max Allan Collins. New York: New American Library, 2002. 73–95.

Cawelti, John. *Adventure, Mystery, and Romance: Formula Stories as Art and Popular Culture*. Chicago: University of Chicago Press, 1976.

Chandler, Raymond. *The Big Sleep*. 1939. New York: Vintage Books, 1992.

_____. "Killer in the Rain." 1935. *Killer in the Rain*. New York: Ballantine Books, 1964. 1–45.

_____. "Letter to Joseph Sistrom, Dec. 16, 1947." *Raymond Chandler Speaking*. Ed. Dorothy Gardiner and Kathrine Sorley Walker. Berkeley: University of California Press, 1997. 130.

_____. "The Simple Art of Murder." 1944. *The Simple Art of Murder*. New York: Vintage Books, 1988. 1–18.

Conan Doyle, Arthur. "The Speckled Band." 1892. *The Adventures of Sherlock Holmes*. New York: Barnes & Noble, 2004. 213–46.

Daly, Carroll John. *The Snarl of the Beast*. New York: E. J. Clode, 1927.

Frank, Nino. "The Crime Adventure Story: A New Kind of Detective Film." Trans. R. Barton Palmer, in *Perspectives on Film Noir*. Ed. R. Barton Palmer. New York: G.K. Hall, 1996. 21–24.

Hammett, Dashiell. "Current Murders" in *Discovering the Maltese Falcon and Sam Spade*. Ed. Richard Layman. San Francisco: Vince Emery Productions, 2005. 98–99. (Originally published in *The Saturday Review of Literature* 21 May 1927.)

_____. *The Maltese Falcon*. 1930. New York: Vintage Books, 1989.

_____. "Poor Scotland Yard!" in *Discovering the Maltese Falcon and Sam Spade*. Ed. Richard Layman. San Francisco: Vince Emery Productions, 2005. 96–98. (Originally published in *The Saturday Review of Literature* 15 Jan. 1927.)

_____. "Too Many Have Lived." 1932. *Nightmare Town*. Ed. Kirby McCauley, Martin H. Greenberg, and Ed Gorman. New York: Vintage Books, 1999. 305–20.

The Kennel Murder Case. 1933. Dir. Michael Curtiz. Internet Archive. 12 November 2007. <http://www.archive.org/details/PhiloVanceTheKennelMurderCase1933>.

Kiss Me Deadly. Dir. Robert Aldrich. United Artists, 1955.

The Maltese Falcon. Dir. John Huston. Warner Brothers, 1941.

Spillane, Mickey. *I, the Jury*. 1947. *The Mike Hammer Collection, Volume 1*. New York: New American Library, 2001. 5–147.

_____. "The Screen Test of Mike Hammer." 1955. *Hard-Boiled: An Anthology of American Crime Stories*." Ed. Bill Pronzini and Jack Adrian. New York: Oxford University Press, 1995. 336–39.

Whitfield, Stephen J. *The Culture of the Cold War*. 2nd ed. Baltimore: Johns Hopkins University Press, 1996.

Woolrich, Cornell. "Deadly Night Call." 1937 as "Somebody on the Phone." *Deadly Night Call (Somebody on the Phone)*. Hasbrouck Heights, NJ: Graphic Books, 1954. 32–37.

Anthropologists as Detectives and Detectives as Anthropologists

James C. Pierson

The fictional detectives who show up in my classes are probably on reading lists for somewhat different reasons than are those discussed in most other essays in this collection. I do not teach classroom courses on detective or mystery fiction but instead use works from that genre to provide certain kinds of information and make the required reading list a bit more entertaining. I am an anthropologist, more specifically a cultural anthropologist, and in several of my classes I assign selected mystery/detective novels to illustrate topics of general interest and reflective of my own specific anthropological interests. Many of the same points can be made by reading writings by professional anthropologists but usually in a less interesting way.

I have directed several independent reading courses that could be titled something like "Learning about Anthropology and Anthropologists through Mystery Literature." This allows me to assign several books based on the specific student's geographic and/or anthropological interests. I will begin this discussion with an overview of some of the detective novels I find useful for this purpose. This will lead into a longer discussion of specific novels that I assign for the classroom and the classes for which I assign them.

Anthropologists appear in a number of contemporary mystery novels, including some very popular series, making the novels a useful mechanism for demonstrating to students how the discipline and its practitioners are perceived and portrayed. Tony Hillerman's novels, set on and around the Navajo Nation (reservation), for example, often include anthropologists in the cast of characters. The fact that some of the anthropologists encountered by Hillerman's Navajo police officers are at least somewhat unsavory (for example in *Dance Hall of the Dead* and *A Thief of Time*) is a lesson for students about the nature of some Navajos' and their Indian neighbors' interactions with and attitudes about anthropologists. It is also instructive that at least some of Hillerman's readers likely carry these perceptions with them after reading the book.

Hillerman's detectives rely on cultural knowledge about their own culture and their abilities to learn about other cultures, including their Indian neighbors, Anglos, and the FBI. They subsequently often function as cultural anthropologists, as I discuss below. Other detective novels with anthropological protagonists introduce readers to the methods and interests of the other anthropological subfields, which include anthropological linguistics, archaeology, and biological or physical anthropology. In most cases, the anthropologist is a dual detective, not only conducting professional research but also helping solve a crime. An explicit example of this is a pair of texts by Adrian Praetzellis, one on archaeological method (*Dug to Death*) and one on archaeological theory (*Death by Theory*), written as mystery novels. The detective/archaeologist defines terms, demonstrates methods, illustrates theories, and solves crimes. The main protagonist in a series by Dana Cameron (the most recent are *More Bitter Than Death* and *Ashes and Bones*) is a young female archaeologist whose activities illustrate archaeological methods, interests, and satisfactions. She attends academic conferences where professional presentations are often overshadowed by professional jealousies that lead to violence and crimes, which she solves with her archaeological knowledge. Like many other fictional accounts, the books make academic settings seem both more dangerous and more exciting than they usually are.

One other series worth noting, but for a different reason, is by Lyn Hamilton. Each book in the lengthy series (recent volumes are *The Moai Murders*, *The Orkney Scroll*, and *The Chinese Alchemist*) is labeled "An Archaeological Mystery," with a main protagonist who is an antiques dealer. Her search for antiquities takes her from her Toronto base (and shop) to places throughout the world. Each book in the series includes at least one exotic locale, related cultural details, and some sort of danger that needs to be detected and sorted out. An integral and somewhat troublesome part of this series is that the recovery of artifacts is not necessarily for research but often for sale to collectors. The potential conflict between this approach and the more academic ones in the Cameron and Praetzellis books can be instructive for students. The detectives/archaeologists have quite different goals.

The first fictional anthropologist with forensic abilities was Aaron Elkins' "Skeleton Detective," Gideon Oliver, who first appeared in *Fellowship of Fear* in 1982. He continues his work, most recently in *Unnatural Selection* and *Little Tiny Teeth*, and remains an instructive example of a well-traveled academic with an impressive background in biology and friends in many parts of the world who frequently contact him to make use of his forensic skills to solve crimes. This gives the novels a cultural component in addition to a biological one, for the settings are integral parts of the story. Gideon Oliver analyzes contemporary human remains (including relatively recent ones) as well as historical and ancient remains. The series includes current events and recent history as well as lessons on important methods and theories in biological anthropology and the evidence on which they are based. Oliver's detective work is always thoroughly explained. The lessons from any one book in the series may be limited to one situation and place, but student readers can be inspired to investigate further on their own.

One of the most popular forensic series, by Kathy Reichs, incorporates biological or physical anthropology into the protagonist's work as a forensic anthropologist in Canada and the United States and wherever else a case may take her. The methods used to recover human remains rely on archaeological techniques as well, and Reichs' anthropologist, Temperance Brennan, provides details, often graphic, about techniques and interpretations. The use of timely events, such as airplane crashes (*Fatal Voyage*), mass graves in Guatemala (*Grave Secrets*), field schools in controversial locations (*Break No Bones*), and solution of cold cases (*Bones to Ashes*), provides a number of settings and sense of relevance that can interest students in the details of and training for forensic work.

Beverly Connor is the author of two series that emphasize the involvement of anthropologists in forensic work. One series features an academic archaeologist whose research in the southern United States regularly uncovers human and cultural remains that are relevant to contemporary people and events (e.g., *Dressed to Die*, *Skeleton Crew*). Her research and academic situations provide a good overview of the nature of academic archaeology, even if the latter tends to be a lot more mundane in real life. The main protagonist in the second series, which includes *Dead Past* and *Dead Secret* among others, is a forensic anthropologist who is both a museum curator and the forensic specialist for the local police department. The danger of this series for readers who are anthropology students is that her museum seems to have many resources and all of the latest technology for her detective work; this can lead to expectations that few museums can fulfill.

Detectives with backgrounds in anthropological linguistics are largely absent in mystery literature although accents and dialects are often subtle clues to one's background. Ian Rankin's Scottish detectives, for example, consistently comment on or think about language, whether that of others or their own. It is not so much a matter of stereotyping as it is a way to explain behavior. The protagonist in a series by Teri Holbrook is involved in linguistic research, most explicitly in *The Mother Tongue*, that emphasizes both contemporary identity and past events. While not explicitly an anthropologist, she is interested in many of the same matters that engage anthropologists, and the novels are instructive in this context for that reason.

Most of the detectives I have mentioned so far are instructive when analyzed for very specific details or when examined as part of an extensive reading list, such as in an independent readings course. The remainder of this paper will discuss specific books that I use or have used in specific courses and how their detectives fit into course goals.

I began to use detective novels as required readings after reading an essay by Ross Macdonald in which he suggests that "a good private detective ... likes to move through society both horizontally and vertically, studying people like anthropologists" (Macdonald xii). Macdonald elaborates by emphasizing the information that results from these intense investigations. This helped explain and rationalize why I read and enjoyed so many mystery novels. It was not an escape from my academic work, it was part of it! I initially explored this in an article titled "Mystery Literature and Ethnography: Fictional Detectives as Anthropologists" and subsequently began to experiment with some of the novels as required readings, for both their cultural content and the "anthropological" activities of the detectives. Some have worked better than others, largely because their detectives provide more ethnographic and methodological detail.

The courses in which I regularly use detective fiction are Peoples of Australia, Great Ideas in Anthropology, Cross-Cultural Child-Rearing Practices, and The Anthropology of Human Development. My primary anthropological field research has been with indigenous people in Australia, and I prefer to use a variety of readings, fiction and nonfiction, on the topic to illustrate both historical and contemporary situations. The second course is my department's required senior capstone course, which tends to include only anthropology majors and encourages new ways to acquaint students with anthropological topics and information. The last two courses are anthropology courses that fulfill requirements in our campus' interdisciplinary Human Development major. They and the Australia course attract many nonmajors, so the readings need to include as much interesting prose and guidance as possible. Several fictional detectives accomplish this quite successfully.

Continent of Mystery: A Thematic History of Australian Crime Fiction by Stephen Knight, published in 1997, demonstrates the large number of fictional detectives at work in Australia. Their numbers are even more impressive a decade later. I have relied, however, primarily on one of the early ones to provide information, insights, and the analysis of a recent historical perspective in my Australia class. Napoleon Bonaparte, the creation of author Arthur Upfield, is a part–Aboriginal, part-white Detective Inspector in twenty-nine novels set mostly in isolated areas of Australia. The first book in the series was published in the 1920s and the last in the 1960s. They cover a long period of time, and that time was quite a while ago, so their contemporary relevance can be questioned. They may not be "documentaries of Australia" at various points in time, as Ray B. Browne (160) describes them, but they do illustrate general themes. Most significantly, they reflect attitudes about Aborigines at the time they were written, both in their content and in the ways Aborigines and Aboriginal cultures are portrayed.

My reasons for assigning books from the series are based much less on their cultural details than they are on the role of the detective of mixed ancestry. This ancestry directs at least some attention in each book to cultural and at least implied biological differences between Aboriginal and white Australians, especially when these differences influence his behavior or thoughts. Bonaparte is an initiated Aboriginal male as a result of knowledge, such as tracking skills and religious rituals, acquired relatively late in life. He was first formally educated in the "white world" from infancy through university after being found by whites with his dead Aboriginal mother. His cultural ancestry is, in other words, as mixed as his biological ancestry. This is a significant advantage in his detective work because he knows how to behave in almost every social setting within which he finds himself in the Outback. In some cases, this means playing the subordinate role many whites expect of Aborigines, although his abilities never fail eventually to impress everyone. His behavior and his recognition of clues, cues, and motivations influenced by various cultural backgrounds contribute to his success as a detective. He is able to deal with all people and solve crimes others cannot.

In many cases, however, Bonaparte's mixed ancestry is problematic for him. His dual heritage often causes him torment as he struggles to decide what to do. This is far too often presented as a struggle to overcome his less civilized Aboriginal ancestry, and he sometimes encourages other Aborigines to assimilate. Some of Bonaparte's experiences, however, demonstrate the positive influence of a traditional culture on someone like him. Two books from the series, *The Will of the Tribe* and *The Bone Is Pointed*, stress the potential impact of "tribal" people and decisions on more assimilated Aborigines. One form of sorcery common in a number of Aboriginal cultures requires the sorcerer to point a bone in the direction of the person to be affected. Bonaparte recognizes this in the latter book as the cause of some illnesses when he is investigating a murder. As he accumulates clues leading to the killer, he begins to feel ill himself. He survives, of course, but only after the spell is lifted by the sorcerer when Bonaparte realizes that the killing was justified. Western medicine did not help him, an important example of the effect of a traditional practice on someone who did not believe it could harm him. Both the illness and the cure symbolize his Aboriginal identity, for better or for worse.

Bonaparte's experiences illustrate a number of issues relevant, but perhaps generally unknown, in Australia at the time the books were written. I'm not entirely convinced Upfield recognized their significance, but his detective can still be used to discuss situations that were in effect long ago but have only recently been widely examined. Bonaparte's upbringing, for example, was determined by an absent white father and the death of his mother. Bonaparte seems to have been rescued and raised in a non–Aboriginal setting. That last sentence could come from the official version of the experiences of thousands of part–Aboriginal, part–white children now referred to as the "stolen generations." The more accurate version is that the children were removed from Aboriginal mothers for purposes of assimilation, many of them in the years during which Bonaparte was detecting in the Australian Outback. Bonaparte's conflicts between his Aboriginal identity and his non–Aboriginal identity suggest what these real-life children experience as adults. Bonaparte's mixed heritage helped make him a successful detective; many members of the stolen generations struggled just to find their real identities.

Napoleon Bonaparte's detective activities have therefore provided a focus on a number of topics relevant to Aboriginal Australia in the Australia class. Tony Hillerman's Navajo detectives, Joe Leaphorn and Jim Chee, have followed in his footsteps and traveled considerably further. They appear separately in some novels and together in most. They may agree on little when they appear in the same novel, but they present the reader with interesting contrasts. They represent different points of view, but not in the way one might think. Leaphorn is older but generally less traditionally-oriented than his colleague, who is training to be a traditional singer/ritual leader. He is at least a bit suspicious of some traditional beliefs but knows them and recognizes how they influence many Navajo people's behavior. Chee, on the other hand, adheres to many of these beliefs but may have to set them aside to perform his job as a detective and Navajo police officer. These two detectives have appeared in more of my classes than all other major fictional characters put together.

Chee is the primary detective in *The Ghostway*, which has appeared on the reading list for my course The Anthropology of Human Development many times. The course, as I teach it, is a cross-cultural survey of life-cycle concepts. The book provides some detailed examples of Navajo attitudes about old age and death and contrasts them with those in general American society. Chee is the main detective in this case, which is appropriate because considerable Navajo ritual is involved. An old Navajo man witnesses a shooting and is treated with great respect, including the use of a kinship term by strangers, because the elderly are valued in Navajo culture. When Chee visits an Anglo retirement home to seek witnesses to a crime, he thinks about how isolation of elders is alien to Navajo traditions.

Navajo beliefs and attitudes about death are illustrated in several ways by Chee's detective work. The death of a Navajo creates a ghost, the negative remains of the person, which is to be avoided. If a person dies inside a building, a traditional Navajo will not go inside in order to avoid the ghost and the illness that will result. Various precautions can be taken to allow the ghost to escape, but this is not always possible so some places are avoided permanently. Ghost sickness, which results from contact with a ghost, can be fatal. Chee is confronted with this belief when he arrives at a dwelling where he believes the old man may have died. His responsibility as a police officer overcomes his beliefs as a Navajo and, after much deliberation, he does enter the dwelling. He is lucky but others in the book do encounter ghosts and are exposed to ghost sickness. Their survival is ensured by their participation in a lengthy and expensive ritual, the Ghostway, led by singers, specialists who have trained for many years to perform this ritual. Chee's knowledge of attitudes toward the elderly and death, and his knowledge of the Ghostway ritual, are integral to the solution of the crimes that led to the shooting at the beginning of the book

I have assigned *Dance Hall of the Dead*, which features Joe Leaphorn as the resident Navajo detective, in two different classes (Cross-Cultural Child-Rearing Practices and Great Ideas in Anthropology) and for quite different reasons. I teach the former two or three times a year and often use the book as the basis for the required writing assignment. Students analyze the learning experiences of the children who are part of the story, using concepts discussed earlier in the class. I teach the latter only when I have to (about every four years) and use the book to demonstrate different styles of presenting cultural information.

Dance Hall of the Dead features a Navajo detective who encounters and explains many Navajo cultural traits, but the title actually refers to an afterlife concept of the Zuni, geographically close but culturally distant Indian neighbors of the Navajo. Zuni people and culture are important actors and clues in the story, and Leaphorn's general unfamiliarity with Zuni culture requires him to learn about it as he goes along. He obtains information about Zuni culture through brief conversations with a somewhat reluctant Zuni police officer, memories of his Zuni college roommate, and a lengthy conversation with a Catholic priest who has lived and worked for many years on the Zuni reservation. His detective work also brings him into contact with members of other groups or subcultures, such as the FBI, archaeologists, Catholic priests, and hippies (the book was first published in 1973). As a good detective and ethnologist, he regularly contrasts these groups' behavior with his Navajo experiences. His involvement begins when a Zuni boy disappears while training for an important winter ceremony; his participation is a significant honor and rite of passage for him, so he is working hard to be able to perform properly. His friendship with a Navajo boy, who is also missing, causes the Navajo police to be contacted. When the Zuni boy's body is found, the Navajo boy's absence causes suspicion. It is Leaphorn's task to find him while trying to understand the somewhat unusual friendship between the boys from different cultures. Leaphorn knows that the Navajo boy is from a dysfunctional Navajo family; he lives in an isolated area with his father and younger brother. His mother lives with her clan on another part of the vast Navajo Nation. This conflicts with the Navajo matrilineal tradition of a married couple living near the wife's clan, from whom a Navajo child should learn family rituals and traditions. The father, an alcoholic, left his wife's area with his sons because he suspected his in-laws were witches. The boy and his younger brother were therefore growing up without some of the important Navajo contacts and information that Leaphorn frequently remembers learning from his maternal grandfather.

Leaphorn's search for the Navajo boy takes him many places on the reservation. He interviews hippies who are living in a hogan (dwelling) abandoned by its Navajo residents when a woman died inside it. He talks to a graduate student in archaeology, who is excavating a site under the direction of a famous professional archaeologist who is seeking evidence for a theory that can bring him even more acclaim. The lack of family ties for some of the young white people he encounters causes Leaphorn to reflect on the importance of kinship, and he begins to see why the Navajo boy may have sought a friendship with the Zuni initiate.

A visit to the Zuni Catholic church provides further evidence. Leaphorn's source of information there is not a Zuni but a Catholic priest who has great respect for Zuni beliefs and supernatural beings. He explains several Zuni beliefs and origin myths to Leaphorn, to whom it is becoming increasingly evident that the older Navajo boy wanted to learn about Zuni culture, which would break a taboo because he would be learning about ritual culture from a source other than his mother's family. The priest suggests that the boy is now missing not because he has killed his friend but because he is trying to find "the dance hall of the dead," where the Zuni believe their afterlife begins. The journey takes several days, so the Navajo boy may believe he can find the location before his friend's spirit arrives and make amends for trying to break the taboo. Leaphorn's search now takes a different focus and is aided by ritual objects he finds symbolizing that a Navajo has recently killed a deer. This indicates to Leaphorn that the priest's suggestion is accurate and that some of his own assumptions are valid. Although the Navajo boy has been missing for several days in rugged country, Leaphorn is confident that the boy could survive on his own. He assumes that the boy has learned survival and hunting skills from his father, for these do not have to be learned from matrilineal relatives. Leaphorn's search is eventually successful although not in time to keep another killing from taking place.

Leaphorn functions as a detective in two ways in *Dance Hall of the Dead*. Both make the book a useful teaching device. He is a police detective as he uncovers clues and evidence in a variety of ways from a variety of sources. These discoveries enable him to track the missing boy and determine who is guilty of murder. He is also a "cultural detective" because he concomitantly introduces and/or learns information about several different cultural groups. The background information he accumulates includes a number of examples of what Navajo children, especially males, learn and from whom they should learn it. Denial of this information can make one's Navajo identity uncertain; Leaphorn recalls how the government boarding school he attended tried to deny the value of Navajo culture. His maternal relatives, however, were still able to teach him many important things; the Navajo boy he sought did not have access to his maternal relatives, causing him to seek an identity elsewhere. Leaphorn also acquires information about some of the things Zuni boys learn and how and why they prepare for important ceremonies. In the process, a number of general Zuni religious beliefs, myths, hunting practices, and rituals are contrasted with those of the Navajo. Contrasts between Navajo and Zuni beliefs about what happens after death are stressed because the latter play a crucial role in Leaphorn's search for the missing Navajo boy. He knew little about them at the beginning of the case.

The contrasts between many Zuni and Navajo cultural traits illustrate one of the most important points that one can learn from Leaphorn's work as a Navajo police officer. This is the simple one that not all Indians are alike. Despite their long history of geographic proximity, the Navajo and the Zuni come from very different cultural backgrounds and traditions and view this world—and the past and next worlds—quite differently. This makes his detective work in this case a matter of learning and diplomacy as much as it is a matter of applying knowledge of his own cultural background. The traditions may be difficult to keep separate for some readers, but Leaphorn tends to be a thorough and patient guide. Many major cultural themes and details appear in the story.

Despite all of the ethnographic information Leaphorn's detective work provides, it is important to keep in mind that *Dance Hall of the Dead* is a work of fiction. The mixture of "fact" and fiction, the context in which cultural details are presented, is the basis for using the same book in the senior seminar. One of the topics when I teach the class is the variety of ways in which anthropologists present ethnographic information. Cultural anthropologists should attempt to present accurate ethnographic accounts while honoring the wishes and privacy of the populations with whom they are conducting research. This is not an easy mission, whether one uses a postmodern approach or not. It has not been uncommon to fictionalize certain information, such as the names of people and places and perhaps certain events. I have used *Dance Hall of the Dead*, a work of fiction with a Navajo detective as a cultural guide, as a contrast to an ethnographic account of the Mescalero Apache that focuses on the cultural context of a female puberty ceremony (*Thunder Rides a Black Horse*). Anthropologist Clare Farrer prefaces her account of the annual four-day ceremony with a lengthy discussion of how the ceremony described in the book is actually a composite of the event in a number of different years. Some people's real names are used; others are not, depending on the person's wishes and status. The author is a character in the book and functions in many of the same ways Leaphorn does in the novel as she describes her relationship with the Mescalero and how she has learned about their culture. Reading this book along with the novel enables the discussion of ethics, personal relationships, and the role of the anthropological fieldworker and writer as a sort of detective.

Finally, I have occasionally used detective fiction in a course titled Urban Anthropology to complement, or perhaps combat, the often obtuse readings in texts on that topic. The best fit was Walter Mosley's *Devil in a Blue Dress*, in which Easy Rawlins begins a detective career in post–World War II Los Angeles. Whatever his success in satisfying his clients and friends, he quite successfully illustrates the milieu of some African Americans in Los Angeles at the time, and the book fleshed out some of the assigned readings on urbanization in the immediate post-war years. Rawlins' friends' backgrounds, as well as his own background, illustrate the ease of geographic mobility and difficulty of social mobility for many of the new urban residents. Some of the potential choices in the urban setting for African Americans are well illustrated by several of the book's characters, and Rawlins, the somewhat reluctant detective, guides the reader through a variety of places and situations.

To close, I will briefly mention two detectives whom I would like to invite onto a reading list in the near future if I can find the appropriate course. One is Ian Rankin's Edinburgh-based but Fife-bred John Rebus, who first appeared in *Knots and Crosses* in 1987. Nearly twenty novels later, he seems near retirement. In between, he has provided a perspective on Edinburgh and Scotland that includes history, society, and culture, with many settings that the tourist board does not advertise. Cases provide Rebus with the opportunity to deal with issues such as recent immigration, the new parliament building and its inhabitants, rural-urban differences, and Scotland's eating and drinking habits. Rebus' most recent case takes place during the G8 conference in Scotland in July 2005 (*The Naming of the Dead*). The second detective is a journalist in the book *Fieldwork* by Mischa Berlinski. While working on some writing projects in Thailand, he learns about an American anthropologist who recently died in a local prison while serving a sentence for murdering a missionary. The specifics seem to be unknown, but he figures there is a story to be told. This begins an investigation that covers indigenous groups, missionaries, and anthropologists—with settings in churches, anthropology graduate schools, and isolated villages. Relying on many sources of information, the journalist is finally satisfied that he has answered most of his questions. It is an interesting mix of fictional detective work and the clash of people from different world views. It subsequently combines many of the topics the detectives discussed above have dealt with and is an appropriate final example for this essay.

WORKS CITED

Berlinski, Mischa. *Fieldwork.* New York: Farrar, Straus and Giroux, 2007.

Browne, Ray B. *The Spirit of Australia: The Crime Fiction of Arthur W. Upfield.* Bowling Green, OH: Bowling Green State University Popular Press, 1988.

Cameron, Dana. *Ashes and Bones.* New York: Avon, 2006.

_____. *More Bitter Than Death.* New York: Avon, 2005.

Connor, Beverly. *Dead Past.* New York: Onyx, 2007.

_____. *Dead Secret.* New York: Onyx, 2005.

_____. *Dressed to Die.* Nashville: Cumberland House, 1998.

_____. *Skeleton Crew.* Nashville: Cumberland House, 1999.

Elkins, Aaron. *Fellowship of Fear.* New York: Popular Library, 1982.

_____. *Little Tiny Teeth.* New York: Berkley, 2007.

_____. *Unnatural Selection.* New York: Berkley, 2006.

Farrer, Clare R. *Thunder Rides a Black Horse.* 2nd ed. Long Grove, IL: Waveland, 1996.

Hamilton, Lyn. *The Chinese Alchemist.* New York: Berkley, 2007.

_____. *The Moai Murders.* New York: Berkley, 2005.

_____. *The Orkney Scroll.* New York: Berkley, 2006.

Hillerman, Tony. *Dance Hall of the Dead.* New York: Avon, 1973.

_____. *The Ghostway.* New York: Avon, 1984.

_____. *A Thief of Time.* New York: Harper and Row, 1988.

Knight, Stephen. *Continent of Mystery: A Thematic History of Australian Crime Fiction.* Melbourne: Melbourne University, 1997.

Macdonald, Ross. *Ross Macdonald's Lew Archer, Private Investigator.* New York: Mysterious, 1977.

Mosley, Walter. *Devil in a Blue Dress.* New York: Norton, 1990.

Pierson, James C. "Mystery Literature and Ethnography: Fictional Detectives As Anthropologists." *Literature and Anthropology.* Ed. Philip A. Dennis and Wendell Aycock. Lubbock: Texas Tech University, 1989. 15–30.

Praetzellis, Adrian. *Death by Theory: A Tale of Mystery and Archaeological Theory.* Walnut Creek, CA: AltaMira, 2000.

_____. *Dug to Death: A Tale of Archaeological Method and Mayhem.* Walnut Creek, CA: AltaMira, 2003.

Rankin, Ian. *Knots and Crosses.* New York: St. Martin's, 1987.

_____. *The Naming of the Dead.* Little, Brown, 2006.

Reichs, Kathy. *Bones to Ashes.* New York: Scribner, 2007.
_____. *Break No Bones.* New York: Scribner, 2006.
_____. *Fatal Voyage.* New York: Scribner, 2001.
_____. *Grave Secrets.* New York: Scribner, 2002.
Upfield, Arthur W. *The Bone Is Pointed.* New York: Garland, 1947.
_____. *The Will of the Tribe.* New York: Scribner's, 1962.

"Just the Facts"

Detective Fiction in the Law School Curriculum

ROBERT C. POWER

Law schools provide professional education. Graduates need to be able to translate legal rules into solutions for the problems of their clients. To do that, an attorney must be able to identify relevant facts, analyze the legal ramifications of those facts, and propose a course of action that serves the client. Unfortunately, traditional legal education does not do a very good job of teaching "fact" skills. Clinical programs and skills courses have improved the situation to some degree, but the gap between academic theory and law practice remains an obstacle to the type and quality of education the profession demands.

Bringing fiction into law school classrooms is an effective and enjoyable way to help bridge that gap. Fiction makes it feasible to go quickly from abstract and general legal rules to concrete and specific applications. Books and movies present issues in many areas of law, such as Sales, where a colleague uses portions of the film *Tin Men,* and Professional Responsibility, where another uses the novel *To Kill a Mockingbird.* In his Evidence course teaching materials, George Fisher of Stanford University provides a DVD of movie scenes (*Evidence*). I use fictional examples in both Criminal Law (elements of crimes and defenses) and Criminal Procedure (constitutional rights and limitations on police practices). The criminal justice system is the setting of so many books and films that choosing good examples for class (and exam questions) is largely a matter of excluding the less helpful.

Detective fiction brings several things to criminal law courses. First, it brings more reality into the classroom than most traditional course materials do, which is ironic because those traditional materials consist largely of opinions by real appellate courts. Second, the best crime fiction adds social perspectives that are unmatched in academic materials. Complementing these two values is a third: crime fiction allows professors to teach factual analysis on a deeper level than is feasible in most courses. In short, thoughtful use of crime fiction helps students understand complex and seemingly abstract legal concepts by presenting them in more accessible contexts.

Before addressing the positive aspects of using fiction, it makes sense to confront a negative one. Many students come to criminal law courses with erroneous understandings of law based on depictions in popular culture, primarily movies and television. Some misunderstandings exist simply because the law is different from how it is portrayed. For example, the plot of the movie *Double Jeopardy* turns on an erroneous description of double jeopardy law. Another problem is the so-called "CSI Effect," in which the public, conditioned by the three highly successful *CSI* television series, believes that scientific evidence can definitively solve most crimes (Tyler). In fact, scientific evidence is neither as available nor as dispositive as portrayed, but to a jury stocked with *CSI*-watchers, a reasonable doubt is likely unless prosecution experts identify the perpetrator and the means of committing the crime with scientific certainty. Such erroneous conclusions by our students are inconvenient, but at least law professors have a forum in which to correct the errors. Those students, however, will practice law in a world in which the clients, witnesses, and jurors have not had their errors corrected. Part of the law teacher's job, therefore, is to prepare students to correct misunderstandings generated by fiction in order to represent their clients properly.

One response to the dissonance created by flawed notions of criminal law in popular culture is to emphasize to students the need to correct their own misunderstandings, and to learn to warn clients, instruct juries, and educate their colleagues. To the extent that response works, however, it fails to take advantage of the fact that fiction is so influential. The more effective response is to embrace popular culture in the classroom. True criminal cases in the news make excellent class discussion, and fictional portrayals of police officers and lawyers can explain seemingly impenetrable legal doctrines and illustrate how various legal rules work together. In the end, the same features that make crime fiction deceptive when it is treated as accurate about the law make it provocatively informative when used correctly.

My first use of detective fiction is to tell students to read mystery fiction or watch police procedural television shows throughout the semester. After their initial chuckles, I stress that this is a real part of their assignment. The second laugh occurs after I mention that this gives them an excuse when their partner wants them to do chores or attend some unappealing social event. Sometimes students ask which books or shows are the best. The answer depends on the topic. For day-to-day issue-spotting and analysis, action television shows are the best. The first major subject in Criminal Procedure ("What is a search or seizure?") is critical to understanding the fourth amendment. I tell students to watch any police show and simply count the searches and seizures in that episode. Students discover that there are quite a few searches and seizures in most episodes, but that there is also a great deal of intrusive police behavior that is not covered by the fourth amendment because it is not considered to be either a search or a seizure. This is the point at which I remind them to be skeptical of the law described on television shows, urging them to follow Detective Joe Friday's advice in *Dragnet* and learn "just the facts." For example, nothing is more common in detective fiction than getting a warrant based on nothing more than a hunch or a whim. In the real world, getting a warrant is much harder, but the warrant requirement can be avoided in many settings. Law teachers, by using detective fiction that errs in describing the warrant process, may help students discover, first, that warrants cannot just be picked up from the "warrant store," and, second, because it is hard to get a warrant, police officers often look for lawful reasons to search or arrest without first obtaining one. This conflict between myth and reality also provides an occasion to talk about the extent to which society wants judges to oversee searches and arrests through the warrant process and whether it is right to encourage the police practice of looking for exceptions.

Most criminal law courses are taught through an allegedly Socratic dialogue about a series of opinions by appellate courts collected in a "casebook." Most cases contain a truncated description of the factual basis of the decision, usually based on findings by a jury or trial court judge, an analysis of pertinent legal authority, and a conclusion. While this method works for teaching legal rules, it is wholly inadequate at preparing law students to deal with discovering and organizing the factual basis of a legal claim.

Detective fiction helps law teachers make up for some of this deficiency. Criminal Procedure again provides a good example. The sometimes elaborate discussions about investigative techniques in crime fiction make it feasible to do two things that are very hard to do with typical casebooks. First, most novels provide a large set of arguably pertinent facts. This rich factual context encourages students to make their own decisions about which facts are important to legal determinations, in contrast to the prefiltered factual presentation and hindsight of appellate cases, which are then edited down in casebooks. In describing the steps leading up to a search for evidence, for example, novels often include a substantial amount of factual exposition leading to the detective's decision about what to do. The conventions of the novel allow for the presentation of many facts, some helpful, some not, and some red herrings, all of which bear on that decision, just as in real investigations. Appellate decisions, on the other hand, are less realistic about the preparation of a factual case because they rarely look beyond those facts that support the decision to search, and then merely ask whether those facts add up to probable cause, the usual legal standard for a lawful search.

Crime fiction also helps explain police tactics that relate to the fourth amendment. *Angels Flight* by Michael Connelly provides several examples. Detective Harry Bosch twice conducts what is known as a confirmatory search (63, 86), an illegal search to determine if useful evidence is present. If it is, the officer will seek a lawful warrant to redo the search and "discover" the evidence. The usual law school treatment of confirmatory searches is *Murray v. United States.* There the Supreme Court upheld an FBI search with a warrant that was obtained and executed only after agents made an illegal entry and discovered bales of marijuana. The rationale of the court was that the illegal search did not influence the magistrate's decision to issue the warrant. Thus, even though the prior search was an illegal fourth amendment search, the second search was legal because it did not result from the earlier one. The case is confusing to many students, however, because they do not see how or why such "two search tangos" occur. Harry Bosch tells us, however, by revealing that a preliminary search allows the detective to keep the investigation moving forward and prevents him from wasting his (and the judge's) time doing warrant paperwork if a search is not going to produce useful evidence.

Later in *Angels Flight,* Bosch visits a suspect's home with a search warrant. He nevertheless asks the owner for permission to search the house (317). Why does Bosch ask for permission to search when he already had a warrant? The context suggests both the "us versus them" ethos of police work and a good sense of the thinking of criminal lawyers on both sides. The warrant might turn out to be invalid, but consent would then provide an independent lawful basis for the search. The nonconfrontational setting of a consent search would also encourage the owner to cooperate and answer the detective's questions. In the absence of information suggesting this context, the idea of seeking consent to search when a warrant has been issued seems nonsensical. Bosch's actions, however, reveal to law students that applying the fourth amendment is part game theory, part scholarly inquiry. By obtaining a warrant, the officer shows official respect for the occupant's legal rights to a warrant and probable cause. By adding consent to the warrant, the prosecution gets a fallback legal argument, which is both effective gamesmanship and pragmatic law enforcement. They are two sides of one coin, and students need to be able to recognize both. One would be hard pressed to find this acknowledged in any appellate decision, however, which says something about the disconnect between real world law and law in the appellate courts.

A final fourth amendment example involves *The Sopranos.* Throughout season two, Sal Bompensiero, one of Tony Soprano's closest associates, served as an FBI informant. As is often the case in real life, the relationship between Sal and his handler was complex. The FBI agent pressed Sal to reveal more information than he wanted to convey and to do everything he could to get Soprano to implicate himself, finally ordering Sal to "make him love you" ("From Where to Eternity"). Sal rummaged through Soprano's papers, wore a microphone, and tried to elicit incriminating statements, all with realistic difficulty and equivocation. If Sal's actions had been police intrusions, they would have been subject to the fourth amendment. Private searches, on the other hand, even if illegal, are not fourth amendment "searches or seizures," and therefore any results would be legal evidence. Was Sal's snooping public or private? He was plainly a private individual, but he was ordered to act by the FBI, was compensated for his actions with promises of immunity and relocation, and sought the information solely in order to report it to the FBI. The line between public and private action is a constant and notoriously dry topic in law school courses. Considering it in the context of an informant acting under fairly loose law enforcement oversight makes it far more accessible. Doing so with colorful characters who are familiar to the students and who have complex backstories makes for richer arguments on each side and helps students appreciate the difficult nature of this important legal issue.

Sometimes one brief extract from fiction can provide material for two courses. In an episode of *CSI*, Captain Brass tries to intimidate an employee at an auto salvage yard into cooperating by telling him, "You towed a car for a serial killer. That makes you an accomplice" ("Dead Doll"). Does it? Probably not, unless the employee knew the person he helped was a serial killer. This two-sentence assertion thus provides material for a discussion of accomplice liability in the Criminal Law course. The follow-up is that Captain Brass would probably berate us for not recognizing that he knew all along that the person was not an accomplice, but he was just trying to manipulate him into providing information. Brass's statement thus becomes a false accusation intended to coerce cooperation, which takes us to interrogation law, a staple of the Criminal Procedure course.

Popular culture is central to constitutional law about interrogations because of the importance of *Miranda v. Arizona*, which applied the fifth amendment's protection against compelled self-incrimination to police questioning. Any regular consumer of crime books or movies since the mid–1960's should be able to recite the Miranda warnings without prompting, and therefore law students know their Miranda rights before they begin the course. What is often lost, however, in both crime fiction and real life, is that Miranda warnings were required for a very specific reason, the creative manipulation of suspects by skilled police interrogators. The Miranda decision is based on the fact that police questioning takes advantage of psychological techniques of pressuring suspects to cooperate. Such techniques include "good cop, bad cop," which has become so ubiquitous that it is commonly parodied in fiction, and falsely accusing a suspect of a serious crime in hope of getting a confession to a lesser one. Students understand many of the implications of these techniques because they are acquainted with police interview techniques from detective fiction.

Providing students with police interrogations in context allows them to evaluate both specific questioning techniques and the more generally coercive aspects of interrogations. When students recognize how and why interrogation techniques work, they can better analyze the constitutional rules concerning interrogations. Questions for discussion concern whether warnings are legally necessary to enforce constitutional rights, whether warnings are effective in preventing coerced confessions, and whether it is appropriate for law enforcement officers to take advantage of foolish or arrogant suspects who might not confess if reminded of their constitutional rights. While it is possible to discuss these questions using only the *Miranda* opinions and the truncated materials in casebooks, it is far richer for students to examine interrogations and then make their own judgments.

Perhaps surprisingly, videotapes of real interrogations are not good teaching vehicles. Real interrogations tend to be very long and to spend large amounts of time on what turn out to be extraneous matters. Good interrogators know, in fact, that time is on their side, and the longer the interrogation, the more likely it is to bear fruit. Moreover, both parties tend to be aware of the camera. Students are also unable to evaluate the context of the interrogation, such as how much the officers knew before it began and the extent of the suspect's prior history with law enforcement.

Good crime novels, on the other hand, often contain concise passages concerning interrogations that focus on the dynamics of the process and present the issues in ways that law students can grasp. The better authors communicate to the reader the facts of an interrogation in ways that make the legal issues transparent. By revealing the police officer's thinking, they remind us of what the Supreme Court in *Miranda* wanted the suspect to understand — that the police officer is trying to collect evidence against the suspect. By also revealing the suspect's thinking, they reveal the vulnerabilities of a person undergoing questioning. Good writers can boil the interrogation down into a short discussion that highlights a few techniques that manipulate a suspect into cooperating. These examples can serve as teaching vehicles for discussing the effectiveness of warnings and the constitutional values underlying the fifth amendment.

An excellent author for this purpose is Archer Mayor, who writes a series about Vermont detective Joe Gunther. Detective Gunther's greatest strength may be his skill at obtaining information from people who would prefer not to provide it. In *St. Albans Fire*, his investigation takes him to New Jersey, where he seeks to interview Peggy, who is romantically involved with Gino, a key suspect. In a very few pages, Mayor paints the picture of Gunther's interview (196–202). Peggy is not in custody, so warnings are not necessary, an important legal point for class discussion. She expresses reluctance to provide information, so Gunther realizes he must make her believe it is better for both her and Gino if she cooperates. He does this by "talking" his way from outside the house, where he can be shut out, to a seat in the living room, where he becomes a "guest." He then minimizes the importance of the interview, suggesting that "we're just here trying to make sense of a few things" (199). Throughout the scene, Gunther encourages each tentative opening and tries to deflect Peggy's hesitations, and his facility is contrasted with the clumsiness of his colleague. Students who read this short extract, substantially shorter than most court decisions addressing the propriety of a single interrogation technique, get a deeper understanding of the dynamics of police questioning than is provided in any criminal procedure casebook.

This selection from Mayor can be supplemented with scenes from *Homicide: Life on the Street*, one of the best televised police procedurals. Several episodes include interrogations in the "box"— the Baltimore homicide squad's interview room. The encounters in the box are more realistic and informative than factual descriptions in casebooks and raise central issues in a clearer fashion. Two episodes that are particularly well suited for class discussion are "Three Men and Adena" (1993), in which the entire episode is an interrogation, and "Extreme Unction" (1994), which shows manipulation from both sides of the table. Andre Braugher portrays Detective Frank Pembleton as a highly skilled officer who probes suspects in an effort to uncover their weak spots and then uses interrogation techniques to mine those spots with precision. *Homicide* also does an excellent job of telling stories about life in the criminal justice system. Encounters between the police officers and criminals, lawyers, and "civilians" suggest history and subtext, which are almost completely lacking in traditional teaching materials.

Homicide led to *The Wire*, which retains the theme of presenting the rich world of police and crime in Baltimore. *The Wire* uses all of the tools of modern video storytelling to tell a long and intricate story that is the equivalent of the finest literary fiction. Scenes from the series can illustrate numerous factual aspects of legal issues addressed in criminal law courses. The title refers to court-ordered electronic surveillance, which moved the plot for five seasons. There are also police raids with legal and illegal warrants, arrests, *Miranda* warnings, searches, seizures, and interrogations. For teaching the overwhelmingly white middle-class law student population, however, the primary value is in *The Wire*'s portrayal of the community in which criminal law is practiced. Most of the criminals of inner-city Baltimore are African

American, as are most of the victims. So is most of its government, including a substantial portion of the police department, and racial politics works its way into many official decisions. *The Wire* asks whether law enforcement can work in a nation that is so divided by race and which suffers the interrelated problems of poverty and drug use. This is a difficult question for most students, but it is one they need to confront before they begin to work as prosecutors or defense attorneys in the criminal justice system.

An excellent companion to *The Wire* in considering the social issues presented in the criminal justice system is the series of books by Carolyn Wheat that features Cass Jameson, a New York City public defender. Wheat's books are useful not only in criminal law courses but also in Professional Responsibility, as they emphasize the conflicts and pressures of serving as a criminal defense attorney. The book that first got my attention was *Mean Streak*, in which Jameson represents a criminal defense attorney accused of crime. In contrast to most examples cited in this essay, where short selections work, *Mean Streak* is best ingested whole. It presents layered details about the nature of a successful criminal law practice, which in today's world sometimes includes pressure from wealthy clients or their criminal associates to fix cases, intimidate witnesses, or falsify evidence. Wheat does a superb job of exploring how a fine and ethical attorney put himself in a position where he could be accused of misconduct and face serious charges. In *Sworn to Defend*, Jameson tries to help friends who are, like her, middle-class African Americans. They are concerned that their teenage son is oblivious to the dangers of guilt by association and racial fear that afflict young black men in this country and believe that Jameson can explain the problem to their son. Jameson's inner reflections on what she needs to say to the boy tell law students more than most of them can imagine about the racial conflicts in our society and how those conflicts affect the practice of criminal law.

Teaching law is necessarily much more than teaching legal rules. Most rules can be learned from treatises or study aids outside class. How attorneys apply the rules, however, is a more demanding subject. One key to making courses help students become professional attorneys is to supplement rule study with realistic fact problems that illustrate the contexts in which rules will have to be applied. Teachers who use detective fiction to bring those settings into class will see a dramatic increase in the sophistication of their students' thinking about criminal law and procedure.

WORKS CITED

Connelly, Michael. *Angels Flight*. Boston: Little, Brown, 1999.
"Dead Doll." *CSI Crime Scene Investigation*. CBS Television. 2007.

Double Jeopardy. Dir. Bruce Beresford. Paramount Pictures,1999.

Dragnet. NBC Television. 1951–99.

"Extreme Unction." *Homicide: Life on the Street.* NBC Television. 1994.

Fisher, George. *Evidence.* St. Paul: Thompson West, 2002.

"From Where to Eternity." *The Sopranos.* HBO. 2001.

Lee, Harper. *To Kill a* Mockingbird. 1960. New York: HarperCollins, 2005.

Mayor, Archer. *St. Albans* Fire. New York: Mysterious Press, 2005.

Miranda v. Arizon., 384 U.S. 386 (1966).

Murray v. United States. 487 U.S. 533 (1988).

"Three Men and Adena." *Homicide: Life on the Street.* NBC Television. 1993.

Tin Men. Dir. Barry Levinson. Touchstone Pictures, 1987.

Tyler, Tom. "Viewing *CSI* and the Threshold of Guilty: Managing Truth and Justice in Reality and Fiction." *Yale Law Journal* 115 (2006): 1050–85.

Wheat, Carolyn. *Mean Streak.* New York: Berkley, 1996.

_____. *Sworn to Defend.* New York: Berkley, 1998.

The Wire. HBO. 2002–2008.

Margaret Coel's *The Story Teller* in a Literary Criticism Course

Edward J. Rielly

Detective or crime fiction, as Ray Browne has pointed out, is "a vigorous genre" within the field of American Indian literature (3). That genre includes a number of interesting, entertaining, and sometimes enlightening series, most famously the Tony Hillerman novels featuring Navaho policemen Joe Leaphorn and Jim Chee. Jake Page, Aimée and David Thurlo, Dana Stabenow, Louis Owens, James Doss, Robert Westbrook, and Craig Johnson are among the other authors who depict Indians either as crime-solving protagonists or in a featured role.

An important member of this group is Margaret Coel. Her decision to enter the genre of detective fiction grew out of two of her earlier books—*Chief Left Hand: Southern Arapaho* and *Goin' Railroading: Two Generations of Colorado Stories*—which established her interest in western history in general and particularly in Arapaho history and culture. She also enjoyed reading mystery stories, but notes in an interview that she turned to writing fiction with considerable uncertainty, both because she had offers to write additional nonfiction books and because she was not confident that she would succeed in mystery fiction (Kaczmarek).

But Coel wrote *Eagle Catcher* in the mid–1990s and never looked back. A long line of novels followed, with her fourteenth, *Blood Memory*, appearing in September 2008. She also has written a series of ten short stories published separately in book form, each based on one of the Arapaho moral commandments, which are close in wording to the Ten Commandments adopted by Christians from the Old Testament.

Coel's mysteries (both the novels and the short stories) feature two amateur detectives who are pulled into solving crimes through their normal occupations, often either to absolve an innocent person of guilt or to save someone's life (often the life of the other co-protagonist). The two are Vicky Holden and Father John O'Malley. Holden is an Arapaho attorney who left the Wind River Reservation in Wyoming and her abusive husband—and her two children to be reared by her mother—while she went away to further

her education and try to make a success of her life. She ultimately graduated from law school and later practiced law in Denver before returning to the Wind River area to open a law office in Lander, Wyoming, with the intention of helping other Arapahos.

Father O'Malley is a Jesuit priest, former history teacher, and recovering alcoholic. Sent to St. Francis Mission on the reservation (based on the real St. Stephen's Mission) to overcome his alcoholism, he quickly comes to care deeply about the people he serves there. He becomes the mission's superior and renews his vocation by helping not only those who attend church at the mission but Arapahos scattered throughout Wind River.

Coel creates engaging characters, especially Vicky Holden and Father O'Malley, who evolve gradually during the novels, develop deep affection and respect for each other, and partly because of their mutual respect keep an obvious romantic attachment in check. Coel also develops plots effectively with a special skill at creating seemingly disparate story lines that gradually coalesce in ways that bring the two amateur detectives together to solve often complex mysteries.

Coel also presents considerable information about Arapaho culture and history in the novels. It is this attribute of her fiction that has led me to use one of her novels, *The Story Teller*, in my Senior Seminar in Literary Criticism for senior English majors at Saint Joseph's College in Standish, Maine.

Coel is not Arapaho, but she researches her material carefully, has Arapaho friends read her manuscripts, and understands well that history can be conveyed through other than written documents— hence her effective use of American Indian artifacts around which she constructs many of her plots. I distribute to my students an article of mine, "Margaret Coel: Crime and History in the Arapaho World," that provides an overview of Coel's series and especially focuses on her ability to build plot and culture around cultural and historical objects such as an eagle feather, petroglyph, council pipe, or ledger book. I also invite my students to examine Margaret Coel's website, which includes considerable information about her and her stories as well as links to other helpful sources of information, including sites relating to Wind River Reservation.

Coel regularly visits the reservation to continue familiarizing herself with specific details of not only her primary setting for the fiction but even more importantly to ensure that she gets the cultural details of her stories right. Arapahos at Wind River seem to enjoy Coel's stories, and not just because of her obvious respect for their traditions and history. During a visit to St. Stephen's Mission in the summer of 2006, I asked an Arapaho woman working in the mission gift shop about Coel. She replied, in a nice corrective to the unpleasant habit of college teachers to take literature a bit too seriously at times, that she loved reading each new novel to discover bits and pieces of people she knows that Coel has absorbed into the text.

For three reasons, then, I take one of her novels in my course: first, she writes good novels; second, she conveys a great deal of authentic Arapaho culture; and third, the novel dovetails nicely with the critical approaches that we study in the senior seminar.

In the course, students read several literary texts—in my most recent iteration of the seminar Coleridge's *Rime of the Ancient Mariner*, Conrad's *Heart of Darkness*, Stoker's *Dracula*, and Coel's *The Story Teller*—and apply a variety of critical approaches to the works. We study new criticism, reader-response criticism, deconstruction, new historicism, psychoanalytic criticism, gender criticism, cultural criticism, and sometimes other approaches as well, along with exploring the transformation of written literature into film, such as the remaking of *Heart of Darkness* into *Apocalypse Now*. We therefore stay with a particular text for quite a while, applying several approaches to that text. In the case of Bram Stoker's *Dracula*, for example, a much better novel than its multitudinous filmic versions suggest and a book that my senior English majors regularly read and discuss with great enthusiasm, we consider the text especially from the perspectives of gender criticism and psychoanalytic criticism.

In the final portion of the course, we take one text — Margaret Coel's *The Story Teller*— and apply at least most of the critical approaches that we have studied to it through classroom discussions, student presentations, and the final exam. The novel is especially suitable to this end-of-the-term unit. It is probably most relevant to cultural criticism, as Coel weaves into the novel many aspects of Arapaho culture including the ledger book that sets the plot in motion. Vicky is called upon to investigate a ledger book that Charlie Redman, an Arapaho storyteller, claims to have seen many years before and that is now missing from a list of cultural artifacts that the Denver Museum of the West supplied.

I talk about how Plains Indians used ledger books (the kind in which Euroamericans kept accounts of income and expenses) to make pictographic narratives of important historical events. Many of the books were beautiful works of art as well as important historical records, and, fortunately, some have survived intact. Increasing numbers of ledger books are becoming available to scholars, teachers, and students through the Plains Indian Ledger Art Project. We examine some of the ledger books online at the PILA website housed at the University of California, San Diego. The site includes information on the history of ledger art and a description of the scope and purpose of the project as well as the books themselves.

The Story Teller also draws heavily on the Native American Graves Protection and Repatriation Act (NAGPRA), a federal law enacted in 1990 to require and facilitate the return of certain classes of objects to Native American tribes and descendants. These items include human remains, funeral objects, sacred objects, and cultural items. The act is quite detailed regarding the items that must be returned, and a useful website enables my students to gain a good understanding of its purpose and mechanisms for recovery. Within the novel, NAGPRA is the motivation for the Denver Museum of the West supplying the list of artifacts that sets the plot in motion.

A third element in Arapaho history and culture that operates within the novel is the Sand Creek Massacre of 1864, during which Colorado militia under Colonel John Chivington massacred Cheyennes and Arapahos, principally women, children, and the elderly. The precise number killed is unknown, but the figure is usually judged to have been at least 150.

A longstanding debate occurred regarding whether Arapahos as well as Cheyennes were at Sand Creek, although that issue today has largely been resolved, with most historians now agreeing that members of both groups were indeed present. That argument also figures in the novel with a graduate student, Todd Harris, who has agreed to become the curator at a museum Father O'Malley plans to open at the mission, researching the Sand Creek Massacre for his dissertation. His research leads him to the holdings of the Denver Museum of the West and the ledger book, which is supposedly the work of No-Ta-Nee (Knock Knee), an actual Arapaho leader who survived Sand Creek. The ledger book is therefore of great importance to Todd because it demonstrates that Arapahos were present at the massacre.

The ledger book is thus culturally and historically important to Todd Harris, Charlie Redman, and other Arapahos. For others, however, its importance is financial, and that leads to Todd's murder.

As Coel weaves these narrative threads together, with Vicky and O'Malley initially following different threads, the novel invites discussion from multiple critical perspectives. Applying reader-response criticism, we consider how differently specific readers or reading communities might respond to the novel. Would Arapahos, college students, artists, historians, lawyers, and Jesuit priests respond in ways distinct from each other? What aspects of the novel might elicit certain reactions? Then there is the reality that this book is very much about the act of reading itself. Can we read only words, or can we just as legitimately read a ledger book even if it is "only" in pictures?

Using new historicism, we conclude during our examination of *The Story Teller* that history is neither a separate realm nor merely a matter of written documents. The distinctions among literature, history, art, and other "disciplines" are indeed blurry, and we need to involve all of them in our reading of the novel and our consideration of the history and culture that it conveys.

The novel raises a number of dichotomies, for example, between written history and oral tradition, Euroamerican and American Indian, civilized and savage, and women and men. Our classroom deconstructing of some of the polarities always proves interesting and sometimes controversial. Which person is truly civilized, one who essentially robs graves to fill museum cases or one who respects the dead and items associated with the dead? Which document is more historical and reliable, a pictographic ledger book or a letter from a militia officer justifying his murderous actions?

Even the cultural groups to which the two detectives belong are difficult to establish completely. One might think that Vicky Holden (herself an Arapaho) would fit more easily into Arapaho culture and be more readily accepted than a red-haired Irish Catholic from Boston. Yet Father O'Malley has come to be widely respected, even loved, as the "Indian priest," while Vicky Holden, still bearing the stigma of leaving her husband, children, and people to don a white woman's profession and even a white woman's clothes finds it difficult to be accepted back. Membership in cultural groups, it seems, may at times involve social and cultural constructs even more than birth.

Deconstructing the roles of John O'Malley the priest and Vicky Holden the lawyer leads us easily into gender criticism. The priestly garb is essentially a version of feminine skirts, and O'Malley consistently proves sensitive to individuals as well as to Arapaho culture — and skilled at nurturing whether the person is a boy on the mission baseball team he is coaching or a grandparent who has lost a beloved grandchild, in this case Todd. Vicky has become the professional "male" person — independent, headstrong, mindful of career, leaving children to others (although throughout the novels she does strive to reestablish her relationship with her now grown children). Both get into plenty of trouble, alternately playing the saver and saved, the victim and the rescuer.

Both O'Malley and Vicky invite psychoanalytic analysis as well. O'Malley struggles with his alcoholism, not yielding to it but sorely tempted from time to time. He loves Vicky, as she does him, yet their motivations for not consummating the relationship are many, including their perceptions of themselves and their respect for each other. Yet to what extent is Father O'Malley's determination to forgo a romantic (and sexual) relationship with Vicky tied to his struggle to maintain self-discipline concerning his alcoholism?

Both characters seem to have developed powerful superegos, but the id jumps out occasionally, especially when the other is endangered. An example occurs near the end of the novel. As both are held prisoner at the mission, one of the men responsible for Todd's death slugs Vicky, and Father O'Malley, enraged, unthinkingly retaliates by attacking another of the criminals. Here Vicky becomes the rescuer as well. As the man who had hit her aims his gun at O'Malley, Vicky smashes a telephone against his head. My students make many other specific critical applications to *The Story Teller* as well. What I have cited above is a mere sampling.

The novel works effectively not only because of its content but also due to its genre. Our exploration and employment of cultural criticism takes us into matters of genre and the literary canon as we consider (and deconstruct) such supposed opposites as high and low culture, classics and popular literature, good taste and mass appeal, elitism and democracy. How, we wonder, can a nation supposedly established on the will of the people and ready to fight wars in support of democracy in turn reject what "the people" like in favor of the preferences of the few?

Anyone in a college setting who has devoted serious time to studying, teaching, and writing about detective fiction surely has had to confront such issues regarding genre and popular culture. If we are fortunate, we teach at institutions where our work is respected and accepted. If not, we may face deans, colleagues, and sundry others reminding us that what we are teaching and writing about is not Milton or Chaucer, not T.S. Eliot or James Joyce. My senior English majors think about this and discuss the criteria for a book's membership in the honored canon.

Finally, literary criticism is about seeing not just literature but countless aspects of life from different angles. So we should read not just Dante or Pound, Shakespeare or Alexander Pope in our seminar. We do, of course, read Coleridge and Conrad. They count. But so do Stoker and Coel, perhaps Coel more than any of the others. Her novel allows us to dig into something approximating real life (with the necessary admission that even a lawyer-priest combo like Vicky Holden and Father O'Malley would not find themselves in quite so many dangerous adventures) and explore that real world of history, cultural relationships, federal legislation, friendship, and gender roles from many perspectives. We learn how to see in different ways and learn from each seeing.

WORKS CITED

Apocalypse Now. Dir. Francis Ford Coppola. Zoetrope Studios, 1979.

Browne, Ray B. *Murder on the Reservation: American Indian Crime Fiction.* Madison: University of Wisconsin Press/Popular Press, 2004.

Coel, Margaret. *Blood Memory.* New York: Berkley Prime Crime, 2008.

_____. *Chief Left Hand: Southern Arapaho.* 1981. Norman: University of Oklahoma Press, 2000.

_____. *The Eagle Catcher.* 1995. New York: Berkley Prime Crime, 1996.

_____. *Goin' Railroading.* 1985. Niwot: University Press of Colorado, 1998.

_____. *The Story Teller.* 1998. New York: Berkley Prime Crime, 1999.

Coleridge, Samuel Taylor. *The Rime of the Ancient Mariner.* Ed. Paul H. Fry. Case Studies in Contemporary Criticism. Boston: Bedford/St. Martin's, 1999.

Conrad, Joseph. *Heart of Darkness.* Ed. Ross C. Murfin. 2nd ed. Case Studies in Contemporary Criticism. Boston: Bedford/St. Martin's, 1996.

Kaczmarek, Lynn. "Hana je nahadina: An Interview with Margaret Coel." Reprinted from *Mystery News* by A.S.A.P. Publishing, Mission Viejo, CA, no date or pagination. Also available on the *Margaret Coel* website.

Margaret Coel. <http://www.margaretcoel.com/index.html>.

Native American Graves Protection and Repatriation Act. National NAGPRA. <http://www.nps.gov/history/nagpra/MANDATES/25USC3001etseq.htm>.

Plains Indian Ledger Art. University of California, San Diego. <http://www.plainsledgerart.org>.

Rielly, Edward J. "Margaret Coel: Crime and History in the Arapaho World." *The Detective as Historian: History and Art in Historical Crime Fiction.* Vol. 2. Ed. Ray B. Browne and Lawrence A. Kreiser, Jr. Newcastle, England: Cambridge Scholars Publishing, 2007. 186–98.

Stoker, Bram. *Dracula.* Ed. John Paul Riquelme. Case Studies in Contemporary Criticism. Boston: Bedford/St. Martin's, 2002.

Women Detectives
in Contemporary American
Popular Culture

DEBORAH SHALLER

For fans and feminists, the 1980s marked a new golden age of detection, a period when women began to write hard-boiled detective novels— and, more significantly, to create within them women detectives— in a dizzying profusion. The hard-boiled genre (or subgenre, or formula), once considered inhospitable to women heroes, suddenly opened up to a generation of women detectives who seemed ideally placed to take advantage of the social gains women had made and to embody the same narrative centrality long available to men. To have done so in a popular text was especially significant because it suggested not only that women had entered protected territory but that their entrances had been heralded.

In subsequent decades, women detectives made similar, if slower, inroads into television and film. However, two of televisions most successful franchises—*Law & Order* and *CSI*— feature prominent women as detectives, district attorneys, and forensic pathologists, while cable TV's enormously popular *The Closer* offers hero Brenda Johnson as lead detective of a Los Angeles police unit consisting otherwise entirely of men. A kind of Southern American equivalent to Britain's Jane Tennison (*Prime Suspect*'s Helen Mirren), the role of Brenda Johnson has garnered actor Kyra Sedgwick numerous awards and much critical attention. Elsewhere, Mariska Hargitay's portrayal of Olivia Benson on *Law & Order: Special Victims Unit* continues to marry Hargitay's own personal popularity with the sympathetic toughness of the character herself.

As a cultural critic, feminist, and fan of fictional detection, I am compelled to ask the inevitable: what does it all mean? And as I often do with my questions, I write this one into a course, where students enter the conversations, ask questions of my questions, and add their own reading and viewing to the store of knowledge already accumulating. We come, then, to the double-listed Cultural Studies/Women Studies course, "Women Detectives in Contemporary American Popular Culture." The course I teach does not make an argument for or against the role of women in the detective novel. Instead, it provides a process for forming such an argument by looking at those areas crucial to an understanding of any cultural product, but especially a popular one: (1) How does the shape of the product determine its content? (2) How is that content represented? (3) What is the role of the producer and the fan? (4) To what uses is the object put?

Each section of the course could easily be a course in itself. What I hope to do is to use the detective novel and our interest in it to provide a kind of script for other analyses. Such inquiries lie at the heart of how we read, how we experience images, and how we talk about what we consume. I do not want to risk oversimplifying. At the same time, the task is daunting.

The course divides into four sections and moves recursively. That is, parts of the discussion are wrestled loose of one another for convenience and necessary linearity but are all part of another denser, inextricable set of readings. For the purposes of a fifteen-week course, each section occupies about four weeks of discussion as described below. At all four points, novels are allowed to exemplify a kind of analysis while also offering interesting instances of women in cultural narrative. That is, we read both as fans and as cultural critics. In the one instance, we explore the possibilities and pleasures the works allow. In the other, we explore the limits imposed by the various fields we construct.

Gender and Genre

What happens when we add something previously excluded? What, for example, happens when women begin to occupy previously all-male places? Do they simply fit neatly into existing openings, perhaps expanding those openings or forcing them into slightly different shapes? Or does inclusion so radically affect the landscape that the territory becomes unrecognizable, something else entirely? Such questions have long been part of feminist inquiry, particularly when the inclusion of women seems to leave the structure of oppression in place, a structure that, moreover, is capable of generating further structures that work against feminist goals of equality and social justice. Genre is just such a structure. The hard-boiled detective story, long understood as creating a particular masculinity in its hero, further implicates the landscape the woman detective enters. Writers like Sally Munt and Kathleen Gregory Klein have offered extensive critiques of the problem and have concluded that the relationship between gender and genre is at best problematic, at worst a collision from which feminist goals cannot emerge unscathed. Klein writes, for example, "The genre must be completely remade, stripped of some of its most characteristic elements and reinforced by a new ideology and awareness. But will the result be either detective fiction or feminist? Or will it simply be an unsatisfactory, watered-down version of both which has compromised all of their greatest attractions?" (221).

We begin here in film. I ask students first to read Lee Horsley's "Definitions of Film Noir" from *crimeculture.com*, a website that is such a good resource I like to get students familiar with it as soon as possible. Horsley's description of the noir detective is brief and immediately applicable. Because we have to move quickly, I want to rely on the students' ability to read the visual, a more predictable competence than the textual. We watch *The Maltese Falcon* and I ask students to write an analysis based on Horsley's definitions. This analysis becomes the basis for future genre analysis. Like much of the work we do, a genre study is easily another course unless we narrow our preoccupations to a manageable set of questions. Having done so, we are ready to move to Sue Grafton's *"A" Is for Alibi,* a work that is easy to see as entering the conversation begun in the hard-boiled story.

With gestures large and small, Grafton introduces Kinsey as not just the equivalent of, but in many ways the alternative to, Sam Spade. She is like him: tough, alone, wary of human connection. Kinsey speaks to us in the first person, investigates crimes that shift shapes and complexities, and even encounters the male equivalent of the *femme fatale*, a seductively charming man with whom she has a sexual relationship only to discover that he is, in fact, the murderer she seeks. But she is also, Grafton suggests, the detective suited for contemporary circumstances, a revision to the detective text. When Kinsey famously equates detective work with the dull, repetitive tasks given to women in a sexist society, she re-genders the territory. Likewise, her insistence on recording the fear she feels in dangerous circumstances argues that masculine stoicism is a worn-out facade, that the fearless detective is not only a myth but an irrelevant one. In *"A" Is for Alibi* and subsequent entries in the series, Grafton offers an excellent example of a space entered and claimed. The works repeat formulaic elements and talk back to them. Noir's invitation to write social criticism, especially economic critique, is faint here, barely a living pulse. But the works do offer an excellent example of how a previously exclusive genre can respond to changing cultural norms even if they do little to alter the structural terms of inclusion.

Written during the same period, *Sisters of the Road* offers the second installment of Barbara Wilson's now-abandoned Pam Nilson series. I use Wilson to see what happens to the hard-boiled detective genre when the detective is a lesbian and when feminist structural analysis guides the narrative. Because the masculine codes of hard-boiled detection were so closely tied to heterosexuality, a lesbian detective offers the potential for radically destabilizing the figure of the hero. And indeed, Wilson's character both adopts generic conventions and changes them: centrally, Pam Nilson's investigation does not validate her alienation, as Hammett's and Grafton's investigations do, but challenges all the ways she has separated herself from other women, particularly those women in different social positions. When Nilson helps two young prostitutes, one of whom becomes a murder victim, she undertakes a journey that will make a feminist claim particularly resonant at the time: that all women by virtue of their oppression are "sisters" because their embodiment as women will ultimately override any differences they have been able to claim. As the book strips Pam of protective differences, it surrounds her with a network of connections, among them her own sexual identity. Unlike Grafton, who makes little use of social and political critique, Wilson foregrounds a reasonably complex argument about prostitution while also demonstrating the effects of sexism on the everyday lives of women. Pam and her sister (who is off stage here as she and her boyfriend volunteer in Nicaragua) have inherited a print business from their parents. The business runs as a collective, thus offering readers a glimpse of alternative economic practices. Despite its very clear ideological grounding, the novel is deft and reads easily as mystery. But in rejecting the alienation of the detective, particularly as that alienation remains resonant of Romantic retreat, Wilson risks much of the genre's conventional attractions. While Kinsey Millhone mocks the heroics of her macho predecessors, she does not reject the edges that outline their identity. Wilson deliberately blurs those edges in order to create alternate shapes. Taken together, the novels help to ask both parts of Klein's question: is this detective fiction or feminism?

Representation

Sara Paretsky's work offers an invaluable glimpse into the problem of representation when her famously feminist detective becomes the subject of a 1991 film, now itself infamous for the changes made to the character. We begin by reading *Killing Orders*, selected because it was published in the same year as Grafton's *"A" Is for Alibi* and thus allows comparisons uncomplicated by what students, most of whom were not yet born in the mid–80s, often imagine are the results of even small temporal shifts: "Well, back then," they might begin. "Or by that time," they often speculate, assuming that 1985 and 1990, for example, are markers of vast social and historical differences. To look at gender roles requires us to hold steady the object of our gaze so that we can more easily see movement as something the writer makes in similar, if not identical, cultural circumstances. What is possible for V.I., in other words, must also be seen having been possible for Millhone.

Paretsky's explicit feminism, as well as her character's crusade against the Catholic Church as an instrument of social control of women, is easy to track as both innovation and imitation: In V.I., Paretsky creates an unapologetic feminist whose detection allows the quest to become politically rooted in systems of oppression, inequality, and injustice. Where there is patriarchy, V.I. finds, there is trouble. At the same time, her character in *Killing Orders* confronts the mystery of her own identity as the central plot also unravels a mystery of background, a revelation about V.I.'s mother that both toughens and clarifies V.I.'s own sense of self. But what helps us to complicate the issue of representation is the film *V.I. Warshawski.* Having screened it in the past, however, I know that I have to set up the discussion carefully if I want it to go where I need it to go. Because students will come to this course with a range of experience analyzing women's representations, I use *Bitches, Bimbos, and Ballbreakers: The Guerrilla Girls' Guide to Female Stereotypes,* a clear, comprehensive, and readable book for those with little experience; for the more seasoned, it is also fun. Its insistence on the visual is enormously useful in moving us between the word and image, with particular emphasis on how many stereotypes — including, of course, noir's *femme fatale* — rely upon sexualizing women in now predictable ways.

But we also need to think about the images we form when we read. To that end, we read Linda Mizejewski's *Picturing the Best Seller List* to understand her claim that "when authors such as Sue Grafton, Linda Barnes, and Sara Paretsky appear in book jacket photographs with props suggesting their female P.I. characters, they're part of a larger commercial scene involving writers as celebrities" (22). In such a "celebrity-driven culture," Mizejewski continues, "the meaning of the book is inevitably enmeshed with the 'meaning' of the author" (22). In other words, I want students to see that Paretsky (and Grafton) give us few details about their characters' appearance. But fans of both are well aware of what Sue Grafton looks like and that V.I. Warshawski, tall, thin, and often elegantly dressed, probably looks in our mind's eye very much like Paretsky herself. So before students get to see Kathleen Turner as Warshawski, they meet Paretsky in the video *Women of Mystery: Three Writers Who Forever Changed Detective Fiction.*

V.I. Warshawski is the film most often cited when writers lament Hollywood's antagonism to feminist detectives, for indeed, few of them appear in mainstream movies and those who do undergo unsettling transformations. It is the film said to dramatically unsettle Paretsky herself, for example, and to prevent Grafton from allowing Kinsey Millhone to become a movie star. For thousands of readers of Paretsky, the much-anticipated movie became a disappointment bordering on betrayal. Yet with all of that, the film is not that bad — especially if the viewer has never read Paretsky, never "pictured"

Warshawski, has not noticed how the insistently unmaternal Warshawski of print is carefully redeemed in the film by becoming the default mother to an orphaned girl, and is thoroughly inured to the sexualizing representations of women and thus wishes only that such representations at least stand on their own two high-heeled feet. Particularly now, when the images of sexualized girls and women are so persistently equated with women's strength, it can be very difficult for women students— or any students— to picture strong women who do not fall within a very limited visual field. To work successfully with the interplay between book and film, students need to encounter the clash of different representations as these moments reveal the mediated image, the woman created through the eyes of someone other than herself. Here, then, we can begin to ask if popular works can ever be understood primarily as relationships between readers and writers when they are written and consumed within ever narrowing modes of capital production.

A Small Foray into the World of the Popular

Such capital production, argues David Paul Nord, means that formulas like detective fiction are not wholly shaped by their writers, their audiences, or the collaborations between, but are pressured by producers, for whom the formula is the cheapest way to maximum profits (218–27). In this section of the course, then, we consider some elements of the popular as a category of consumption. Students read Nord largely to sketch the parameters of a territory heretofore shaped by writers and readers, whose interactions lead us to read formulas like the detective novel as imaginative artifact. To supplement Nord's short article, we spend class time discussing the phenomenon of the corporate media conglomerate. Websites such as *Take Back the Media* offer useable handouts of the world of media giants (http://www.takeback-themedia.com/owners.html). We spend time examining how much of what we consume as entertainment now resides in the hands of an ever narrowing field of producers. We look at publishing houses grown fat from gorging on what was previously the competition, with the necessary caveat that even as we speak, further gobblings are altering the maps we are using.

Into this discussion, we bring Janet Evanovich, the most popular writer of those we read, the closest to a publishing phenomenon, and a writer who unabashedly acknowledges the business of writing. Evanovich's creation of a family business and her use of separate publishers for different editions of her novels are both noted practices within the publishing community and begin to make visible the relationships among popularity, production, marketing, and money. For many feminists, the books also represent that interesting cultural problem, the guilty pleasure, the enthusiasm for something we do not think we should like, the moment of fandom that seems to challenge the identity we have otherwise nailed into place.

Evanovich's detective, Stephanie Plum, a big-haired New Jersey bounty hunter "from the burg," is a comic creation in the style of director Blake Edwards' *Pink Panther*. Stephanie's successes as a bounty hunter, like Inspector Clouseau's, follow in the wake of an incompetence so dazzling that it becomes sheer comic bravado. When Stephanie solves a crime, readers are both delighted and amazed. A bounty hunter for her Uncle Vinny's bail bonds business, Plum takes the job out of desperation when she is laid off from her job as a lingerie buyer in the first novel of the series, *One for the Money*. We pick up Stephanie in the eleventh book, *Eleven on Top*, chosen in large part because it returns to an underlying theme of the series, the problem of getting work. Indeed, despite elements of fantasy in the series, Evanovich remains as true to the working-class sensibilities of the hard-boiled as any writer we encounter. Stephanie does not want to leave the burg but is content to reside in a relatively small world of attached houses, inelegant concrete apartment buildings, entertainments so limited that the funeral parlor is the burg's primary social space, and a network of gossiping relatives and friends she has known since elementary school.

Throughout the series, Stephanie's mother laments the dangers of bounty hunting, with the recurring reminder that the local button factory is looking for help, a reminder for Stephanie and the reader of the virtues of bounty hunting despite the risks. In *Eleven on Top*, Stephanie finally succumbs to her own exhaustion and takes a series of available jobs, beginning at the button factory, where she is immediately the target of a boss whose determination to sexually harass the women who work for him has created the vacancy Stephanie briefly occupies. From the button factory, she goes to a dry-cleaning business where, among other ultimately insurmountable problems, she reports, cheerfully enough, the exhaustion of standing on her feet all day and tagging clothes. From here she goes to a fried chicken emporium, from which she returns home every day saturated with grease. Amidst the humor and chaos, Evanovich is actually making a serious point: for the majority of Americans, work is limited, poorly paid, and physically exhausting. It also often occurs among bosses whose insensitivities range from the illegal to the merely dispiriting. While the other works we have read keep alive the detective's romantic relationship to autonomy and self-sufficiency, Evanovich's unromantic bounty hunting recasts the terms of the choice by showing it as no choice at all. When Stephanie returns to detection, we are relieved, for in its way, it is the safest choice she can make.

Evanovich's burg culture also challenges the reader to accept a working class esthetic, a challenge both radical and rare, with deep and invisible roots in American class prejudice. Stephanie herself is coded white working class by hair, her eye make-up, and her Lycra shirts. Burg houses embrace the artificial: siding, plastic decoration, faux stone. Stephanie's sidekick, Lula, regularly defies her own girth with seam-stretching Spandex. As the series progresses, Stephanie gathers a recurring group of characters who defy other boundaries: for example, Sally, the gender-unfettered rock singer and wedding planner, and Grandma Mazur, who resists aging not by hiding or altering her body but by cheerfully displaying it at every opportunity. The books conjure a world also imagined by John Waters in film, but unlike Waters, an upper-middle class child of the white suburbs, Evanovich writes Stephanie from the inside, a point Evanovich makes when she allows the similarities between Plum and herself. As readers, we are encouraged to enter that world, not to watch it — but perhaps also, as Evanovich has done, to leave it.

In other words, Evanovich hides a kind of deep radicalism under a surface that appears to collude unselfconsciously with the marketplace. In part, of course, Evanovich is just very funny. Is she also an example of how to slip serious critique past the censors? Of how serious material becomes trivial in popular texts?

Uses of the Popular

The popularity of the police procedural has been growing steadily; as a variation of the hard-boiled formula, it now dominates television detection and accounts for some of the most interesting and critically acclaimed detective dramas of the late twentieth- and early twenty-first centuries. David Simon's *Homicide*, *The Corner*, and *The Wire*, for example, have each been said to offer not only singularly "realistic" glimpses of police work but to do so with an increasing attention to social/cultural critique. This latter characteristic aligns the police with a number of socially progressive perspectives and thus extends the steady rehabilitation of the police that began in the 1970s, gained momentum in the 1980s, and arrived solidly in the 1990s. Along with establishing the police as heroic, the police procedural also defines relationships between suspects and the law, between prosecutors and the defense attorneys who are routinely vilified. Arguably, for instance, most of what we know and think about the Miranda Decision — including our almost universal ability to recite it incantatorially — is shaped within the police procedural, where it is commonly regarded as one of the most egregious impediments to police work. As the organization Human Rights First has recently made clear, television drama contributes significantly to our understanding of interrogation techniques: whenever we see brutal interrogations that lead to confessions, we are not only learning to accept abusive physical interrogation but to see it as a way of eliciting important and accurate information. Such repetitive conditioning easily leads to a tolerance for forms of interrogative torture and to a false belief that torture is a useful way of quickly learning what we urgently need to know.

In its construction of the police as an aggrieved body, the police procedural often presents a rapacious press, intent upon revelations that will further impede an ongoing case; an amoral district attorney whose quest for reelection routinely trumps his or her interest in justice; and an internal bureaucracy so voracious that it consumes all but the toughest, most cynical, and least law-abiding detectives. Such constructions importantly define territories like the public right to know, for example, and increase suspicion of both public institutions and public officials.

Partly because we experience such a constant diet of it, the police procedural is the clearest instance of the relationship between narrative fiction and public consciousness. As a class, we have considered throughout the course the implications of the stories we read. We end here by watching several of the most popular television procedurals, tracking how they play against notions like those I have described above. Because many students choose such television shows as *The Closer* and *Law & Order: SVU*, I outline the generic habits of the procedural earlier in the semester but leave the police novel until the end, where it seems to belong chronologically and, in some sense, ideologically.

Eleanor Taylor Bland's Marti MacAlister avoids much of what characterizes the police procedural elsewhere: it is not prickly or aggrieved, does not regularly violate suspects' rights, is not intent on opposing police work to every other human relationship except the hero's relationship to work and partner. Bland herself seems uninterested in police work as a distinct category of work except insofar as it allows Marti to encounter crimes and in so doing to make visible those people and events often made invisible. Nonetheless, the police station is a workplace that Marti enters as a black woman. Like Evanovich, Bland brings Marti into environs capable of unfriendliness, though when we meet her for the first time in *Dead Time*, she has already established her place. Still, her partner, Vik, has a lot to learn and still prefers dividing police work into men's jobs and women's jobs. Other policemen link Marti's anger to her menstrual cycle. Suspects might not answer Marti's questions but turn to Vik instead. But Marti has come to this smaller police station from Chicago, so she is both more experienced than most of the men around her and already inured to even worse conduct. Bland allows her — and us — the luxury of a Marti who is firmly settled, though unlikely to let sexism pass uncontested.

Bland's novels are relatively short (one of the many virtues for classroom use) and pay little attention to the dense, procedural detail that gives the subgenre its name. Like Wilson's novels, they prefer to foreground characters, victims of crime, who are also victims of social neglect. Children figure prominently in *Dead Time* as they do elsewhere in the series because they are among the least heard, least visible victims: impoverished in staggering numbers, neglected and abused by parents and institutions alike, unable to fight for themselves. But Bland is careful to keep Marti's interest in children and other disempowered groups distinct from anything that might be attributable to biology. Not only is Marti vigilant against charges of "maternalism" and "instinct," she also has children who necessarily spend a great deal of time without her. When we first meet them, they have recently lost their father. Theo, the younger child, is especially wounded and remains here, as elsewhere in the series, difficult for Marti to read or to help. Nevertheless, while she worries that she cannot give her children the kind of safety she herself had growing up, she is aware of what she does give them: a solidly middle-class life.

Bland writes in the third-person omniscient, with a point of view that follows Marti closely most of the time. The narrative distance, however, departs from the hard-boiled convention, removing the reader from the immediacy of Marti's voice while allowing the focus to shift away from the individual as the sole source of knowledge. This shift is significant, for like Wilson's narrative pattern, Bland's suggests the primacy of connections rather than separations. The individual here is important, even heroic, but never operates alone. To be alone is to be abandoned, forgotten. Bland's many characters in *Dead Time* — children, homeless people, mentally ill people — must form supportive networks in order to survive. It is Marti's ability to move among those networks that facilitates detection and solution.

Are Bland's works ultimately police procedurals at all? Like Wilson's novels, they unsettle the form with substantial variation, as we have seen. They offer a version of policing that is closer to social work, in homage perhaps to the beat cop MacAlister remembers fondly from her childhood. And they demonstrate little or no interest in policing as a set of either ritualized relationships or activities. Instead, the novels use crime and its aftermath as a way of writing about systemic neglect, of illuminating small corners of neglected territories. But Bland's enormously likeable hero inevitably invites the same revision, the same rehabilitation of image that seems so central to the police novels of the 1980s and subsequent decades. It is impossible to imagine Bland's success without a narrative context that repositioned the police from objects of suspicion to heroic subjects.

In the last two classes, we return to the original question: is this detective fiction or feminism? We end with Robin Truth Goodman's essay "Dick

Lit: Corporatism, Militarism, and the Detective Novel," which specifically implicates Sara Paretsky, the most conscious feminist of the writers we read, in the work of economic neoliberalism, increased militarism, and the loss of both civic and civil liberties. Goodman's work extends the cultural politics of the form into the international relationships undertaken by the United States as "world cop" and loops fascination with the police back into a domestic scene full of post–September 11, 2001, fears and phantasms. Embedded in such ideological workings are stories like those told by Paretsky in *Tunnel Vision,* a novel that, Goodman claims, establishes an ethics of surveillance, a regular abridging of legal codes, and a reliance on the private detective to do the work that cannot be accomplished in effective public institutions. These gestures collude with the very circumstances that Paretsky might otherwise explicitly oppose through Vic's feminism: that is, inequality, injustice, violence, and political oppression. Goodman's article is dense and would take longer to summarize here than is necessary to make this point: that even for a writer like Paretsky, whose feminism shapes her detective and the stories she tells, the detective novel may encode — or indeed, reanimate — the very instruments of control that oppose any true transformation, any real imaginings of a world in which all humans participate equally.

Ending on such a note inevitably suggests the culmination of an argument, but in fact, the various parts of the course could easily be rearranged for any number of purposes. As a literary critic, I move reflexively toward analyses that begin with genre and literary history. But I suspect that other disciplinary orientations might want to locate the object socially, culturally, or in the field of the reader. Certainly when, before reading Goodman, I asked students to talk about the changes in their world since September 11, 2001, they offered a list of differences — more surveillance, greater fear and anxiety, less tolerance for dissent, loss of civil liberties — that strongly suggest their own deep knowledge of the kinds of subjects Goodman and others find implicated in contemporary culture, hidden in the plain sight of our everyday pleasures.

Logistics

Students take an exam for each of the four units so that I can see how core concepts are being applied. They also provide interim reports on the progress of their final project, an application of the course material to an object we have not studied: they may choose one of the writers we read, but they must read works distant enough in time and placement to provoke different questions from those we have answered in class. Or they may choose other women writers with women detective heroes. Television shows are excellent choices because while we may see single episodes of the most popular series, watching a whole season's worth or comparing seasons allows a depth and complexity we are not able to give in single class sessions. I do not ask for a paper but rather a collection of notes that are then shared for the final exam. In not requiring a paper, I hope to keep students on a more fluid path of invention: I do not want the need to present a coherent paper to overdetermine their research or avoid the complexities that I believe to be central to cultural analysis. Sharing work with other classmates allows us to expand the reach of the course while it gives students an opportunity to apply and analyze independently.

WORKS CITED

Bland, Eleanor Taylor. *Dead Time*. New York: St. Martin's Press, 1992.

Evanovich, Janet. *Eleven on Top*. New York: St. Martin's Press, 2005.

Goodman, Robin Truth. "Dick Lit: Corporatism, Militarism, and the Detective Novel." *Education as Enforcement: The Militarization and Corporatization of Schools*. Ed. Kenneth J. Saltman and David A. Gabbard. London: Routledge, 2003. 259–76.

Grafton, Sue. *"A" Is for Alibi*. New York: St. Martin's, 2005.

Horsley, Lee. "Definitions of Film Noir." *CrimeCulture.com,* 2007. <http://www.crime culture.com/Contents/Film%20Noir.html>.

Klein, Kathleen Gregory. The *Woman Detective: Gender and Genre*. Urbana: University of Illinois Press, 1995.

Mizejewski, Linda. *Hardboiled & High Heeled: The Woman Detective in Popular Culture*. New York: Routledge, 2004.

Munt, Sally. *Murder by the Book: Crime Fiction and Fem*inism. London: Routledge, 1994.

Nord, David Paul, "An Economic Perspective on Formula in Popular Culture." *Popular Culture Theory and Methodology*. Ed. Harold E. Hinds et al. Madison: University of Wisconsin Press, 2006. 214–27.

Paretksy, Sara. *Killing Orders*. New York: Signet. 1985

Walton, Priscilla, and Manina Jones. *Detective Agency: Women Rewriting the Hard-Boiled Tradition*. Berkeley: University of California Press, 1999.

Wilson, Barbara. *Sisters of the Road*. Seattle: Seal Press, 1986.

Reading Students
Reading Detectives

Rosemary Weatherston

"I am an omnivorous reader with a strangely retentive memory for trifles."
— Sherlock Holmes, "The Adventure of the Lion's Mane"

In today's United States college classrooms, detective fictions can be found on the syllabi of courses ranging from advanced feminist theory and ancient Greek drama (*Oedipus Rex*, anyone?), to narrative poetics and forensic chemistry. They are taught in a remarkably wide array of disciplines and from an equally wide array of theoretical perspectives. For the instructor, then, who wants to incorporate one or more detective fictions into a syllabus, the issue is not one of precedence, but of prioritization: what text or texts to choose and through what critical lens or lenses best to teach?

In thinking through these questions it can be useful to realize there is at least one element all detective fictions, courses, and critical approaches to detective fictions have in common: a foregrounding of readers and the reading process. To state the obvious, all courses that teach detective fiction involve students reading detective fiction, and regardless of whether those fictions are approached from historical, cultural, sociological, psychoanalytic, reader-response, gendered, racial, generic, or narratological perspectives, issues of readers and reading come into play.[1] What earns these truisms a closer examination is that detective fictions and many of their critical frameworks can be seen foregrounding readers and the reading process in ways that generate unique pedagogical challenges and opportunities for the instructors who teach them. Moreover, finding ways to enable students to reflect on their own reading processes and positions as consumers of detective fiction can serve as a very effective means for them to think through the larger issues surrounding detective fictions—whatever particular issues an instructor chooses to highlight.

As a means of illustrating these challenges and opportunities, in this essay I describe some of the main ways in which "readers" and "reading" factor into several prevalent critical approaches to detective fiction. I then discuss the dynamics at play in a classroom of student readers of detective fictions, as well as the way these dynamics shaped my students' and my experience in a 400-level literature course entitled "Topics in Genre: Detective Fiction." Finally, I detail several assignments and activities instructors can use to facilitate students' reflections on their own reading.

Detective fiction's explicit reader orientation can be seen in everything from the longstanding expectation that authors play "fairly" by making sure readers have the same access to clues as do their detectives to the ubiquitous references characters and narrators make to reading detection fiction within the texts themselves. Not surprisingly, then, in the most common theoretical approaches to detective fictions we also see a strong emphasis on readers and the reading process. Some critical approaches, such as historical, cultural, and sociological, focus primarily on the relation of readers and the context in which detective fictions are created or consumed. These approaches regularly try to account for the popularity of particular subgenres of detective fiction with particular audiences at particular points in time. They frequently ask questions about what type of cultural work is or was being completed by a specific text or group of texts and what social anxieties common to readers of the time period in which it was created can be seen reflected in the texts' form or content. For example, as Lee Horsley explains in his useful study *Twentieth-Century Crime Fiction*, "golden age" or classic detective fictions produced in the interwar period by authors like Agatha Christie and Dorothy Sayers often are characterized as "feminized," reflecting both a general shift in British literature after World War I to a female readership and the subgenre's specific "containment of violence" within frequently domestic settings (38). In contrast, the U. S. hard-boiled detective stories of the same period are seen, in part, as reflecting U.S. readers' anxieties about the spread of social, political, and economic corruption within an increasingly urban and violent landscape and the destabilization of traditional models of American masculinity (69–73). Approaching detective fictions from these critical perspectives brings to the foreground the participation of readers and texts in larger cultural and historical discourses.

Other approaches to detective fiction, such as psychoanalytic and reader-response theories, focus more on the relation of the reader to the texts themselves. Emphasis routinely is placed on readers' experiences of and motivations for reading detective fictions: Are readers more likely to identify with the detective, the criminal, the narrator, or the author? To what extent do readers consume detective fictions for the sense of closure the solution of a mystery provides? To what extent do they read for a sense of transgression as they submerge themselves in the often violent worlds of criminals and their pursuers? Are these motivations best explained in terms of psychological drives or membership in discursive communities? "Apparently," observes

CSI: Miami star David Caruso, "people will watch forensics seven nights a week" (qtd. in Doherty B15). Do we think today's *CSI*-junkies are more motivated by a voyeuristic fascination with the violated body-as-spectacle or the implied infallibility of technology in its pursuit of a fully knowable truth? With a focus on individual readers' experiences of detective fictions, these critical perspectives emphasize readers' active construction rather than passive consumption of detective fictions' meanings.

Approaches to detective fiction that use lenses of identity (race, gender, class, nation, sexual, orientation, etc.) regularly transverse all manners of relations among context, text, and reader. In examining the relations of readers and categories of identity, scholars commonly focus on the ways in which representations of characters from particular identity groups promote or critique readers' ideologies of identity. Also of much interest is the relation of marginalized readers and mainstream texts: Are subversive readings of such texts possible? If, as some critics such as Kathleen Gregory Klein have suggested, in his or her victimhood and embodiedness the victim of a crime is always feminized regardless of his or her bio-sex, in what position does this leave the female reader? With whom does she identify and to what textual effect (173–74)? Conversely, these scholars debate whether texts that feature marginalized detectives such as Walter Mosley's African-American detective, Easy Rawlins, or Mary Wing's lesbian detective, Emma Victor, can unsettle dominant readers' preconceived beliefs by using their conventional desire to identify with the detective to undermine those beliefs. They question whether the centrality of race and sexuality in such texts can reveal to readers the habituated invisibility of white and heterosexual privilege (Horsley 200, 204, 250). Critics' answers to such questions are as diverse as the texts, identities, and reader relations they study.

The critical approaches to detective fiction with perhaps the most significant implications for reader-centered pedagogies are generic and narratological. Both approaches traditionally focus on the structural elements of texts: the literary conventions or "codes" that determine how detective fictions are identified as such and how stories of detection are told. These elements can include narrative point of view, narrative structure, character types, plot patterns, diction, degree of narrative closure or ambiguity, degree of self-reflexivity, and so forth. These approaches also study how such conventions change over time and between subgenres. Interestingly, there has been a growing tendency in the critical literature to define generic and narratological conventions as strategies of reading as well (or rather than) as strategies of writing. In this view, Peter J. Rabinowitz explains, literary conventions and codes are seen as "[b]undles of operations which readers perform in order to recover the meaning of texts rather than as sets of features found in the texts" (419).

This has interesting implications for both the definition and consumption of detective fictions. For example, as "genre fiction," detective fictions frequently are dismissed as formulaic and as a form of low or popular art. They are contrasted with the high art of "literary" literature which, supposedly, is characterized by the uniqueness of individual texts. In what ways, if any, might this evaluation influence the interpretive strategies readers employ when reading detective fictions? How would "popular" readers approach a text like Paul Auster's *City of Glass* (1985), which has been hailed both as one of the great works of postmodern twentieth-century literature and one of the great metaphysical or "anti" detective fictions of all times?[2] Some genre and narratology scholars analyze the ways in which readers' levels of familiarity with the conventions of detective fiction factor into their enjoyment of it. Others argue that this pleasure is augmented by readers' enjoyment in devising and employing new reading strategies in response to the vast formal and thematic variations among different subgenres and periods of detective fiction.

Further complicating readers' relation to the genre of detective fiction is a well established critical thread that identifies detective fiction as "the narrative of narratives" (Brooks 25). In contrast to a low form of literature, through this critical lens detective fiction is viewed as a type of "meta-literature" that "presents the most basic elements of narrative (sequence, suspense, and closure) in their purest form, but that also explicitly dramatizes the act of narration in the relationship between its narrative levels and its embedded texts. In other words," Susan Elizabeth Sweeney claims, "the detective story reflects reading itself" (7).[3]

The act of detection depicted in and enacted by detective fictions, then, is seen as paradigmatic of the act of reading any text. Thus, just as a detective must continually identify, interpret, and connect clues in order to discover the story of the crime, readers must continually identify, interpret, and connect textual elements in order to build a cohesive understanding of any narrative. If we follow the turn in much critical theory to expand definitions of "text," "narrative," and "reading" beyond the confines of the literary, we might indeed claim, like Brian McHale, that detective fiction is the "epistemological genre *par excellence*" (147). Thus, in any discipline where issues of knowledge and interpretation come into play, detective fictions might find relevance. Of course, in what disciplines could one possibly say that issues of knowledge and interpretation are not in play?

When we consider the ideas discussed above in relation to our own classrooms of student readers a number of interesting pedagogical dynamics become evident. As a way of illustrating some of these dynamics, I want to describe an incident that took place in a 400-level literature course I taught entitled "Topics in Genre: Detective Fiction."[4] In this class students surveyed nineteenth- and twentieth-century Anglo-American short stories, novels, and films that featured detective characters. A wide range of secondary readings provided theoretical models through which they examined the texts' literary and cultural frameworks. Although we discussed the tendency on the part of readers and critics to dismiss detective fictions as mere guilty pleasures, in this course I was presenting them to students as ideal sites of artistic and cultural investigation. We focused on the ways in which the texts could be seen to be motivated by questions of identity (Who is it? Whodunit?), epistemology (How do we know? What do we know?), and hermeneutics (How should we interpret and understand?). We debated the ways in which detective fictions could reflect, critique, and/or recuperate their cultural and historical milieus. Some of the students were die-hard detective fiction fans; others were taking the class simply because it fit into their schedules or they needed another 400-level course to complete their majors. These latter students had all heard of Sherlock Holmes and might have seen a few episodes of *CSI* but certainly were not familiar with the conventions or history of detective fiction as a genre.

For the first eight weeks of the semester the course went smoothly. Then, as they say, the plot thickened. The class was reading Sara Paretsky's novel *Burn Marks* (1990), which features her famous and famously female private investigator, V. I. Warshawski. Up to this point in the class students had read several short stories by Edgar Allan Poe and Sir Arthur Conan Doyle; *The Murder of Roger Ackroyd* (1926), by Agatha Christie; *The Big Sleep* (1939), by Raymond Chandler; and seen the film *The Maltese Falcon* (1941), based on Dashiell Hammett's 1929 novel by the same name. *Burn Marks* was meant to be their introduction to the "chick dick" subgenre that exploded onto the U.S. detective fiction scene in the 1980s and 90s. Combining hard-boiled generic conventions with female protagonists and, some would argue, feminist generic and social critiques, a "chick dick" novel like *Burn Marks* seemed to offer a rich opportunity for the class to investigate relations of genre, gender, and the progressive reworking of literary conventions.

And it might have — if the class had not, almost to a single student, hated V. I. Warshawski's guts. They hated the baths she took, the shoulder-padded clothes she wore, the sardonic references she made to other fictional detectives. They hated that she was "hung up" about her family, spent so much time talking to her old neighbor, and had relationship problems. They thought the case she was working on was boring, they considered her investigative methods mediocre at best, and that, in sum, *Burn Marks* was a badly written relic of the time period in which it was set and created.

Now, most if not all instructors have suffered the experience of the text or project that flops. Nothing in teaching works every time for every class.

You learn how to turn flops into "teachable moments" and to salvage a discussion. Sometimes you just move on. So vehement, however, was my students' loathing of poor V. I. that I found myself more fascinated than flustered. Instead of moving on I stopped our discussion and asked them to try and explain their aversion. After two full class periods and an online forum's worth of discussion, they boiled it down to this: V. I. Warshawski wasn't "cool."

In coming to this terse conclusion my students conducted a surprisingly sophisticated examination of their own reading processes and positions as consumers of detective fiction. They looked at the ways in which *Burn Marks* differed from the texts they had read and viewed up to this point and the ways in which V. I. Warshawski differed from the male detectives with whom they were familiar. They analyzed their own motivations and generic expectations as readers of detective fiction. They argued whether Sara Paretsky has succeeded in a feminist reworking of hard-boiled detective conventions or merely created a "Philip Marlowe in drag."[5] They hotly debated whether detective fiction was inherently coded as conservative, white, middle-class, and/or male. They discussed their underlying beliefs about the relevance (or lack thereof) of an author's or reader's gender. They argued whether contemporary U.S. culture was intrinsically misogynistic and to what extent V. I. occurred as an "outdated" second-wave feminist in a third-wave- or postfeminist world. As a whole they agreed that *Burn Marks* should not be considered "great literature" but then disagreed whether any of the detective fictions they had read up to this point should either.

Sometimes students referenced ideas and critical vocabulary from their theoretical readings; at other times their group or individual discussions were more casual and/or naive. In essence, however, when the class proclaimed V.I. was not as "cool" as the other detectives, they were asserting that she failed to meet their cultural and generic expectations. Based on their readings of pre–1945 U.S. and British detective fictions in class and their viewings of contemporary U.S. television and filmic detectives out of class, they believed a detective should be an exceptional rather than ordinary individual, someone removed from the circumstances and criminals being investigated. Coolness was equated with superiority, independence, and distance — characteristics the students came to recognize as depending on certain degrees of masculine and class privilege. V. I. Warshawski, deeply enmeshed in visible structures of community, family, class, and gender, had no chance of being "cool."

Burn Marks did end up offering the class a rich opportunity to investigate relations of genre, gender, and the progressive reworking of literary conventions, but not because of the students' and my reading of the text; rather, because of the students' and my reading of them as readers of detective fiction. "Cool" remained an active critical category through which students evaluated each detective we studied and each reading or viewing experience they had for the rest of the semester.

I have spent many years teaching students to reflect on their own reading processes and I have a good familiarity with the centrality of readers and reading in the detective fiction genre and its literature. However, it was not until this incident that I really began to look at the dynamics at play in a classroom of student readers of detective fictions and recognize them as, in some ways, distinct from those in other classrooms. Again, since "students reading detective fiction" is one of the things all courses that teach detective fictions have in common, it can be very useful for the instructor who wants to add one or more detective texts to his or her syllabus to keep the following dynamics in mind:

First, our U. S. students live in a culture where detective fiction is both ubiquitous and devalued. Authors like Patricia Cornwell and James Patterson regularly make the *New York Times*'s best-seller lists while detective series such as the multiple *Law & Order*s and *CSI*s dominate television programming. Films that feature detective characters are equally pervasive. At the same time, these print and visual fictions commonly are thought to hold only entertainment value, and a somewhat sordid one at that. Thus, when students find a detective fiction on an academic syllabus they are just as likely to react with confusion and skepticism (a trashy novel?!) or delight (an easy read!). Instructors may need to spend time discussing, even justifying the text's purpose in the class and the larger discipline of which the course is a part.

If an instructor chooses to use critical readings in the class's examination, he or she might face resistance from the confused and skeptical students, who may question whether a detective fiction warrants close critical study, and from the delighted students, who can resent having to study the text rather than just read it for "fun." At the same time, however, the addition of critical readings can serve as an excellent opportunity to expand students' appreciation for complexities inherent in the genre. However, in using secondary sources, instructors have to be conscious that most student readers of detective fictions are largely motivated by a desire to figure out the "mystery" along with or ahead of the detective. They can be quite resentful of any critical texts that contain "spoilers." The design of the reading schedule may require adjustment to accommodate this fact. The students' strong desire for the type of closure comfortingly and regularly delivered by most popular detective fiction can also mean they are less likely to embrace detective fictions that "violate" these conventions, such as metaphysical, postmodern, or anti-detective texts. The same students who might readily appreciate the "playful ambiguity" of Tom Stoppard's *Rosencrantz and Guildenstern Are Dead* (1967) might feel rudely cheated by the no-ending ending of Auster's *City of Glass.*

It also is useful to keep in mind students' potential affective as well as intellectual responses to detective fictions. These responses can include pleasure, titillation, and satisfaction; they also can include boredom and annoyance, as well as shock, revulsion, and outrage. The majority of detective fictions engage with and depict violence; many contain graphic renderings of violence committed against human bodies and beings. Their characters and plots frequently are driven by powerful conflicts of sex, desire, death, power, rationality, insanity, crime, law, order, guilt, innocence, marginality, agency, politics, gender, class, and race. As David M. Stewart observes, however, most academic criticism has maintained a long-standing ambivalence — even anxiety — about pleasure, and a "special resistance to affect" in general that is only magnified by reference to bodies (677). Instructors will be well served to think through the relevance that affect and the somatic are granted in their own disciplines as well as ways in which they may enable students to think through their own affective or somatic reading experiences.

Once conscious of the distinctive challenges and opportunities represented by our students as readers of detective fiction, we instructors are in a better position to facilitate our students' reflection on their own reading processes and positions. We also can draw connections between their reading and the larger formal, thematic, and contextual issues surrounding detective fictions. I close this essay by describing several activities and writing topics instructors might consider in this process. Some may be more relevant to a course devoted entirely to detective fiction; others can be used in the study of individual texts. In the words of one of my students, "I think that the coolest detectives [are] the readers.... We are all amateur detectives looking for clues...."[6]

Activities and Writing Topics

1. Before reading a detective fiction ask students to describe the "ideal" detective and on what they are basing this definition (Books? Television? Movies? Real life?). As a follow-up question ask them to consider what models of detection (techniques used, motives for), crime (nature of, causes of, motives for), and justice (form of, possibility of) are represented by this ideal.

2. Many models of detective fiction draw parallels between the relationship of the detective and criminal and between the reader and the author. In this view both detective and reader attempt to outsmart their criminal/authorial adversary by solving the mystery. Other critics suggest

readers identify more readily with the criminal or author. Ask students to evaluate with whom they most identify and why.

3. Halfway through a text ask students to predict the solution to the mystery or crime. Have them identify the textual "clues" and generic or extra-textual assumptions on which they are basing their predictions. This can be done individually or in the form of a class debate.

4. Have students discuss or write about one of the following reading scenarios and argue how it might impact the meaning of their text/s. Have them consider which elements of the text become most important, how their experiences of the formal features of the text and their relation to the detective or detection process are altered, etc.:

    a. Reading for the restoration of order offered by formal closure versus reading for the ambiguities or uncertainties enacted and/or represented by the text;

    b. Reading as an inexperienced reader versus a reader familiar with the genre of detective fiction;

    c. Reading the text the first time versus reading it the second time.

5. With historical detective fictions, have students research prevailing attitudes toward and controversies about crime, law, and social order.

6. In classes where the nature of the course's discipline is one of the subjects under examination, have students compare the detection process or processes depicted in the text/s to their discipline's own models of defining, obtaining, interpreting, and evaluating "knowledge."

7. As a final project, have students write their own detective story. This can be done as an individual or small-group exercise.

NOTES

1. This list is not meant to be exhaustive; there also are semiotic, poststructuralist, postmodern, postcolonial, queer, biographical, legal, socio-economic, and religious studies of detective fictions. However, the approaches listed represent some of the most common critical lenses used in U.S. college classrooms in the study of detective fictions written in English.

2. As defined by Patricia Merivale and Susan Elizabeth Sweeney, editors of *Detecting Texts: The Metaphysical Detective Story from Poe to Postmodernism* (1999), metaphysical and/or anti-detective detective stories are a distinct genre, "in which the detective hero's inability to interpret the mystery inevitably casts doubt on the reader's similar attempt to make sense of the text and the world" (back cover).

3. Depending on the detective fiction, these relationships between narrative levels and embedded texts can become quite multifaceted. For example, every detective fiction includes the narrative levels of (a) the story of the crime (what happened) and (b) the story of the investigation (how the detective finds out what happened). However, some fictions also include (c) the narrative of the character who is telling the story of the investigation (e.g., Sherlock Holmes's Dr. Watson), (d) metafictional references by characters to other detective fictions, and/or (e) direct references to the real reader's consumption of the text. Circulating through these narrative levels can be a wide range of

embedded texts—clues—that the different characters and the actual reader must interpret correctly to solve the mystery: diary entries, letters, wills, newspaper articles, police reports, eyewitness accounts, bills of sale, computer records, e-mails, confessions, ticket stubs, train schedules, memos, etc. To this list we easily can add the "texts" of the body of the victim or victims, trace evidence, the body language of witnesses and suspects, and so forth. For excellent discussions of these issues see Peter Hühn"s "The Detective as Reader: Narrativity and Reading Concepts in Detective Fiction," Laura Marcus's "Detection and Literary Fiction," Susan Elizabeth Sweeney's "Locked Rooms: Detective Fiction, Narrative Theory, and Self-Reflexivity," and Tzvetan Todorov's classic essay, "The Typology of Detective Fiction."

4. The course reading list and assignments for ENL 462: Topics in Genre: Detective Fiction as well as excerpts from several students' online discussions of *Burn Marks* can be found at <http://weatherr.faculty.udmercy.edu/secure/index.html>. Although these excerpts are quoted with permission of the students, the page is password protected to further ensure their privacy. Readers of this essay can access the page using the username and password "reader."

5. This phrase is often found in critiques of texts featuring female hard-boiled private investigators. I first noted it in Manina Jones's essay "'Philip Marlowe in Drag?': Performing Gender and Genre in Lesbian Detective Fiction."

6. J—. "Who's the Coolest Detective?" Online Posting. ENL 462: Topics in Genre: Detective Fiction.

WORKS CITED

Auster, Paul. *City of Glass*. New York: Penguin, 1987.

Brooks, Peter. *Reading for the Plot: Design and Intention in Narrative*. Cambridge: Harvard University Press, 1984.

Chandler, Raymond. *The Big Sleep*. New York: Alfred A. Knopf, 1939.

Christie, Agatha. *The Murder of Roger Ackroyd*. New York: Dodd, Mead & Co., 1926.

Conan Doyle, Arthur. "The Adventure of the Lion's Mane." *The Case Book of Sherlock Holmes*. Ed. W. W. Robson. New York: Oxford University Press, 1994. 172–91.

Doherty, Thomas. "Cultural Studies and 'Forensic Noir.'" *The Chronicle of Higher Education* 24 Oct. 2003: B15-B16.

Hammett, Dashiell. *The Maltese Falcon*. New York: Random House, 1929.

Horsley, Lee. *Twentieth-Century Crime Fiction*. New York: Oxford University Press, 2005.

Hühn, Peter. "The Detective as Reader: Narrativity and Reading Concepts in Detective Fiction." *Modern Fiction Studies* 33.3 (Autumn 1987): 451–66.

J—. "Who's the Coolest Detective?" Online Posting. 22 April 2007. ENL 462: Topics in Genre: Detective Fiction. 12 Dec. 2007 <http://weatherr.faculty.udmercy.edu/DetectiveFiction.html>.

Jones, Manina. "'Philip Marlowe in Drag?': Performing Gender and Genre in Lesbian Detective Fiction." *Pop Can: Popular Culture in Canada*. Ed. Lynne Van Luven and Priscilla L. Walton. Scarborough, ON: Prentice Hall Allyn and Bacon, 1999. 56–65.

Klein, Kathleen Gregory. "Habeas Corpus: Feminism and Detective Fiction." *Feminism in Women's Detective Fiction*. Ed. Glenwood Irons. Toronto: University of Toronto Press, 1995. 171–85.

The Maltese Falcon. Dir. John Huston. Warner Brothers, 1941.

Marcus, Laura. "Detection and Literary Fiction." *The Cambridge Companion to Crime Fiction*. Ed. Martin Priestman. New York: Cambridge University Press, 2003. 245–67.

McHale, Brian. *Constructing Postmodernism*. New York: Routledge, 1992.

Merivale, Patricia, and Susan Elizabeth Sweeney, eds. *Detecting Texts: The Metaphysical Detective Story from Poe to Postmodernism*. Philadelphia: University of Pennsylvania Press, 1999.

Paretsky, Sara. *Burn Marks*. New York: Delacorte Press, 1990.

Rabinowitz, Peter J. "The Turn of the Glass Key: Popular Fiction as Reading Strategy." *Critical Inquiry* 11.3 (Mar. 1985): 418–31.

Stewart, David M. "Cultural Work, City Crime. Reading, Pleasure." *American Literary History* 9.4 (Winter 1997): 676–701.

Stoppard, Tom. *Rosencrantz and Guildenstern Are Dead*. London: Faber and Faber, 1967.

Sweeney, Susan Elizabeth. "Locked Rooms: Detective Fiction, Narrative Theory, and Self-Reflexivity." *The Cunning Craft: Original Essays on Detective Fiction and Contemporary Literary* Theory. Ed. Ronald G. Walker and June M. Frazer. Macomb: Western Illinois University Press, 1990. 1–14.

Todorov, Tzvetan. "The Typology of Detective Fiction." *The Poetics of Prose*. Trans. Richard Howard. Ithaca, NY: Cornell University Press: 1977. 42–52.

Detective Fiction in the
First-Year Seminar

ROBERT P. WINSTON *and* JUDY GILL

Dickinson College, as its *First-Year Seminar Handbook* (2007) states, "established its First-Year Seminar Program in 1981 as a way to cultivate and encourage positive attitudes toward academic work and to stimulate appropriate mental habits" by introducing "new students to the standards and expectations of academic life at the College." Seminars should therefore "introduce students to the habits of mind essential to critical inquiry and liberal learning. They include the ability to read with discernment; to formulate important questions; to locate and bring to bear on these questions reliable evidence from a variety of sources; to recognize that all disciplines have specific modes of inquiry and that real understanding may require the application of information from across a variety of disciplines." A First-Year Seminar is thus intended to be "one of the courses that lay the foundation for the development of skills that allow students to formulate imaginative, analytic arguments; and to express such thoughts clearly in written, spoken, and visual communication."

Dickinson faculty are free to teach seminars on a wide range of topics in order to meet the goals of the First-Year Seminar Program. While some teach in areas outside their core field(s) or have consciously created interdisciplinary or cross-disciplinary courses, others use multiple approaches within their disciplines to introduce first-year students to the rigors of academic study. Opting for the latter approach, Professor Winston has regularly taught — and team-taught — seminars on genre fiction since the early 1980s; Professor Gill has done so for the past decade.

The current iteration of the Winston/Gill Seminar has multiple pedagogic goals in keeping with the overarching goals of the program as a whole. First, the course introduces students to the concept of genre and critical methods applied specifically to formula literature such as detective fiction, a critical approach codified by John Cawelti in *Adventure, Mystery, and Romance* as well as in books and articles by George Grella ("Murder and Manners: The Formal Detective Novel"; "Murder and the Mean Streets: The Hard-Boiled

Detective Novel"), George Dove (*The Police Procedural*), and others. Cawelti contends that "throughout its long-lasting tradition, literary crime serves as an ambiguous mirror of social values, reflecting both our overt commitments to certain principles of morality and order and our hidden resentments and animosity against these principles" (77). Thus, for example, because the "domestic circle" was a primary focus of "moral and social authority" in the nineteenth century, crimes against family members "fascinated the public" (77). By the second decade of the twentieth century, however, "the ideology of individual success and rising in society became the prevailing ethos" (77). What we now think of as classic detective fiction responded to the former, and a new genre, hard-boiled detective fiction, arose in response to the latter. Each genre of detective fiction, then, is built upon a series of elements that, taken together, constitute a formula that enables both author and reader to come to grips with the social concerns of the day. When a particular genre is no longer sufficiently flexible to incorporate cultural changes, a new formula will displace it or develop alongside it. George Dove's work, for example, analyzes the rise of the police procedural after World War II, suggesting that the post-war world is so complex that no individual can cope; thus the police squad supplants the solitary investigator.

Second, the class seeks to demonstrate the links between popular and dominant national cultures. In order to make such connections as clear as possible, the course uses examples of detective fiction from beyond the United States, thus requiring students to explore the contexts in which the novels are written and take place. While students may know — or at least think they know — Raymond Chandler's California in 1933, they will need background information in order to discuss novels from foreign countries as cultural texts that reiterate and/or challenge dominant ideologies, both social and political (Conan Doyle's defense of the British class system, Sjöwall and Wahlöö's direct intervention in Swedish politics, and Van de Wetering's discussion of the impact of Dutch colonialism when "natives" immigrate to the Netherlands, for example). Third, the seminar raises questions about the complexities of race, class, and gender as they are constructed and articulated over time and across cultures.

A typical reading list for a First-Year Seminar consists of the following: Sir Arthur Conan Doyle, *The Hound of the Baskervilles*; Raymond Chandler, *The Big Sleep*; Chester Himes, *A Rage in Harlem*; Sara Paretsky, *Bitter Medicine*; Maj Sjöwall and Per Wahlöö, *The Laughing Policeman*; Janwillem van de Wetering, *Outsider in Amsterdam*; Carl Hiaasen, *Stormy Weather*; Denise Mina, *Garnethill: A Novel of Crime*. This order, roughly chronological, starts the discussion with two well-known examples of traditional forms of detective fiction, classic and hard-boiled. The primary task here is to insist that students derive their analysis from the texts rather than from popular conceptions—and misconceptions—of Sherlock Holmes or Philip Marlowe (often as embodied by Humphrey Bogart). Students tend to be surprised at the very conservative nature of the depictions of class, property, and gender articulated in Conan Doyle's novel, and they are likewise taken aback by the depictions of gender and sexual orientation in Chandler's. Reading Himes provides the opportunity to discuss a writer whose novels, produced in the late 1950s and 1960s, deliberately and openly challenge the racial structures of the United States, while Paretsky invites a very different discussion of gender as she attempts to revise the hard-boiled form to serve feminist ends.

An important purpose of discussing these novels is to make them "strange," even "foreign," by highlighting the cultural work they perform. Shifting to Europe makes the foreign obvious and enables students to consider the ways in which the populations of other countries view (and articulate) issues of class, race, and gender. Sjöwall and Wahlöö's Marxian critique of Sweden's socialist state is the antithesis of Conan Doyle's defense of class and property; van de Wetering's sympathetic presentation of the impact of former colonial subjects on contemporary Amsterdam in particular and Dutch culture more generally is strikingly at odds with Chandler's use of negative stereotypes to depict anyone in Los Angeles in 1933 whose sexuality, for example, falls outside the cultural mainstream. A writer like Hiaasen returns students to the United States, but his satirical, even surreal, vision of contemporary Florida pushes students to re-examine their thinking about contemporary U.S. society just as Himes's anger and sarcasm had done for an earlier era. Denise Mina's novel returns to questions of class and gender in yet another foreign city, Glasgow, and the grittiness of her portrait of Maureen O'Donnell's trials and tribulations raises questions about the relative ease with which V. I. Warshawski, Paretsky's female private investigator, at least superficially occupies the role of the traditionally male hard-boiled detective.

Because the members of a typical First-Year Seminar are a mixed group, their presence in a seminar focusing on a popular literary form does not necessarily mean that they intend to go on to further study of literature. Thus, using critical jargon to describe such a seminar for incoming students would hardly be productive. Instead, it is important to articulate these course goals in language that will appeal to a relatively broad segment of an incoming class but is also intellectually honest in its presentation of both the subject matter and the questions it raises. Course descriptions like the following have been successful in drawing more than enough students.

> What could mystery novels set in Victorian England, 1930s California, 1950s Harlem, 1960s Stockholm, and 1970s Amsterdam have in common? How do they reflect or interrogate the cultures that produced them? Why did Conan Doyle set

much of *The Hound of the Baskervilles* on remote Dartmoor? Why does Philip Marlowe constantly encounter sexual "deviancy" in *The Big Sleep*? What does Sjöwall and Wahlöö's *The Laughing Policeman* suggest about Swedish politics in the 1960s? What is van de Wetering saying about Holland's colonial past in *Outsider in Amsterdam*? These are some of the questions we will explore as we study one of the most popular forms of genre fiction: detective novels. If time allows, we will also look two or three film adaptations to see how a different medium transforms works of literature. Last, but not least, we'll tackle the big question just why have these sorts of novels remained so popular?

It is important to note that descriptions like this one, concentrating on a popular and well-known form, will sometimes attract the student who assumes that "popular" is synonymous with "easy." Even a recent course title, "Theory and Praxis of Detective Fiction," did not provide a fool-proof filter; some students said they simply read past "Theory and Praxis" and only took in "Detective Fiction." It is crucial to emphasize the rigor of the course from the first meeting.

One way to do this is to emphasize the skills students will need to develop in order to succeed in the seminar. Dickinson College requires that students be introduced to library research and that writing (and revision) be major components of all First-Year Seminars. Each seminar is assigned a library liaison who works closely with faculty to improve students' information literacy. Although the library component need not count heavily in calculating grades, it has been the College's experience that unless library instruction is followed by required — and evaluated — exercises, the skills are never internalized and quickly slip away. Exercises such as the following have proven successful.

EXERCISE #1:

Find six (6) critical books (secondary sources) that discuss detective fiction. At least two of the books should be general studies of the genre; at least two of the books should study a specific author of detective fiction (not necessarily one of "ours"). At least two of the books should be held by Dickinson; at least two of the books should be held by libraries other than Dickinson. Write a citation for each of the books using correct MLA style. Indicate the books NOT held by Dickinson by using an asterisk (*) at the beginning of the citation.

Submit your completed assignment to the seminar's library liaison as a Microsoft Word attachment to an e-mail no later than class time, Friday.

EXERCISE #2:

Find six (6) critical articles in scholarly journals that discuss some aspect(s) of detective fiction. Articles can discuss some general or theoretical principle of detective fiction or can study some aspect(s) of a particular author's work. Write a citation for each of the articles using correct MLA style. If an article is available in print at Dickinson, mark the entry with a pound sign (#); if an article is not available in print at Dickinson but is available electronically through the College, mark the entry with a percent sign (%); if an article is available only through Interlibrary Loan (ILL), mark the entry with an ampersand (&).

Submit your completed assignment to the seminar's library liaison as a Microsoft Word attachment to an e-mail no later than class time, Monday.

EXERCISE #3:

Write an entry for an annotated bibliography on an article you discovered in Exercise #2. Your entry should include the citation in MLA format, followed by the annotation in which you summarize the author's thesis, methodology, and conclusion; you should also evaluate the source's usefulness for a paper appropriate to this seminar. Your entry should be about 150 words (half a page).

Submit your completed assignment to the seminar's library liaison as a Microsoft Word attachment to an e-mail no later than class time, Monday.

Dickinson's librarians, all of whom work with First-Year Seminar students and faculty, generally are willing to evaluate these assignments, so these exercises need not become a burden to the instructor.

The sequential nature of the library component can and should be linked to the writing component of the seminar, and so the third exercise, writing a sample annotation, prepares students for a final project, the production of an annotated bibliography and a short critical research paper. First-Year Seminars are meant to build their writing assignments incrementally. One method is to build from a short close-reading assignment of a single text to a comparison/contrast essay on two works to the final project. Each of the three papers goes through a drafting, feedback, and revising process. The grade on the final version of each paper takes into account the extent and effectiveness of the student's revision as well as the overall quality of the final product. To demonstrate to students that revision is worthwhile, they must have ample time for writing the first version of their essays and, equally important, for revising after receiving feedback on the draft. In addition to feedback from other students in the seminar and faculty members, students also are encouraged to visit the college's Norman M. Eberly Writing Center at any point in the writing process. The Center is staffed by trained peer tutors, and each seminar has a linked tutor who works closely with the professor to ensure that seminar students understand the nature and goals of any given writing assignment. As a matter of general policy, students are required to meet with their linked tutor on at least one paper.

What follows are examples of writing assignments that have proven successful.

Paper #1

Draft due: in class, Friday...
Final Version due: in class, Friday, two weeks later

Write a two to three (2–3) page essay on the following topic:

Explain the significance of Dr. Watson in *The Hound of the Baskervilles*.

OR

Explain the significance of sporting imagery in *The Hound of the Baskervilles*.

Your first task is to devise a *thesis* that articulates the *critical argument* you will make about the topic. Your essay should make the case for your argument. Generalize freely, but be sure to provide *concrete textual evidence* — and your analysis of that evidence — to support your claims. Much of the success of your essay will depend upon the judicious choice and *careful discussion* of these materials from the text. Remember, papers are to be submitted on the dates indicated. Papers (drafts or final versions) submitted after the deadlines will be penalized at least a full letter grade and may be failed outright at the discretion of the instructor.

Paper #2

Draft due: in class, Friday...
Final version due: in class, Friday, two weeks later

Write a three to four (3–4) page essay on the following topic:

Is it accurate to label Sara Paretsky's *Bitter Medicine* a hard-boiled detective novel? Why or why not? In order to answer this question, you should compare Paretsky's novel to Raymond Chandler's *The Big Sleep*.

This topic is deliberately broad. Your first task, therefore, one that will in many respects determine the success of your essay as a whole, is to devise a *thesis* that articulates the *critical argument* you will make about the topic. Your essay should make the case for your argument. Generalize freely, but be sure to provide *concrete textual evidence* — and your analysis of that evidence — to support your claims. Much of the success of your essay will depend upon the judicious choice and *careful discussion* of these materials from the text. Remember, papers are to be submitted on the dates indicated. Papers (drafts or final versions) submitted after the deadlines will be penalized at least a full letter grade and may be failed outright at the discretion of the instructor

Final Project (Papers 3 and 4)

Paper #3: The Annotated Bibliography

Produce an annotated bibliography that consists of six to eight entries. You must use a variety of kinds of critical sources (articles in scholarly journals, books or chapters in books, etc.). Each entry should include the citation in MLA format, followed by the annotation in which you summarize the author's thesis, methodology, and conclusion; you should also evaluate the source's usefulness for your paper. To accomplish these tasks, each entry should be about 150 words (half a page).

PAPER #4: THE CRITICAL RESEARCH PAPER

Write a critical research paper of seven to eight (7–8) pages, excluding Works Cited page. Please double-space, use one-inch margins and a 12-point Times New Roman font, and please follow MLA guidelines for format, citations, and list of Works Cited. As with the first two papers, you should have an arguable thesis appropriate to a paper of this length and a logical and well-developed argument with evidence from both your primary and secondary sources. Please come see me so that we can discuss your topic, make sure it's appropriate to a paper of this length, and discuss strategies and methods; this is a required meeting.

Students have chosen to write on topics as diverse as Sjöwall and Wahlöö's depiction of the negative impact of vigilante justice on Swedish society, the use of animal imagery in Chandler to characterize women as dangerous sexual predators, Paretsky's criminalization of corporate behavior, and Conan Doyle's use of atavism as a key to solving the mystery of *The Hound of the Baskervilles*.

As should be obvious by now, Dickinson College expects a good deal from its First-Year Seminar program, and attempting to fulfill all the goals of the Seminar program requires careful balance among the various components. The college policy that precludes having work due for a seminar after the last day of classes imposes a further constraint. Nonetheless, it is possible to construct a syllabus that weaves the various components together into a reasonably coherent whole. Winston's syllabus for a Seminar entitled "Detecting Cultural Narratives," taught in the autumn of 2007, follows this essay.

Detective fiction therefore can be an effective focus of a first-year seminar that engages students and introduces them effectively to the rigors of academic study in colleges and universities, but a cultural perspective is only one of many approaches that could be applied to the genre. Recent critical studies on gender in detective fiction, including those by Kathleen Gregory Klein (*The Woman Detective: Gender and Genre*, 2nd ed., Urbana: University of Illinois Press, 1995), Sally R. Munt, (*Murder by the Book? Feminism and the Crime Novel*, New York: Routledge, 1994), Gill Plain (*Twentieth-Century Crime Fiction: Gender, Sexuality and the Body*, Edinburgh: Edinburgh University Press, 2001), and Priscilla L. Walton and Manina Jones (*Detective Agency: Women Rewriting the Hard-Boiled Tradition*, Berkeley: University of California Press, 1999), provide critical and theoretical bases for a seminar based in feminist criticism. Works on race such as those by Frankie Y. Bailey (*Out of the Woodpile: Black Characters in Crime and Detective Fiction*, New York: Greenwood, 1991) and Maureen T. Reddy (*Traces, Codes, and Clues: Reading Race in Crime*

Fiction, New Brunswick, NJ: Rutgers University Press, 2003) do the same for a seminar using detective fiction to ask — and answer — questions on race in the United States and elsewhere. Studies like those by Ernest Mandel (*Delightful Murder: A Social History of the Crime Story*, Minneapolis: University of Minnesota Press, 1984) and Robert P. Winston and Nancy C. Mellerski (*The Public Eye: Ideology and the Police Procedural*, London: Macmillan, 1992) offer starting points for a course from a Marxian perspective. The possibilities are literally as diverse as the novels that constitute the genre — and the faculty and students who read them.

WORKS CITED

Cawelti, John. *Adventure, Mystery, and Romance*. Chicago: University of Chicago Press, 1976.

Dove, George. *The Police Procedural*. Bowling Green, OH: Popular Press, 1982.

Grella, George. "Murder and Manners: The Formal Detective Novel." *Novel* (1970): 30–48.

_____. "Murder and the Mean Streets: The Hard-Boiled Detective Novel." *Contempora* 1.1 (1970): 6–15.

APPENDIX

Course Syllabus

DETECTING CULTURAL NARRATIVES (SYLLABUS)

WEEK 1:	M	Introduction: reading the syllabus
		Reading classic detective fiction: "The Adventure of the Speckled Band" <http://www.bakerstreet221b.de/canon/spec.htm>
	W	Defending the Status Quo: Conan Doyle, *The Hound of the Baskervilles*
	F	Conan Doyle, *The Hound of the Baskervilles*
WEEK 2:	M	Conan Doyle, *The Hound of the Baskervilles*
	W	Information Literacy: An Introduction and Finding Books; Getting Materials from Off-Campus (ILL) (Meet in the Information Commons Classroom on the lower level of the library)
	F	Paper Workshop
		Information Literacy Exercise #1 due
WEEK 3:	M	Reading hard-boiled detective fiction: Chandler, "The Simple Art of Murder"
	W	Detective Fiction and Social Criticism: Chandler, *The Big Sleep*

	F	Chandler, *The Big Sleep*
		Draft of Paper #1 due
WEEK 4:	M	Chandler, *The Big Sleep*
	W	Chandler, *The Big Sleep*
	F	Information Literacy: Using Scholarly Databases; Physically Locating Journal Articles (Meet in the Information Commons Classroom on the lower level of the library)
WEEK 5:	M	Detective Fiction and Race: Himes, *A Rage in Harlem*
		Information Literacy Exercise #2 due
	W	Himes, *A Rage in Harlem*
	F	Himes, *A Rage in Harlem*
		Final Version of Paper #1 due
WEEK 6:	M	Himes, *A Rage in Harlem*
	W	Detective Fiction and Feminism: Paretsky, *Bitter Medicine*
	F	Paretsky, *Bitter Medicine*
WEEK 7:	M	Paretsky, *Bitter Medicine*
	W	Paretsky, *Bitter Medicine*
	F	Group advising workshop
		Draft of Paper #2 due

MIDTERM PAUSE

WEEK 8:	W	Information Literacy: Scholary Journals vs. Popular Magazines; Evaluating Websites (Meet in the Information Commons Class room on the lower level of the library)
	F	Information Literacy: Critically Analyzing Sources; Writing an Annotated Bibliography (Meet in the Information Commons Classroom on the lower level of the library)
WEEK 9:	M	Reading the police procedural
		Information Literacy Exercise #3 due
	W	Detective Fiction and Politics: Sjowall and Wahloo, *The Laughing Policeman*
	F	Sjowall and Wahloo, *The Laughing Policeman*
		Final Version of Paper #2 due
WEEK 10:	M	Sjowall and Wahloo, *The Laughing Policeman*
	W	Detective Fiction and the Colonial Legacy: van de Wetering, *Outsider in Amsterdam*
	F	van de Wetering, *Outsider in Amsterdam*

WEEK 11:   M   van de Wetering, *Outsider in Amsterdam*

            W   Detective Fiction as Satire: Hiassen, *Stormy Weather*

            F   Hiassen, *Stormy Weather*

WEEK 12:   M   Hiassen, *Stormy Weather*

            W   Workshop on draft of final paper

            F   Workshop on draft of final paper

WEEK 13:   M   Workshop on draft of final paper

                 THANKSGIVING VACATION

WEEK 14:   M   Workshop on draft of final paper

            W   Workshop on draft of final paper

            F   Workshop on draft of final paper

                 Paper #3 (Annotated Bibliography) due

                 Course evaluation

WEEK 15:   M   Detective Fiction and the Contemporary: Mina, *Garnethill*

            W   Mina, *Garnethill*

            F   Mina, *Garnethill*

                 Final Version of Paper #4 due

The Mystery of Composition
A Detective-Themed Composition Course

CHRIS YORK

Any number of pedagogical approaches in composition courses is possible, but in over ten years teaching composition I have come to subscribe to a pretty basic equation: time plus effort equals improved writing. This is unfortunate for the teacher of college composition because a semester is both an artificial and an extremely short amount of time for a student's writing skills to grow. Only the students who really invest themselves in the course tend to show any substantial development.

From a student's perspective, a sustained effort in the composition classroom is a struggle. Writing is an arduous process filled with ambiguities and this leads to frustration. Furthermore, on most college and university campuses, composition is a required course. Students, therefore, often come to the class with the presumption that they should not be there (either because they are already a good writer or because it has, in their words, nothing to do with their major), or they come to class riddled with anxieties because writing is a talent they feel they do not possess. In short, students would prefer to be elsewhere.

Considering these drawbacks, the first challenge for a college composition instructor is to find a way to invest more students in the course. The detective-themed composition course "The Mystery of Composition" emerged from brainstorming ways to accomplish this task. This volume's focus on detectives in the classroom has a dual significance when considering "The Mystery of Composition" course. First, the course replaces traditional composition textbooks with a variety of detective narratives. Doing so keeps more students engaged in the course readings for a longer period of time and, simultaneously, allows the class to approach traditional composition topics from new perspectives. The concept of "detectives in the classroom" can also be interpreted as a reference to the students themselves as detectives. This is true in the sense that critical thought and research, two essential tools of the detective trade, are also two outcomes often expected of composition students. This is also true in a more literal way, as the "Mystery of Composition" curriculum asks students to don the sleuthing cap in several themed assignments and actually exercise their critical thinking skills.

Detective Narratives as Composition Texts

When it comes to engaging the student in the course materials, the standard composition textbook is certainly more a part of the problem than the solution. Most are in some way structured around writing modes and include explanations of modes, examples of successful essays within given modes, and a variety of supplementary materials including questions for consideration, writing exercises, and grammar review. In spite of all of these well-designed and useful components, by the end of the semester a large portion of the class stops reading the text. The result is that fewer students are participating in discussion or group work, fewer students are reading about writing strategies and seeing how successful writers employ those strategies, and students' writing tends to regress, or at best plateau, over the last 20–25 percent of the semester.

This recurring problem with student reading led to my consideration of texts, any kind of text, that might engage the student more effectively than standard composition materials. Mysteries came to mind as a popular genre, and the more consideration I gave the genre, the more teaching opportunities became apparent. The first opportunity was in the nature of genre fiction and the balance it strikes between formula and creativity. Particularly in terms of character and plot, the detective genres follow distinct patterns. Classic detective narratives, for instance, follow a pattern in which the reader is introduced to the detective and the crime, confounded as the investigation of clues seems to make the case more confusing than clear, surprised by the detective's announcement of the solution, and enlightened in the denouement by the detective's explanation of the case. Readers of the genre recognize this pattern and begin to develop certain expectations about the way a mystery will develop.

It is important for students to understand, though, that a set of expectations between audience and writer based on precedent is true of most kinds of writing, whether it be a mystery, an interoffice memo, or a recipe. The academic essay is no exception. While most composition instructors find the five-paragraph essay too rigid and somewhat archaic, a standard academic essay still has essential components such as a thesis and evidence that supports this thesis. As with the mystery, the audience expects these things.

Discussion of structure and formula in essays leads some students to ask how their own voice makes its way into their writing. Again, mysteries provide a case in point. Students need to understand that there is a lot of room for creativity within seemingly rigid formulas. No two classic detective stories are exactly alike. It is illuminating to compare a Sherlock Holmes mystery like *The Sign of the Four,* rich in the atmosphere of London and a sense of adventure as Holmes and Watson pursue the criminals down the Thames, with a more contemporary example. In order to avoid overburdening the students with reading in order to make this point, I usually use an example from television or film. In the USA Network series *Monk,* for example, the picturesque streets of San Francisco and an emphasis on humor over adventure stand in stark contrast to the dark moodiness of Holmes' London. Similarly, in academic essays the thesis and supporting evidence are held together by introductions, conclusions, and transitions to provide context and flow for the essay. It is in the way the students put all of these pieces together that their unique voices are articulated.

Detective narratives also allow a class to address writing modes in interesting and illuminating ways. Analysis, for instance, is a very difficult concept for students to process. An instructor can tell them that it is breaking down a complex subject into its core components or processes, but that is not necessarily helpful to students. Inevitably, many students fall back on summary when analysis is required. Here detective fiction can be particularly helpful. Early in *The Sign of the Four,* Watson challenges Holmes to analyze a watch that he has recently acquired from his late brother and reveal the "character and habits" of its former owner. When Holmes is able to do so with great precision Watson is shocked. Holmes explains that he takes "small facts" and from them makes "large inferences." An effective in-class strategy at this point would be to ask the class to go to the text and describe the watch. They would be able to say that it looks like "a fifty-guinea watch" but is dented in places and also has cuts and marks all over it. Once the class has a description of the watch, it can then turn back to the text and see how Holmes moves from description to analysis:

> It is customary for pawnbrokers in England, when they take a watch, to scratch the numbers of the ticket with a pin-point upon the inside of the case.... There are no less than four such numbers visible to my lens on the inside of this case. Inference — that your brother was often at low water. Secondary inference — that he had occasional bursts of prosperity, or he could not have redeemed the pledge [11].

Holmes' analysis is a bit fantastic to be sure, but in being so it is perhaps that much more memorable and will be an example that will endure with students.

Mysteries can also be rich examples of narration, description, cause and effect, comparison and contrast, and many other modes of writing. And it is not a Herculean challenge to turn these examples into writing assignments.

One of the first assignments I use in "The Mystery of Composition" focuses on description. Detective novels are excellent examples of how the description of a setting or a character can create a distinct tone in the writing. To return to *The Sign of the Four*, Holmes and Watson travel with their client, Mary Morstan, to a rendezvous with a mysterious informant. As they ride in their cab, the description of London sets a tone that is dark and foreboding:

> Down the Strand the lamps were but misty splotches of diffused light which threw a feeble circular glimmer upon the slimy pavement. The yellow glare from the shop-windows streamed out into the steamy, vaporous air and threw a murky, shifting radiance across the crowded thoroughfare. There was, to my mind, something eerie and ghostlike in the endless procession of faces which flitted across the narrow bars of light — sad faces and glad, haggard and merry [21].

To illustrate the extent to which this description colors the reader's impression of the Strand in London, it can be helpful to provide a contrasting description. This one is from a walking tour description on *The Made in Atlantis* website:

> If any thoroughfare is to rank as chief street of all London, it is the Strand, till the other day choked by double tides of business and pleasure, but now opened out more roomily, and its channel seconded by the broad Thames Embankment, on to which a fleet of tramcars has at last broken way.

Both descriptions portray a crowded street, but this second description lacks the moodiness of the first as terms like "murky," and "slimy," which help create tone in the first, are absent in the second. Discussing the contrasts in approach and purpose helps students to understand more clearly how writers manipulate language for a specific purpose. This lesson transitions nicely into a descriptive writing assignment like the following:

> Choose a place with which you are very familiar and with which you associate very specific feelings. Write two descriptions. Description #1 should be an *objective* description of this place. In other words, describe it in a neutral way, as if you had never been there before. Be thorough and precise and describe what you see, smell, hear, and taste as clearly as possible. Then write Description #2, which will be a description of the same place. Only now use descriptive words that convey your personal feelings toward the place. Be careful. Don't *tell* your audience how you feel. Show them. Let the feeling come from the descriptive words you use.

Because detective fiction includes a number of different subgenres, it is an excellent text for teaching comparison and contrast. After spending time with the classic detective genre, the course then moves on to the hard-boiled genre. Again, it is best to use a fairly prototypical example of the genre like Raymond Chandler's *The Big Sleep* or Dashiell Hammett's *The Maltese Fal-*

con. But there are other interesting ways to use mystery texts for the teaching of modes. As detective novels, the hard-boiled and the classic share many characteristics. First, they follow similar story arcs, moving from introduction through investigation, and on to revelation. They also share a similar cast of characters: the detective, the damsel in distress, the police and other law enforcement officials, and, of course, criminals.

Within these similarities, however, there are also radical differences. While the classic detective's investigative process includes the revelation and analysis of clues, a largely intellectual exercise, the hard-boiled detective's investigative process involves a give-and-take of threats and intimidation until the detective stumbles upon the solution. Similarly, his relationship with the law is quite different. Though both genres tend to portray the police as inept or, at best, inefficient, in the hard-boiled detective story officers are much more likely to be openly hostile toward the detective, often because the department or elements within the department are corrupt. That so many differences exist within apparent similarities allows for quality in-class discussions on the extent of the genres' similarities, which in turn leads to interesting paper topics. For example:

> The emphasis of the classic detective story is the solving of a complex puzzle, while for the hard-boiled detective story the emphasis is in seeing criminals brought to justice (and, in particular, the detective's own moral vision of what is just). Focusing either on the detective or the portrayal of the actual crime or crimes, explain how this is demonstrated in *The Sign of the Four* and *The Maltese Falcon*.
>
> Compare and contrast the portrayal of police officers and other public officials in *The Sign of the Four* and *The Maltese Falcon*. Are they portrayed in a similar way? Another question you may want to ask as you think about this topic is why they are portrayed in a certain way.

This approach to teaching writing modes does require more work on the part of the instructor. Where traditional composition texts often define and explicate the individual modes, in this curriculum the sole responsibility lies with the instructor to generate these elements either through discussion, lecture, or group work. In the end, though, having a larger percentage of the class that has read the text and, beyond that, actually enjoyed it, far outweighs the small addition the instructor will encounter in his or her prep time.

The Student as Detective

Student feedback coupled with personal observation certainly suggests that the detective narrative generates more student interest than traditional composition texts without sacrificing content that is essential to the course. Perhaps the greatest advantage to "The Mystery of Composition," however, is the opportunities it provides for developing a more student-centered classroom.

One of the ways this is accomplished is through an exercise and assignment sequence based on the five-minute mystery. Five-minute mysteries are short stories, generally two to four pages long, that provide enough evidence in the text itself for the reader to solve the mystery. A key at the end of the book provides solutions against which readers may check their conclusions. There are a number of series currently being published, but my course uses selections from a series written by Ken Weber and published by Running Press.

This assignment sequence is generally spread out over the semester, with phase one repeating itself two or three times during the term, and phase two introduced toward the end of the term. In phase one, a mystery is distributed to the class. Students are asked to read the mystery individually and try to solve the mystery. If they arrive at a solution, they are asked to write it in their notebooks along with the evidence they used to arrive at their conclusion. If they cannot come to a conclusion, they are asked to identify and explain what they see as key pieces of evidence.

Students are divided into small groups to compare answers and discuss possible solutions. They are asked to come to a consensus about a solution within their group. Once they have done so, they are asked to write the group's solution in their notebooks. Finally, the class reconvenes to debate and discuss solutions. The discussion both in small groups and in the full-class discussion does tend to get lively, but almost invariably the class is able to arrive at some kind of consensus by the end of the session.

This is a particularly useful exercise to distribute early in the semester for a couple of reasons. First of all, as noted above, it does generate a lot of participation, and establishing a high level of interaction early sets a positive tone for the class. Students now expect the class to be discussion oriented even on days when there are no mysteries to solve. Second, it shows students that they do have the ability to read and think critically. Even students who are not able to come up with the correct answer on their own are generally able to identify key pieces of evidence. Furthermore, it gives students confidence in the group dynamic when they are able to contribute to a conversation and ultimately agree on the solution to the mystery.

During the course, this exercise is repeated two or three times to reinforce the objectives mentioned above and also to familiarize the students with the style of the five-minute mystery. This familiarity becomes particularly important in the second phase of the sequence. In this phase students are again broken down into small groups, but this time they are asked to write their own five-minute mystery. This group project serves two very practical purposes. First of all, at the end of the semester it is a refreshing change of pace, and most students, even those suffering from burnout, tend to embrace this assignment and make a concerted effort to write an effective narrative. Second, anyone who has worked in a corporate environment knows that much of the writing done in the business world is collaborative, and the taste of group dynamics, both good and bad, that they experience here will serve them well should they encounter it professionally.

Another mystery-themed assignment sequence that "The Mystery of Composition" employs is based on the board game Clue. College instructors are naturally apprehensive about bringing a board game into the classroom. Students tend to be skeptical as well. But Clue needs to be thought of as nothing more than a text, although an interactive text that the students help create through playing the game. And it is a game in which students need to engage in critical thinking to win. Again, the ability to think, read, and write critically is a common outcome institutions expect from their composition course. This is yet another opportunity to practice critical thinking in a venue where a large percentage of students, after their initial reluctance, will engage in the process.

In addition to using Clue as a critical thinking exercise, it is possible to attach several writing assignments to the game itself. The first is directly related to yet another mode: process. After students have familiarized themselves with the game and played it a couple of times, the students write a process paper detailing a winning Clue strategy. Before students play, it is helpful to distribute an assignment sheet with three or four writing assignments asking them to use the game that is about to be played as a text. Some examples are below:

> You are an aggressive journalist from *The National Inquirer.* The editor of your tabloid has received a tip that someone involved in the Mr. Boddy investigation is, indeed, an alien. Based on the events of the game write an article that reveals one of the suspects to be an alien.
>
> You are a Clue fan and also happen to write a column for *ESPN, the Magazine.* After seeing poker, chess, and spelling bees all make their way onto ESPN and ESPN2, you are outraged that Clue competitions have not been televised. Using specific details from today's competition, make a case for televising Clue tournaments. How does Clue stack up to these other competitions?
>
> Miss Scarlet is a Hollywood starlet and you are the editor of the Miss Scarlet Fan Club online newsletter, *The Scarlet Letter.* Miss Scarlet as a suspect in the death of Mr. Boddy is a potential publicity disaster. Based on the actual events of the game, write an essay that puts a positive spin on her involvement in the murder.

Before play begins, the class needs to have a discussion concerning each selection. While the assignments are fanciful, the publications in them either

are real publications or, with *The Scarlet Letter*, fit a realistic formula for publications. The questions students need to consider include: What type of narrative do these publications generally tell? What kind of tone will their
audience expect? What kinds of biases will the audience want to read? The
concept of audience is difficult for composition students to understand, but
students easily discuss the kinds of writing in these publications and also
readily discuss the stereotypical readers of the publications. After a thorough
discussion of the assignments, students have a much better understanding of
the changing nature of their audience relative to the kind of writing they have
to do.

Conclusion

This essay has not tried to be comprehensive and take readers through
a day-by-day account of "The Mystery of Composition" curriculum. Rather,
it highlights some texts and approaches to those texts that make a detective-
oriented composition classroom both viable and dynamic. It is possible to
learn about writing from any kind of writing. The challenge for instructors
is to find texts that will engage their students and then draw teaching opportunities from those texts.

WORKS CITED

"Along the Strand." *Atlantis International.* 22 Dec. 2007 <http://madeinatlantis.com/lon
    don/along_the_strand.htm>.
Chandler, Raymond. *The Big Sleep.* New York: Vintage, 1992.
Conan Doyle, Arthur. *The Sign of Four.* New York: Penguin, 2001.
Hammett, Dashiell. *The Maltese Falcon.* New York: Vintage, 1992.
Weber, Ken. *Absolutely Amazing Five-Minute Mysteries.* Philadelphia: Running Press,
    2002.
_____. *Five-Minute Mysteries.* Philadelphia: Running Press, 1989.

Notes on Contributors

Pamela Bedore is an assistant professor of English at the University of Connecticut, where she teaches undergraduate and graduate courses in several areas of popular literature including detective fiction, science fiction, and horror. She was recently awarded a Provost Grant to develop a new course in popular literature that will become part of UConn's general education program. Bedore coordinates the dime novel area of the Popular Culture Association and is currently completing the manuscript of her first book, *Detecting Dime Novels*. Her recent articles can be found in *Dime Novel Round-Up*, *Studies in Popular Culture*, and *Foundation: The International Review of Science Fiction*.

Stephen Brauer is associate dean for first-year programs and associate professor of English at St. John Fisher College. He teaches courses in American literature and culture, especially of the nineteenth and twentieth centuries, including classes on the American dream, the Harlem Renaissance, the gangster and the detective, and modernism and the city. He has published articles on *The Great Gatsby*, Faulkner's *Sanctuary*, and the film *Fight Club*, among others.

Patricia P. Buckler is on the English faculty at Indiana University Northwest in Gary, Indiana. Her teaching has ranged from courses in first-year composition to detective fiction and Chaucer. Her two main research interests are detective fiction and the rhetoric and history of scrapbooks. She co-edited (with Susan Tucker and Katherine Ott) and contributed to *The Scrapbook in American Life*. She authored the essay "Scrapbook" in *American Icons*, "From the Personal to the Historical" in *The Mary Baker Eddy Library Magazine*, "Owen Keane, Failure and Detective" in *Journal of Popular Culture*, and "From Edwin to Games: Early Character Development in the Sharon McCone Novels" in *Echoes from a Wild and Lonely Place: Marcia Muller and American Literature*. For many years she has been an active member of the Popular Culture Association's mystery and detective fiction area caucus and served as its co-chair in 2004 and 2005.

Benjamin Fraser is assistant professor of Spanish at Christopher Newport University in Newport News, Virginia. He has published on the topic of Latin American detective fiction in Spanish in *Studies in Latin American Popular Culture*. His essays on other topics have appeared in publications from a range of disciplines including such journals as *Sign Language Studies*, *Environment and Planning D: Society and Space*, *Studies in Hispanic Cinemas*, *Social and Cultural Geography*, *Mosaic*, *Chasqui*, the *Bulletin of Spanish Studies*, and the *Arizona Journal of Hispanic Cultural Studies*.

Genie Giaimo is a lecturer at Clark University and Becker College in Worcester, Massachusetts. Her teaching ranges from freshman-level expository writing and literature courses to continuing education seminars on the detective genre in popular culture. She has published an article on the ethnic detective in *Mystery Readers Journal*.

She has recently entered a Ph.D. program in English literature at Northeastern University in Boston.

Judy Gill directs the Norman M. Eberly Writing Center at Dickinson College where she also teaches in the English Department. She regularly offers courses in contemporary American literature, expository writing, the first-year seminar program, and tutor training. Her research and writing interests include writing pedagogy and writing center history, theory, and practice. She has published in *The Writing Center Journal* and *The Writing Lab Newsletter*.

Derham Groves is a senior lecturer in architecture at the University of Melbourne. He is the author of several books on popular art, architecture and design, including *You Bastard Moriarty, In the Privacy of Their Own Holmes* (with David Harris), and *There's No Place Like Holmes: Exploring Sense of Place Through Crime Fiction*. One of Groves' most satisfying accomplishments was becoming the first Australian member of the Baker Street Irregulars in 1985.

Mary Hadley is an associate professor teaching creative crime fiction and composition at Georgia Southern University in Statesboro. She has produced two nonfiction books on detective fiction (both for McFarland): *British Women Mystery Writers* (2002) and *Minette Walters and the Treatment of Justice* (2008), the latter co-edited with Sarah D. Fogle. In addition, she has co-authored four crime novels with her husband, Charles Martin — *Casey's Revenge, The Reluctant Corpse, Nightmare in Savannah*, and *Savannah Scores* — under the pseudonym Mary Charles.

Steve Hecox teaches English at Averett University in Danville, Virginia. He is also the director of the university's writing center. He has taught courses and given numerous presentations over the years in the field of mystery fiction. His most recent scholarly publication, "Sherlock Holmes Pastiches," appears in the new *Critical Survey of Mystery and Detective Fiction*.

Ellen F. Higgins is an independent scholar of English and women's studies specializing in women and detective fiction. Her work focuses on gender and the history, theory, and criticism of the genre. She created one of the first courses focusing on women's detective fiction, which serves as the basis for her article in this volume. Other articles she has written include "The Female Rivals of Sherlock Holmes," on female authors and detectives contemporaneous with Arthur Conan Doyle and his sleuth; and "*Gaudy Night* Revisited," on the contributions of Dorothy L. Sayers' masterpiece to literary, detective fiction, and Interwar period studies.

Alexander N. Howe is an assistant professor of English at the University of the District of Columbia, where he teaches courses on American literature, detective fiction, and film. He is the author of *It Didn't Mean Anything: A Psychoanalytic Reading of American Detective Fiction* (McFarland, 2008) and the co-editor of *Marcia Muller and the Female Private Eye: Essays on the Novels that Defined a Sub-Genre* (McFarland, 2008).

Rosemary Johnsen is assistant professor of English at Governors State University. Her book, *Contemporary Feminist Historical Crime Fiction*, was published by Palgrave Macmillan in 2006. She has published on crime fiction and on twentieth-century British literature, and her current book project is on non–Modernist English literature between the wars.

Virginia Macdonald received her Ph.D. in Renaissance studies from the University of Texas at Austin and is an associate professor of languages and literature at Nicholls State University, Thibodaux, Louisiana. Her Prentice-Hall writing textbook, *Mastering Writing Essentials* (co-authored with Andrew Macdonald), came out in 1996. She has published widely in ESL, popular culture, film studies, Renaissance studies, and pedagogy. Her books with Andrew Macdonald include *Shapeshifting: Images of Native Americans in Recent Popular Fiction, Shaman or Sherlock: The Native American in Recent Detective Fiction, Jane Austen on Screen,* and *Scott Turow.* She edited volume 276, *British Mystery and Thriller Writers Since 1960,* in the *Dictionary of Literary Biography,* and has published books on Robert Ludlum and James Clavell.

Deane Mansfield-Kelley is a professor in the Department of English at the University of Texas at El Paso. Mansfield-Kelley teaches a variety of undergraduate and graduate courses in detective fiction and uses the genre in other classes. Along with Lois A. Marchino, Mansfield-Kelley has edited *Death by Pen: The Longman Anthology of Detective Fiction from Poe to Paretsky,* published as a trade paperback edition the textbook *The Longman Anthology of Detective Fiction,* co-authored essays on detective fiction, and presented papers in the mystery and detective fiction area at the annual Popular Culture Association conference.

Lois A. Marchino, a professor in the Department of English at the University of Texas at El Paso, teaches a variety of undergraduate and graduate courses in detective fiction and uses the genre in other classes. Along with colleague Deane Mansfield-Kelley, she has edited *Death by Pen: The Longman Anthology of Detective Fiction from Poe to Paretsky,* published as a trade paperback edition the textbook *The Longman Anthology of Detective Fiction* (2005), co-authored essays on detective fiction, and presented papers in the Mystery and Detective Fiction area at the annual Popular Culture Association conference.

Meg Matheny is an assistant professor of English at Jefferson Community and Technical College-Southwest in Louisville, Kentucky, where she teaches composition, business writing, and detective fiction. She presented a paper entitled "The Elusive Gervase Fen" (Edmund Crispin's 1940's detective) at the Popular Culture Association conference in Boston in April 2007. She previously taught writing and literature at Eastern Kentucky University in Richmond and the University of Kentucky in Lexington.

Stanley D. Orr is associate professor of English at the University of Hawai'i, West O'ahu. He teaches American literature, writing, film studies, and cultural studies, including courses on the history of detective fiction and film noir. Orr has published in journals such as *Literature/Film Quarterly, Paradoxa: Studies in World Literary Genres,* and *Jouvert: A Journal of Postcolonial Studies.*

Christine Photinos is associate professor in the Department of Arts and Humanities at National University, San Diego, where she teaches American literature and film courses. Her most recent articles have appeared in *Women's Studies: An Interdisciplinary Journal, The Journal of American Culture, The Journal of Popular Culture,* and *AmeriQuests.* Her current project examines crime writer Cornell Woolrich's 1940s "black series" and film adaptations of these stories.

James C. **Pierson** is professor emeritus of anthropology at California State University, San Bernardino, where he continues to teach courses in the Anthropology and Human Development programs. His research and publications focus primarily on recent and contemporary Australian Aboriginal populations. A current project is a case study of selected members of the "Stolen Generations" of Aboriginal children removed from their families and cultures as part of official government assimilation policies from about 1900 to 1970. His courses regularly compare these children's experiences with those of the residents of American Indian boarding schools of the same era.

Robert C. **Power** is a professor and the H. Albert Young Fellow in Constitutional Law at Widener University School of Law. He previously served as vice dean and senior academic officer at the Harrisburg Campus of Widener University. He holds degrees from Brown University and Northwestern University. Prior to becoming an educator he served for five years with the United States Department of Justice prosecuting organized crime and official corruption cases.

Edward J. **Rielly** holds a doctorate from the University of Notre Dame and is a professor of English at Saint Joseph's College of Maine. He previously edited *Baseball in the Classroom: Essays on Teaching the National Pastime* for McFarland (2006). He has edited three other collections of essays, two on baseball and one on Jonathan Swift's *Gulliver's Travels*. Other publications include biographies of F. Scott Fitzgerald and Sitting Bull, a book on the popular culture of the 1960s, and eleven collections of his own poetry, most recently *Old Whitman Loved Baseball and Other Baseball Poems*. He is currently writing a book on football and American culture and an analysis of American Indian resistance leaders.

Deborah **Shaller** teaches English, cultural studies, and women's studies at Towson University. She directs the writing program and has co-directed the Cultural Studies program. She writes about popular literature, youth culture, and subcultural practices. She has taught courses in detective fiction for many years, including women detectives in contemporary American culture.

Rosemary **Weatherston** is a professor of English and the director of the Dudley Randall Center for Print Culture and UDM Press at the University of Detroit Mercy. Her areas of interest include twentieth- and twenty-first-century U.S. literatures, critical theory, and gender and cultural studies. Her essays, interviews, and reviews have appeared in *AUMLA, Discourse, Theatre Journal,* and *ARIEL* as well as in such anthologies as *Body Politics and the Fictional Double, Queer Frontiers: Millennial Geographies, Genders, and Generations, Critical Mappings of Arturo Islas's Fictions,* and *A Different Image: The Legacy of Broadside Press,* which she co-edited.

Robert P. **Winston** is professor of English at Dickinson College. He specializes in American literature before 1914, especially the development of the early American novel. His current research focuses on the relationships between popular literatures and national cultures. He is the co-author, with Nancy C. Mellerski, of *The Public Eye: Ideology and the Police Procedural.* He has published articles on detective fiction in *Clues, Studies in Scottish Literature, Texas Studies in Literature and Language,* and elsewhere.

Chris **York** has an eclectic publication background that includes essays on pedagogy, baseball literature, and Batman. His papers include "Sifting Native Grounds:

Academia in the Detective Fiction of Tony Hillerman" and "Twin Killing: The Convergence of Baseball Literature and Detective Literature in the Late Twentieth Century," both presented at Popular Culture/American Culture Association conferences. He is currently an instructor of English and American studies at Pine Technical College.

Index